The Dragons versus St G
England versus Wales in rugby league 1

CW01511019

Graham Williams

London League Publications Ltd

The Dragons versus St George
England versus Wales in rugby league 1908 to1996
© Graham Williams
Foreword © Jim MIlls

The moral right of Graham Williams to be identified as the author has been asserted.

Front & back cover design @ Stephen McCarthy.

All photographs are credited to the photographer or provider of the photo. No copyright has been intentionally breached; please contact London League Publications Ltd if you believe there has been a breach of copyright.

Front cover photo: Trevor Foster (Wales) and Ernest Ward (England) toss up before an international (Courtesy Robert Gate); Jonathan Davies (rlphotos.com – David Wiliams)
Back cover: Don Gullick (Wales) challenged by Alan Davies – England versus Wales at St Helens 16 September 1953 (Courtesy Robert Gate); 1970s Welsh squad (Courtesy Gary Slater)

This book is copyright under the Berne Convention. All rights are reserved. It is sold subject to the condition that it shall not, by way of trade or otherwise, be lent, resold, hired out or otherwise circulated without the publisher's prior consent in any form of binding or cover other than that in which it is published and without a similar condition being imposed on the subsequent purchaser.

A CIP catalogue record for this book is available from the British Library.

Published in October 2023 by London League Publications Ltd, PO Box 65784, London NW2 9NS

ISBN: 978-1-909885-34-9

Cover design by Stephen McCarthy Graphic Design
46, Clarence Road, London N15 5BB.

Editing and layout by Peter Lush

Printed and bound in Great Britain by CPI Group (UK) Ltd, Croydon CR0 4YY

Foreword

I was always proud to play for Wales. Pulling on the red shirt – especially if we were playing England – was always special. My first experience of playing for Wales against England was when I played for the Wales Youth team and we played against England Schools at Twickenham. It was the only time I played at Twickenham. Earlier that season, I captained the Welsh Youth team when we played a Combined Midlands Colts XV at Moseley. We won 16–0 and that was a great experience.

After I switched to rugby league, I played 17 times for Wales. Seven of those matches were against England.

The one that stands out was in the 1975 World Championship. On 10 June, we played England in Brisbane and won 12–7. Before the game, the England team manager, Alex Murphy, was interviewed on television and said that not one of the Welsh players was good enough to play for England. That created a bad feeling between the sides. Afterwards, some of the England lads told me that he should not have done that, winding up the opposition.

Trouble kicked off in the game straightaway. Mick Morgan was knocked out. He came back, was knocked out again and again a third time. He did finish the game, but would not have been allowed back on today. When Widnes had played Warrington in the Challenge Cup Final, Dave Chisnall had hit me in the last few minutes of the game, so I owed him one! I hit him in the first scrum, payback for Wembley

We were also playing against some of our club mates. I hit George Nicholls, a great player for England and one of my best mates. He was very upset and didn't speak to me for a while.

I played with some great players for Wales. David Watkins was brilliant; also John Bevan, John Mantle, Kel Coslett, Colin Dixon, Bobby Wanbon, Mike Nicholas, Tony Fisher, David Willicombe, Clive Sullivan and many others. It didn't surprise us when we beat England. But that 1975 side was getting old, and there weren't enough younger players coming through.

England had some great players at that time as well. Roger Millward stood out, as did George Nicholls and Steve Norton.

After beating England, we played Australia, but we only had four days rest and they beat us 30–13. England had a longer break and held them to a draw.

I enjoyed playing back in South Wales, usually at Swansea. However, I remember one match when the snow was so bad that the game had to be cancelled. The snow was so deep it was up the rugby posts. The officials wanted us to travel to the ground, but the weather was so bad we couldn't get the coach out of the hotel car park.

After I retired, I later became the Welsh team manager. I was told by Maurice Lindsay that if we beat France and Papua New Guinea we would be in the 1995 World Cup. We did win the games, but Maurice said there had been a change and we would not be in the World Cup. I had told the players that we would, so I resigned in protest. Trevor Foster was offered the job, but after speaking to me turned it down. Mike Nicholas took it on and I'm pleased to say that Wales did play and reached the semi-final.

I still chair the Wales Past Players Association. We meet twice a year – on St David's Day and around Christmas. And recently I was inducted into the Welsh Sports Hall of Fame, which is a great honour for me, to be alongside the famous sports people from both rugby codes and many other sports.

Jim Mills

Introduction

The Welsh team's challenge in the 2022 World Cup and its brave fight to overcome the likes of the Cook Islands, Papua New Guinea and Tonga, made me think back to how different Welsh Rugby League is now from how it was 60 years ago when I first became interested in the wider game and its history. Those thoughts provided the inspiration to start work on this book.

The battle between 'professional' rugby league and 'amateur' rugby union raged in south Wales for a century. For most of that time, rugby league faced high levels of opposition and prejudice. Choosing the 'honest' professional option, whether as a player or as an official, was a step not to be taken lightly. There were obvious affinities between the two games but northern recruitment in particular created bitterness and distrust between the Rugby Football League (RFL) and the Welsh Rugby Union (WRU) which at times brought out the worst in both bodies.

Mostly playing in exile in the northern counties of England, Welsh rugby league players were often viewed nostalgically but the official reaction to them even if they returned home was to shun them. Some would choose to vilify them as people who had betrayed their country and its 'national game'. According to their detractors they were people who could or would only play for money. Their achievements in the north of England, if acknowledged at all, would be belittled. And yet these were athletes, many of them of the best of their generation, who with limited means did the best for themselves and their families despite the brickbats thrown at them.

There were never that many Welshmen playing regularly in the north, but at times with a commanding figure to the fore they 'punched' way above their weight. They may have gone north but they gave their all when they pulled on the red shirt. Above all they remained proud, passionate Welshmen always keen to do the best for their country, especially if that meant by getting the better of an England team that always looked much stronger on paper. Sadly, for those Welshmen, the highly anticipated chance to get one over on the Anglo-Saxons was not always shared by the RFL's officials.

Acknowledgments

Thanks are due to the publishers, Peter Lush and Dave Farrar, for encouraging me to start and then finish this book and subsequently so ably turning into the finished product. Robert Gate's writings on Welsh rugby league have been invaluable as have the research efforts of Trevor Delaney. Along the way, I have been fortunate to receive help and advice from Harry Edgar, Simon Foster, Graham Morris, David Thorpe and John Pitchford. I have also been fortunate to draw upon the work done by members of both the Rugby League Record Keepers' Club and the Rugby Memorabilia Society. As on many occasions before, Moira Doolan has kept me focused and corrected more typescript than I had a right to expect. Any errors that do remain are of course entirely my own.

Graham Williams
September 2023

London League Publications Ltd would like to thank Steve McCarthy for designing the cover, Gary Slater, Dave Williams, Alex Service, Robert Gate and Harry Edgar (*Rugby League Journal*) for providing the photos.

Contents

Ernest Ward (England) and Trevor Foster (Wales) – two legends of the sport in the 1940s and 1950s. (Courtesy *Rugby League Journal*)

England versus Wales at Central Park, 20 September 1947. (Courtesy Alex Service)

1. In the beginning

England versus Wales may not be rugby's oldest rivalry, but it certainly has generated more than its fair share of passion and commitment over the years. The first meeting was not until February 1881, when a team picked by the South Wales Football Union (SWFU) was invited to play England at Blackheath. The outcome was a disaster for the Welsh who conceded 13 tries. That embarrassing drubbing shocked Welsh rugby supporters and led to the formation of the Welsh Football Union (WFU) at Neath the following month. The change of name did not, however, reflect a wider membership. The WFU, like its predecessor, remained confined to a handful of often fervent counties in south Wales.

It was not the closest of contests for the rest of the decade. By the end of the 1880s, however, an improving Welsh XV was posing a real threat to English supremacy. The Welsh recorded their first victory over England at a snowy Dewsbury in February 1890. Three years later, once again in severe cold weather, they repeated that feat but this time in Wales, at Cardiff Arms Park. After an inauspicious start the Welsh team had established itself as more than worthy opponents.

English rugby splits

Wales was not the only threat to the supremacy of the English team in the spring of 1895. A group of clubs in northern England were approaching the end of their third season of organised league competition in the Yorkshire Senior Competition and the First Division of the Lancashire Club Championship. To improve their competitive position, those clubs devised a plan to spread beyond their county boundaries and create a new body, the Lancashire and Yorkshire Rugby Union of Senior Clubs that could ultimately match the Football League. Unfortunately, the Rugby Football Union (RFU) rejected that plan in May 1895 as prejudicial to the interests of the game, forcing those senior clubs to take stock of their situation.

Once it became clear to them that the RFU was planning to introduce even more stringent regulations on amateur status later that year, those senior clubs had to face up to some hard choices. Over the close season the debate raged – a small minority arguing to stay with the RFU and fight their case. The majority determined that rather than be picked off individually they would leave as a group and create their own independent regional union.

On the evening of Thursday 29 August, 21 senior clubs met in Huddersfield to determine the course they would take. Eventually, 20 of those present agreed that they would submit their resignations to the RFU and form a new Northern Union (NU). Two clubs from Cheshire applied immediately and were accepted into membership. To meet the needs of its members, a Northern Rugby League (NRL), comprising all 22 clubs, was formed to harness their competitive ambitions.

To cope with the increased travel distances on match days, expense payments for leaving work early, known as 'broken-time', were approved. These payments were fixed at 6/- (£0.30) per day with only one day being payable in relation to any match. Such payments had been rejected two years earlier by the RFU as being contrary to its amateur regulations. Subsequently, all those involved in the NU, having agreed to a more liberal 'amateurism' in their terms, were declared professional.

The WFU supports the RFU

Although there were some sympathies in south Wales for the northern rebels, the WFU was not under any comparable threat to its unity. Rumours of abuses of the amateur regulations were kept in check and the WFU was able to report a growth in membership. Nevertheless, Welsh players would be drawn northwards and the WFU would make clear in its support for the RFU over its ostracism of the NU and its aims. There would be no welcome in the valleys for the NU if the WFU had anything to do with it.

The NU embraces professionalism

From the start, critics were adamant that the only basis for the NU's future success was professionalism. They did not have to wait long to be proved correct. At the NU's AGM in July 1898, the honorary secretary opened a debate on the subject by telling those present that it was "an admitted fact that professionalism is now carried on by the majority of clubs in membership". When it came to the vote the majority of clubs voted to adopt professionalism although on a very restricted basis; all professionals would be expected to hold down a 'proper job'.

The rise of international rugby

As the 1890s drew to a close, the British Rugby Unions were showing signs of getting their game back into shape. Despite losing a large number of its northern clubs, the RFU had managed to survive largely intact in the midlands and southern counties of England. Meanwhile, across the River Severn, the Welsh Football Union (WFU) had brought its own rebellious currents sufficiently under control to enable it to grow in stature both on-and-off the field. Wales, the youngest of the four home unions, had shown itself able to deal with the other three in the committee rooms and was on the verge of proving itself superior on the field. Scotland had been England's first and for many years its staunchest opponent. As the new century loomed, the increase in Welsh prowess meant that their meeting with England was close to becoming the new main event. As a contest it not only unleashed the age-old passions of Anglo-Saxon and Celt rivalry, but also was a showcase for the growing tactical maturity of the handling game, as developed by the innovative Welsh XV in particular.

Having decided to retain only six players from the previous season, introducing five new caps into the pack, and recalling the James brothers after a seven-year absence, the Welsh selectors tried, at the last minute, to improve their team's chances ahead of the opening match against England on Saturday 7 January 1899. They brought the players together at the Arms Park on the Thursday before the match so that, in the words of 'Old Ebor' in the *South Wales Daily News* for Friday 6 January, they could gain "some knowledge of each other's peculiarities of style". Tom Graham, the now retired Newport and Wales forward, was on hand to drill the pack's newcomers.

It proved to be a day well spent. The James brothers were the mainspring of the Welsh team, launching their backs on a six-try spree as Wales inflicted England's heaviest defeat to date in a 26–3 win. A reporter stated proudly that "no international team England put in the field had ever been more routed." That victory was even more emphatic when it is realised that Evan James had suffered a dislocated shoulder and, while he stayed on the pitch until the end of the match, he was effectively a passenger. The rout was all done in front of a higher than expected Swansea crowd of over 25,000 who paid £1,500. The rising attendance reflected the growing interest among Welsh supporters in the fortunes of their national team.

The James brothers

Twelve days after England had been overrun, on Monday 19 January, the celebrated James family – 16 people in all – abruptly left Swansea and accompanied Harry Rebitt, a future director of Broughton Rangers, back to Manchester. David and Evan, the half-back partnership that were credited with laying the basis for the Welsh victory, had agreed to rejoin Broughton Rangers for £200 each in gold sovereigns, £2 per match and housing provided. In the party which included mother, father, grandmother and grandchildren were David and Evan's three younger brothers – Sam – who had appeared for Swansea's first team, Willie – 14 at the time – and Claude who was aged 10. All three would go on to play for Broughton Rangers.

How good were the northern recruits?

Following the split in the RFU's ranks, the Home Unions had ruled on how selection for their respective national sides would operate in future. Association football, while recognising the separate status of amateur and professional, had kept their national sides as fully reflective of the whole game in each nation. Rugby union did not follow that path. It would banish all those deemed not amateur enough from its representative teams. Along with many of England's best players who followed their clubs into the NU, others would follow. Even before the NU officially adopted professionalism in 1898, Welsh talent had begun to take the road north in significant numbers to give the rebels a highly talented player pool. They constituted a parallel professional world. For most of the first decade the only representative rugby on offer to those players was the NU's County Championship and a number of Welshmen found their way into the county teams.

Some journalists were keen to play down the quality and impact of the NU's recruits. One of them was 'Welsh Athlete' who dismissed the impact of their departure on the Welsh game in the *Western Mail* on Monday 9 January 1899: "The Northern Union need not enter particularly into our calculations, except so far as to suggest that England's strength undoubtedly lies in their ranks. Fortunately, we in Wales are not in the same position although the Northern Union now and again touch us in a tender spot by attaching a few of our players. They have not, however, been fortunate enough, except perhaps in the case of Cooper, to draw from us any player of merit – that is in the slightest degree likely to weaken our international chances." The Cooper in question was Fred who had left Newport in 1893 to make a name for himself in Bradford.

Two days later writing in the *Yorkshire Evening Post*, 'Old Ebor' drew a slightly different conclusion on the impact of the NU on Welsh rugby. It appeared to him that some observers "ignore the extent to which Welsh football itself has suffered by the formation of the Northern Union. Numbers of Welsh players have been drafted Northwards, and comparing the size of the Welsh and the English Unions, it is a moot point whether Wales has not been relatively more crippled than England." There was only one real way to answer such questions – and that was on the field of play, but the Home Unions would never allow such a thing to happen. With no 'official' options open the question of whether or not a departing player was a loss to the RFU or WFU would largely remain in the realm of spectator banter for the next 100 years or thereabouts.

Keeping those players of merit sometimes required a little financial assistance. One who appeared for Wales in the victory at Swansea in 1899 was Cardiff's Gloucestershire-born Gwyn Nicholls. His skills and leadership qualities were exactly what the NRL's clubs were looking for. The *South Wales Daily News* in October 1900 linked Nicholls with a move to Oldham for a fee of £400 and a year later the *Yorkshire Post* reported him turning down an offer of £500 and "a substantial weekly salary" from Hull FC where elder brother Sydney, a former Welsh international, was honorary secretary. Thanks to benefactors he found lucrative employment before developing his own business interests with their support. Gwyn Nicholls was one of those who would never be tempted by the NU.

Unofficial imitations

There was nothing to stop the NU harnessing the keen rivalry of England and Wales under its auspices. Where the rebel leaders feared to tread, others boldly stepped in to use the rivalry as a vehicle for raising funds for good causes. Around Manchester there was no shortage of available talent to call on; a few who had international caps, some who had been on the verge of international recognition and some who would undoubtedly have won international caps but for the split. Re-assembled as England and Wales, few doubted that the district's rugby fans would fork out the admission price to watch the action.

After months of wrangling, teams representing England and Wales met at Salford's New Barns ground on Wednesday 19 April 1899. Held as part of a testimonial for Jim Valentine's benefit, the match raised around £60. Valentine, Swinton's former England international centre, captained the English XV to a 12–8 victory over a Welsh team captained by his club-mate and former Welsh international forward Jack Evans, in front of 6,000 spectators.

When the NU Cup Final was held at Fallowfield a year later the Welsh exiles were conspicuous. There was probably a dozen of them representing either Salford or Swinton that day although only two of them – Jack Evans and Jack Rhapps – had gained a cap before coming north. Two days later, England met Wales unofficially once again at New Barns. This time it was in a benefit match for the wives, widows and orphans of the Salford Volunteers who were fighting in South Africa.

Life could be harsh in those days as Evan James discovered after catching a severe cold playing for Broughton Rangers reserves in October 1900. Weakened, he subsequently contracted consumption and decided to move back to Bonymaen in South Wales with his family. The Lancashire NU committee sanctioned a testimonial match for Evan which was held on Tuesday 30 April 1901.

The format was the same as the one used the previous year except that this time the teams would be reduced to XII-a-side. Wheater's Field, the home of Broughton Rangers in Lower Broughton, was the venue. It would not prove to be a happy homecoming for Evan who would die of consumption, aged just 33, four months later.

The chance for teams drawing on the two regions of the United Kingdom where the rugby game was most popular and thought about most deeply – the north of England and South Wales – to meet on the field seemed an obvious development and promised a great potential showcase for the handling code.

The Other Nationalities

Surprisingly, official matches between the two countries took time to come about. The NU preferred initially to put together an Other Nationalities team which faced an English-born side on three occasions. Bad weather forced the original fixture, scheduled for Oldham on New Year's Day 1904, to be postponed. It was eventually held at Wigan's Central Park on the afternoon of Tuesday 5 April 1904. An Other Nationalities team which included a couple of Scots, an Englishman of Irish descent and nine Welshmen proved too good for the Englishmen on the day and won 9–3. The attendance of 6,000, on a rainy Tuesday afternoon, was considered disappointing.

Speaking at the NRL's AGM on Tuesday 28 July 1904, JH Houghton, the honorary secretary, said that the international was a game worthy of the occasion, was very much appreciated by the players in the winning of caps and would eventually prove a success financially. There was much to be done if his opinion was to become fact.

The *Yorkshire Evening Post* in its report of England's 26–11 defeat of opponents who included 11 Welshmen at Bradford's Park Avenue on Monday 2 January 1905 was not that impressed: "The Northern Union, not being able to indulge in the luxury of a genuine international game has invented an amusing variant." It went on to add that "It may have been an international fixture, but it remained, nevertheless, a pale ghost of the genuine thing." The third and final match, when the Other Nationalities included two Scots and 13 Welshmen, ended in a draw on New Year's Day 1906.

After that the Other Nationalities were mothballed for the next 15 years. In their place came a new opponent, Wales, which looked more than capable of providing England with a genuine international challenge. By the time that challenge came along a significant change had taken place in the rules of NU football.

A brave new game

Out of necessity, the NU ended its long agonising debate over professionalism. It threw the game open by removing all its restrictions on outside employment at its 1905 AGM. Twelve months later, it drew a line under nearly 10 years of experimentation and made its definitive break with three key elements of the Laws as framed by the RFU. After a difficult gestation, significant changes in how the game was played were made at the AGM held on 12 June 1906. There was no overall master plan, but three unrelated resolutions created the basis for the emergence of a very different game.

That AGM represented a test of the confidence and vision of the NU's membership, marking as it did a choice between two distinct paths, one towards a new game, the other championed by Bradford taking the organisation back towards rugby union. Essentially, the first path answered three main needs: to keep the ball on the field, in play and visible as much as possible, thereby providing space and opportunity for individual skills to shine. Of those three, ball visibility was thought to be particularly important as it was considered to be a major contributor to the growing popularity of association football.

First, the meeting discussed various proposals covering team size. Nearly everyone present recognised that such a move had to be made and from the list of options tabled at the meeting chose, by 43 votes to 18, Warrington's proposal, supported by Leigh, to reduce the number of players in a team from XV to XIII with the expectation that this would shift the emphasis of play from weight to speed and produce a more open, spectacular game.

There was no stipulation in the law change as to how this should be achieved and William McCutcheon of Oldham hoped that it would mean a reduction in the forwards to seven. In practice, however, it meant removing two forwards.

Second, the AGM agreed to Bradford's proposal to change the method of returning the ball back into play after the tackle. Since the 'split' the NU's and the RFU's laws governing the tackle had diverged with the former requiring a scrummage when the ball was fairly held in the tackle. As there was a lot of lying on the ball this change produced rather a lot of scrums, which were adjudged to be monotonous and waste time. At the AGM it was agreed to return to the RFU law in a bid for greater continuity of movement. When the ball was held the RFU law governing a standing tackle required the tackled player to "at once put the ball down between himself and his opponent's goal line", after which either side could play it with their feet.

The RFU law was adopted, before an amendment was moved by Oldham's representative, William McCutcheon. In a bid to reduce accidental injuries McCutcheon proposed the tackled player, if on the ground, be prohibited from just releasing the ball and rolling away. Instead, the game would momentarily stop while the tackled player got to his feet before placing or dropping the ball.

Third, the meeting adopted a proposal from Oldham, moved by William McCutcheon, that in future for a team to gain territory any kick to touch other than a penalty would require the ball to bounce in the field of play. If it went into touch on the full then play would resume with a scrummage, not at the point at which it went into touch, but in line with the point at which it was kicked. This change forced teams to employ more skilful tactical kicking thereby curbing the aimless defensive punting to touch that had previously blighted so many games. It also meant the ball was kept in play for longer.

The Welsh XV at Leicester

English rugby's split had reduced the number and attraction of the remaining loyalist venues in northern England for the RFU. To take their place, the RFU had found in Leicester a sufficient level of support and it would become its most northern venue. The Welford Road ground hosted its second England international on Saturday 9 January 1904. Having not ventured northwards since the heavy defeat at Birkenhead a decade earlier, the Welsh came to Leicester and as expected they proved a great attraction. The *Leicester Daily Post* report noted that excursions were run from all parts of England. There was a contingent of two to three thousand from Wales in an attendance estimated at 16,000 who paid £1,100. It was according to the report "the largest crowd ever assembled in Leicester to witness a game."

2. The Welsh XIII appears

When the NRL's fixtures were published on 29 July 1907, they included two Welsh clubs – Ebbw Vale and Merthyr Tydfil – for the first time. Those two pioneers faced a huge challenge – to become professional and proficient at a distinctly different form of rugby virtually overnight. Keen to build on the momentum generated by the arrival of the first NU tourists from New Zealand, the NU agreed to offer its Welsh-born and Welsh-raised players the chance, if they wanted it, to represent Wales. It would be a major challenge for the NU's new combination to reach an equivalent level to the rugby union Welsh XV, but it offered the rebel game the chance to shed its reputation for being solely interested in Wales as a recruiting ground.

Several Welsh players, whose time in the north had not worked out and had returned home, took the chance to continue playing top-class rugby for either Ebbw Vale or Merthyr Tydfil. For a couple of them, the opportunities would be much greater. Tom Paddison, briefly once of Salford, built on his performances with Merthyr to gain Welsh NU honours. Hull had not provided 'Chick' Jenkins with the chance to develop his talents, but once in Ebbw Vale's colours he shone and went on to represent both Wales and the NU in the years ahead.

The first dual code international

While the NU was openly professional, clandestine professionalism was believed to exist in parts of Wales. Allegations of serious breaches of the professional laws by clubs in the South Wales valleys first reached the press in January 1907. More and more stories followed, forcing the WFU to act and an inquiry was launched. Fearing the outcome of that inquiry, some clubs began to look at other options.

When the inquiry finally reported in September, it found accusations of widespread professionalism not proven, but it did confirm that the paying and receiving of excessive expenses was the norm at certain clubs. Having received the report, the WFU ordered the suspension of six Aberdare players, warned Merthyr for a number of breaches of the rules and suspended for life both the Aberdare and Treorchy committees and eight players, one of whom was Dai 'Tarw' Jones, while suspending seven others for periods from three to 12 months.

Jones, considered a giant of a man standing over six feet and weighing over 15 stones, was the best known, having made his debut for the Welsh XV against England in January 1902 while with Treherbert.

In the summer of 1905, he appears to have joined Aberdare and it was while a member and captain there that he played for Wales against the 'original' All Blacks in December 1905. It was as a member of Aberdare that Jones made his 13th and final appearance for the Wales rugby union team against South Africa in December 1906.

According to allegations made public by the former secretary of Aberdare, the following month, Jones had reverted to Treherbert when Aberdare cut his wages from 10/- (£0.50) to 7/6 (£0.38) per week. Having refused to give evidence, the 26-year-old collier was found guilty of "receiving a money consideration for playing football" and permanently suspended by the WFU. Jones eventually threw in his lot with the new Merthyr Tydfil NU club in October.

The first clash

Within six months of the first Welsh clubs switching to the NU, a Welsh international team was assembled ready to take on the touring New Zealanders on New Year's Day 1908 at the Ynys Field, the Aberdare Athletics Ground. A last-minute try brought Wales a narrow victory, 9–8, but it was enough to thrill a crowd estimated at 12,000. Reflecting on the match on 11 January, the *Aberdare Leader* was clearly impressed: "Those who witnessed the Wales versus New Zealand match at the Athletic Grounds on New Year's Day were given a good insight into the method of playing the game under Northern Union rules. Personally, I admire the new method for it gives the spectator full value for his money, which I believe, is the secret of obtaining a substantial credit to any club's balance sheet at the end of the season. The spectators were greatly impressed with the new game, especially as the ball was always kept in play by virtue of the quickness in breaking up the scrummages with the abolition of the lineout. In truth it is a faster game than the old-fashioned amateur method." Similar views would provide a constant backdrop to the next 85 years.

Monday 20 April 1908: Wales 35 England 18
Tonypandy, 12,000

An England victory 10 days later meant both home nations had beaten the New Zealanders. A meeting between the two old rivals seemed the obvious next step. With the rugby season drawing to a close, the NU committee selected both English and Welsh teams to meet at the Mid-Rhondda Social and Athletic Club's "commodious and well-appointed" Athletic Ground in the village of Penygraig, just to the south of Tonypandy, on Easter Monday.

It meant that a Welsh XIII showing five changes from the one that took on the New Zealanders at Aberdare was again taking to the field, this time to take on an England team that retained only four of the men who had defeated the tourists at Wigan. Dai Jones was the only rugby union cap in the first ever Welsh XIII to take on England. Six of the team were playing for either Ebbw Vale or Merthyr Tydfil. The team, listed with their original Welsh rugby union clubs, was 'Chick' Jenkins (Pontypool); Llew Treharne (Tredegar), Bert Jenkins (Mountain Ash), Phil Thomas (Neath), Dai Thomas (Aberdare); Rhys Rees (Merthyr Tydfil), Johnny Thomas (Maesteg); Arthur Buckler (Pill Harriers), George Ruddick (Brecon), Dai Jones (Merthyr Tydfil), Dai B. Davies (Merthyr Tydfil), Oliver Burgham (Abertillery), Bill Saunders (Ebbw Vale).

The selectors had bent the rules somewhat by including a Scotsman, Andy Hogg, in the English line-up. The Welsh were also crossing borders. Oliver Burgham, an early specialist hooker, was born in Cinderford in the Forest of Dean and played for Gloucester before he moved to Abertillery in 1907. Later that year he joined Ebbw Vale NUFC. He had become an adopted Welshman and was making his second appearance for the Principality at Tonypandy. It was a clash that offered the prospect of an intriguing contest if the two teams, both nurtured in similar harsh industrial landscapes, were able to establish a strong national rivalry.

Eastertime was always a busy time for rugby in South Wales and all the top clubs were at home to entertain the usual range of tourists. On that Easter Monday the Barbarians were at Swansea (10,000) and Leicester Tigers were at Cardiff (12,000). Newport welcomed the Monmouthshire League champions Abertillery who brought with them a large contingent from the valleys. At that time the Rhondda valley was a rugby hotbed and the NU had to hope that fans in the nearby towns and villages – Pontypridd to the south, Llwynypia, Treorchy and Treherbert to the north – would support the venture. With the Welsh club scene being so partisan, the NU had to hope that the national team would offer the possibility of a unifying force for their game.

Both sides had to make late changes. For England, Billy Batten was brought in to replace Jim Leytham and Bill Holder for Hunslet's Harry Wilson. Bill Saunders replaced Warrington's Frank Shugars in the Welsh line-up. With the international being held so late in the season only four players – Billy Batten, Bill Holder, Harry Taylor and Tom White – had any meaningful game-time to come. For the rest of the players the summer break beckoned.

On a fine day for playing rugby, Wales scored first, a try by winger Llew Treharne. Although play was close England held the initiative and worked four tries, two of them from Jack Fish in what would prove to be the great winger's last international appearance. What Fish could do so could Treharne who got over for his second try, a brilliant length of the field effort, to leave Wales trailing by three points at the break.

Once the match resumed the Welsh were immeasurably superior. England could not contain the Celts who added another four tries – a brace from Bert Jenkins and one each from Oliver Burgham and Dai Thomas. All seven Welsh tries were converted to provide a comfortable victory for the Welsh. There was an immediate record of seven goals against England for Wigan's Johnny Thomas which has never been beaten. Perched on the surrounding grass banks, a crowd of 12,000 – only slightly down on the one at Aberdare – indicated the fixture had potential for the future. The Mid-Rhondda Social and Athletic Club's management clearly thought there was potential – they formed a club and were accepted into the NRL on 14 July.

Before returning to their clubs, the Welsh XIII travelled over to Merthyr on Easter Tuesday to play a friendly against the town's NU club. It was a relaxed affair which the national team won by a single point.

The first 'Golden Era'

Just three months prior to the match at Tonypandy, the Welsh XV had inflicted a fourth consecutive defeat on the English to move ahead 12 to 11, with two drawn, in the series of matches. This showed the increasing prowess of Wales on the rugby field. Life was always going to be difficult for the Welsh NU XIII, having been launched at a time when the Welsh XV was enjoying a period of unparalleled interest and success.

Later dubbed the 'Golden Era', the Welsh XV had just completed a clean sweep of the home nations, the Triple Crown, on the way to becoming champions for the fourth time. They repeated that success the following year and then added another championship by 1911 when the first sweep of the home nations plus France, the Grand Slam, is generally agreed to have brought the 'Era' to a close. It was a period also marked by an unbeaten run of 10 matches against England. A major factor in the success of the 'Golden Era' was the settled nature of the Welsh XV despite the best efforts of the NRL. While the background of many of the first-choice Welsh XV meant it was unlikely they would ever switch to the NU, some such as Gwyn Nicholls and Dickie Owen were reckoned to be susceptible to northern offers, but none of the side's big-names ever took the money. Keeping those prize assets safely at home provided the WFU with the stability and stature it desperately needed if it was to keep filling its major rugby grounds. The Welsh XV had made the nation proud and become synonymous with the rugby game at its best. Could the Welsh XIII do likewise for itself and the NU?

Victory at Tonypandy had provided the best possible start for the rebel XIII. The old rivalry could be harnessed and some valuable visibility in south Wales gained, but to build on that the NU had to ensure that its Welsh team appeared in Wales reasonably regularly from then on. Just appearing in South Wales, however, was not enough on its own; the venue needed to be prestigious if possible and the location had to have good rail links. Hopes of such a venue, which had risen at the start of the year when there was news of possible NU clubs in Cardiff and Pontypridd, faded to nothing when ground problems scuppered both projects. The lack of suitable grounds in South Wales would bedevil the northern game for nearly 90 years.

To go or not to go north

An offer to turn professional was not to be treated sentimentally. In the days before the welfare state, a sizeable signing-on fee could be life-changing for the player and his family. It needed to be addressed in a thoroughly commercial manner.

When Billy O'Neill announced he was leaving the Cardiff club after a decade and throwing in his lot with Warrington, there was condemnation from some quarters. O'Neill stoutly defended his decision in the *South Wales Daily News* on Tuesday 13 October 1908: "I go to better myself. I have a wife and child, and I am only a working man. I was offered £100 down, and I couldn't resist it – indeed I felt at the time and I now feel it too, that I would have failed in my duty to my wife and my young child if I had not taken the chance – it takes a working chap a long time to save £100 you know."

When asked the terms of his engagement, he replied: "Well, it cannot be a secret long and there's no reason why it should be now. The terms were £100 down, £2/10/- (£2.50) for every match I play that's won, and £2/5/- (£2.25) when I am in the team and we lose. But that's not all I am guaranteed – it's in black and white – a job at £2 per week, winter and summer, and also remuneration for broken-time. It may be all right for well-to-do people to say they prefer amateur sport – I have been satisfied with that myself until now – but let them put themselves in my position."

He concluded by saying that "I had to wrestle with myself before I could put pen to paper to sign myself to go North because of the happy days I have spent in Cardiff, but we – my wife and I – think it was the best thing to do, and I hope my old football friends will try to place themselves in my position before condemning me."

Manchester

Obviously keen to build on the support shown for the international match at Tonypandy, the NU committee at its meeting in Manchester on 14 July decided to set the date that the date for the next meeting – it would be held on Monday 28 December 1908 and it chose Broughton Rangers' ground as the venue. Before the 'split' in the RFU, Manchester had played a key part in popularising international rugby without ever hosting a visit from the Welsh national team. A dozen years on the city would at last have its chance. Both the old international venues were ruled out of contention. Whalley Range, the old home of the RFU-loyal Manchester club, had been lost to housing developers while the Manchester Athletic Club's stadium at Fallowfield was probably thought too expensive to hire for the match.

Many of the NU's later problems were caused by the date being selected five months earlier. The touring Australians had just begun their three test match series against the NU. In addition, England was due to meet the tourists at the start of January. Sandwiched in between was the meeting of England and Wales which struggled to get the priority it deserved, being scheduled in the middle of the busy festive period. Situated 10 minutes walk from the city centre, Wheater's Field, the location chosen for the first ever meeting of professional English and Welsh teams in the north, was a popular venue and had been packed with 20,000 spectators just before Christmas for the Lancashire Cup Final. On the downside, it was hemmed in by factories and had limited spectator facilities.

The Welsh XIII, which was selected by the committee of the Welsh League, showed eight changes from the team that had won eight months earlier. Two of the men brought in were returnees to the international stage. Tom Llewellyn who had captained the Welsh XIII against the New Zealanders was brought back at centre and Will Hopkins, who had previously spent a brief time with Wigan during which he had played for the old Other Nationalities side against England in January 1905.

The Welsh XIII included four from South Wales – Tom Paddison and Dai B Davies (Merthyr), Jack Foley (Ebbw Vale) and Will Hopkins (Aberdare) – who travelled north to take their place in the team. They may well have been accompanied by their team's two new dual internationals, Billy Dowell and Billy O'Neill, who had only joined Warrington earlier in the season and had not yet relocated to Lancashire. It seems quite likely as normally the Warrington pair would travel northwards after work on the evening before a match and then return home either directly afterwards or on the following morning if that was a Sunday.

Monday 28 December 1908: England 31 Wales 7
Broughton, 4,000

Although protected by straw, the almost grassless pitch was very hard. The frosty weather took the blame for a seriously disappointing attendance; the report in the *Manchester Courier* estimated 3,000 at best. According to Tuesday's *Nottingham Evening Post*, the crowd included "a little band of Welsh enthusiasts sporting scarlet favours and some sporting the leek" who had made the long journey from the Rhondda to Manchester.

Both teams took the field as chosen although it had been a close-run thing for England. Alf Mann, the NU Test forward, had failed to show up at Parkside before Christmas which led Bradford Northern to suspend him and inform the NU of that fact. It seemed odds-on that Mann would be forced out of the England line-up, but late on Northern lifted the suspension and he took his place on the field.

England made a good start with an early try from George Dickenson, converted by Lomas. A second try by Billy Longworth, again converted by Lomas, enabled the home side to turn round 10 points to the good. Welsh attacks had shown promise, but had broken down just before the try-line was reached. One minute after the restart, Asa Robinson was allowed to drop on the ball in the in-goal area and England had a third try. After that setback Welsh errors began to mount, their enthusiasm dipped and England went on to add a further four tries. The best touchdown of the day, however, was Welsh. When his side looked well-beaten, Dai Thomas intercepted and held off the defence for a magnificent 75-yard try which was converted by Johnny Thomas. Thanks in large part to a massive performance by the forwards, who accounted for five of their side's tries, backed up by James Lomas who scored a try and kicked five conversions, England had equalled Wales's performance earlier in the year, winning comfortably, 31–7.

A captain's lot

In the days before club and national coaches came on the scene, responsibility for the team was split. The NU selectors picked the team while the captain, who had been largely excluded from that task, was expected to look after their subsequent performance. Operating as a sort of early player-coach, the captain's first job was to set up training sessions in whatever time was available and to draw on his experience and that of his senior players. Taking their input, he had to appraise the strengths of his team, develop the appropriate tactical plan before finally inspiring his team throughout the course of the match. In reality, the captain was unable to go much beyond the basics of what passed as standard club style.

The best laid plans

Home and away international matches were arranged for the coming season by the NU committee at its meeting on 13 July 1909. While no dates appear to have been set, the venues were selected. England's home match was allocated to Huddersfield. Wales's home match would be hosted by either Merthyr or Mid-Rhondda. A re-consideration was soon necessary. At the August committee meeting, the England home match was switched to Wakefield. By then financial problems had forced Mid-Rhondda out of the NU so they were no longer an option. News would soon reach the NU committee that Merthyr had relocated to a newly developed ground at Rhydycar whose basic facilities fatally undermined its attraction as an international venue.

A year on, the burgeoning power of professional association football had effectively strangled three of the NU's pioneering Welsh clubs – Aberdare, Barry and Mid-Rhondda – after a single season and left Treherbert in a parlous state. Control of the first three grounds, two of which had hosted international matches – Aberdare and Tonypandy – was in the process of passing over to the round-ball game.

Bridge End Field, Ebbw Vale

The NU's most secure ground and therefore its international venue of choice going forward was in Ebbw Vale, even though as a small town its location at the head of the Ebbw Fawr valley always made it an awkward place to visit from the north of England. It did, however, offer the 25,000-capacity Bridge End Field, the home of Ebbw Vale's NU club, which was just a short walk from the railway station.

The first international duly went ahead at Wakefield's Belle Vue ground on Saturday 4 December 1909. In its preview, the *Manchester Courier* commented that "hitherto these encounters have not been taken seriously" but it hoped that that was about to change. An attractive Welsh team had been selected and there were hopes of a large crowd. When word arrived that Leigh's Ellis Clarkson missed his train, Hunslet's Herbert Place was called in. A serious injury had ruled out Trinity's AK Crosland and his place in the pack was taken by Fred Hill. A family bereavement forced 'Chick' Jenkins out of the Welsh threequarter-line and Phil Thomas was called up to fill in for him.

Saturday 4 December 1909: England 19 Wales 13
Wakefield, 4,000

On a dull December afternoon, both nations proved willing to move the ball about on a heavy pitch. For some reason, Frank Young took the field wearing a white England shirt. There was bound to be confusion and it happened within a couple of minutes when a nonplussed George Tyson failed to close down Young who sent Howell de Francis over for a try. Confusion reigned until Young donned a Trinity shirt much to the delight of the crowd. Both sides played well, each scoring a couple of tries, and were only separated by a Frank Young conversion, Wales leading 8–6, when it came time to change ends.

When play restarted Trinity's scrum-half, Tommy Newbould, came into his own. He scored the first try and had a hand in the second scored by Joe Ferguson. His half-back partner, Fred Smith, set up a third try for James Lomas. Lomas added the conversions for the final two tries. There was still some fight in the Welsh XIII, but they could only add a try by Jack Foley, converted by Young, to their total leaving the final score as a comfortable win for England.

It was clear that a disappointing crowd, estimated to be less than 4,000, meant that the NU had been left with a small deficit on the proceedings. Sadly, the missing thousands had missed a close match with plenty of open play. In Monday's *Yorkshire Post* the sports editor directed a harsh assessment of the match at the NU. After doubting whether there were any onlookers present at Belle Vue who had seen real international matches in which the Welsh XV had taken part in the last two decades, the writer could only commiserate with any present who had for "they must have missed the palpitating enthusiasm of the crowd, the deadly earnestness of the forwards, and the high skills of the backs, which make matches in which Welsh international teams take part the great events of the Rugby season." There was clearly much for the NU to address if it was to convince northern fans of the importance of the internationals and raise their standing to the same level as those organised by the RFU and the WFU.

Saturday 9 April 1910: Wales 39 England 18
Ebbw Vale, 4,000

The season's second match, arranged for Saturday 9 April 1910, coincided with a critical phase of the NRL's season and clubs with a chance of honours were none too keen on losing their best players. Proudly, three of Ebbw Vale's players – 'Chick' Jenkins, Lew Llewellyn and Jack Foley – took their place alongside three representatives from Merthyr and one from Treherbert in the Welsh XIII. There were a couple of late changes. After being included in the morning's team photograph, Billy O'Neill cried off and had to be replaced by Dan Lewis in the home side. Tom White stood in for Tommy Newbould in the visitor's line-up.

The members of the NU's first tour party bound for Australasia had already been selected and many were booked in the first group due to sail in just over a week's time. Twelve of them were on duty for England – Albert Avery, Billy Batten, Francis Boylen, Bill Jukes, Jim Leytham, James Lomas, Dick Ramsdale, Joe Riley, Jim Sharrock, Fred Smith, Billy Ward and Fred Webster – and six for Wales – Bert Jenkins, 'Chick' Jenkins, George Ruddick, Frank Shugars, Johnny Thomas and Frank Young.

On a fine day, a Billy Williams try put Wales ahead after just two minutes play. England regained the lead through its powerful pack, but a 'Chick' Jenkins try just before the whistle cut their lead to just two points, 13–11, at the break. Once again, the side that had the better of the first half went on to lose the match. Part of the reason for that was the recurrence of a knee injury that forced Billy Batten onto the sidelines. The Welshmen returned to the field full of vigour and Billy Williams got a second try after just two minutes. After that, the Welsh cut loose running in a further six tries to set up the sort of win that normally could only be found in Welsh dreams. Near the end, James Lomas got over the line for a converted try to record England's only score of the half.

Remarkably, all nine Welsh tries had been scored by their threequarters. One of that quartet, Billy Williams, had managed to add a third to record the first hat-trick in these matches. Nine tries against England was a Welsh record in both Northern and Rugby Union matches and has so far not been equalled. At first Batten's knee injury looked like it would cause him to miss the upcoming tour, but he recovered in time to join the second group of players who departed at the end of the month.

So, after the first four matches the series stood at two wins apiece, with home advantage appearing to be the deciding factor. It seemed clear that the corps of Welsh players, nearly all of whom were previously overlooked by the WFU's selectors, could be marshalled into a strong side and not only take on, but beat, the NU's best English combination.

Exiled, but not forgotten

Players that had left for the north of England were often remembered fondly and their careers in the professional code followed with interest in South Wales. Frank Shugars who had played for Wales at Ebbw Vale had joined Warrington from Penygraig in August 1904. Almost six years and two Welsh NU caps later, he was one of seven Welshmen selected for the NU's first party to tour Australasia in 1910. Shugars had not been forgotten in his hometown of Tonypandy and a collection there raised sufficient money to buy a gold watch, which was presented to him in honour of his selection.

Another member of the Welsh contingent was Leeds's Frank Young. For him the tour was memorable, but for all the wrong reasons. Unfortunately, Young twisted his knee so badly that he was forced to leave the field in his second outing against Metropolis in mid-June. His cartilage was so badly damaged that he was unable to play for the rest of the tour. Ultimately, that injury restricted Young to just nine more appearances for Leeds and forced him into early retirement in March 1911. Young returned to South Wales and joined the ranks of agents working on behalf of the northern clubs. His successes as an agent would mean he would not be forgotten either.

The Welsh agent

Welsh rugby's strength was based on a strong layer of senior clubs that was fed by a buoyant junior game. From the outset of professional rugby in the NU, Welsh players were interested in being signed and the northern clubs were interested in signing them.

The size and nature of the Welsh player pool in both the NU and the NRL varied depending on how the northern clubs were using their cash at any given time. Recruitment was driven by either the need to fix a weak spot in the team when no northern-based player could be sourced, or a big-name signing was deemed necessary to buoy up the supporters' morale. Sometimes, the two overlapped. Those motives meant that recruitment from Wales was always skewed by short-term club needs leading to occasions when there was a glut of

14

players in some positions and a dearth in others. The most desirable positions for many years were stand-off halves, wingers and scrummaging prop forwards.

The players that were subsequently signed owed much to the activities and credibility of their agents on the ground in South Wales. Many agents worked on behalf of more than one club and were paid by results. Most of the scouting and first contacts were carried out by those agents who then passed recommendations on to one or more NRL clubs. Generally, the final negotiations and payment were overseen by a club representative. Whatever agreement was reached between the club and player, there was never any guarantee that it would work out for the latter. Of course, there was no road back to rugby union.

For many of those young men the journey northwards would be their first time out of Wales. Those from Cardiff and Swansea would not find cities like Bradford and Manchester too overwhelming. Neither would they be out of place in a smaller mining town. But, those from west Wales appeared to have been more affected by a loss of certainties of home, chapel and community or the necessity to live life in English which could stoke a homesickness that could erode a player's determination to cope in a new game up north.

Agents would try to get the best men they could for the money and their success rate would fluctuate from season-to-season in terms of both numbers and quality. Each major signing from among the 20 or so who went north each season increased the chances of the NU team beating the Anglo-Saxons. It was, however, a process that left the Welsh selectors with a very limited player pool of disparate talents to work with and meant some converts enjoyed very rapid promotion to the national team. A limited pool was also very susceptible to disruption by injuries.

Coventry

Following an RFU inquiry into 'veiled professionalism' in its Coventry club, NU sympathisers formed their own club which was included in the NRL for 1910–11. They also managed to secure The Butts, previously used by the rugby union club, as the NU club's home. That ground, in the old heart of the city of Coventry, had been a regular venue for Midland Counties Cup finals. Rugby returned to the site with the opening of the Butts Park Arena in 2004.

Public interest in the NU's pioneering Midlands club remained strong, but considering that practically every Saturday they would have competition from one or sometimes both of Coventry RUFC and Coventry City, holding this interest was not going to be easy. To aid those local pioneers in their fight, the England versus Wales match was arranged at The Butts on Saturday 10 December 1910, when the NU had the city to themselves.

Saturday 10 December 1910: England 39 Wales 13
Coventry, 4,500

There was an interesting selection in the Welsh team when the much-travelled Dai Davies was chosen as one of the half-backs. Twelve years earlier Davies had grabbed the chance to leave Llanelli for Swinton in the spring of 1899. Three years later, he packed in rugby to join nearby Bolton Wanderers as a goalkeeper. At the start of 1910, having played in goal for Wales, Davies returned to Swinton and reclaimed his place in the Lions' team. He caught the eye of the selectors and aged 30 became the rarest dual international, being capped by both the Welsh FA and NU. He remains the only player ever to appear in both an FA and a NU Cup final. For another Welsh debutant, Ben Gronow, the match offered the chance to get some redress against the old enemy – he had been part of the Welsh XV that had been surprisingly defeated by England at Twickenham the previous January.

Both captains withdrew late in the day. James Lomas's place went to Billy Lynch while the captaincy passed to Jim Leytham. His opposite number, Johnny Thomas, was replaced by Jim Davies, Bert Jenkins assuming the captaincy. Alongside Lynch in the English centres was another Yorkshireman making his first appearance against the Welsh. He was Harold Wagstaff, just 19 years old, who would go on to become one of the NU's all-time greats. For added local interest, England included Jack Tomes from Coventry in the pack – making him that club's first, and, as it turned out, only international representative. With the exception of Tomes and the three Ebbw Vale representatives the remaining players travelled south on the morning of the match – the Yorkshire contingent leaving Leeds at 8.22am and their Lancashire counterparts departing from Manchester at 10.15am.

The ground, which was in a poor state after recent bad weather, was made worse when the morning of the match was marred by wretched weather. Unfortunately, this extended into the afternoon, keeping the attendance down to 4,500 which was well below expectations. Lew Llewellyn opened the scoring, but the points were all one way after that, which allowed England to lead 16–3 when the teams turned round.

Heavy rain marred the second half. The Welsh pack battled on against England's heavier six and Jack Foley and DB Davies added tries. Both were converted by Ben Gronow, but despite his efforts he ended up once again on the losing side. England emerged as easy winners, 39–13. After an early dinner the players and officials headed homeward.

In January 1911, the Merthyr club announced that financial difficulties meant it could no longer pay the rent on their ground and that they would have to close down. Ebbw Vale was left as the sole Welsh NU club. This meant that the Bridge End Field would once again host the return match on Saturday 1 April 1911.

There were a number of late team changes. The only one for England saw Billy Kitchin take the place of Jim Leytham. Wales had to make three changes – 'Chick' Jenkins, who took over as full-back in place of Frank Young, was in turn replaced in the centre by Willie Thomas and Hull's Alf Francis was replaced by WT Davies. Only two of the Welsh team were locally based. All the other players and officials left Leeds and Manchester on the Friday afternoon. Following an overnight stay in Newport, they completed the journey to Ebbw Vale early on Saturday morning. It was hardly ideal preparation and the *Liverpool Evening Express* noted that NU supporters tended to prefer club matches where "the quality of the fare provided is frequently equal to, if not better than that presented by mixed sides where the players are ignorant of each other's moves and intentions".

Saturday 1 April 1911: Wales 8 England 27
Ebbw Vale, 4,000

Although the English backs grabbed the headlines with six of their side's seven tries, 'Forward' reported in the *Athletic News* that the English victory was down to their pack which held a virtual monopoly in the scrums. On a splendid day for rugby, the English XIII were immensely superior. Four tries in the first half before Bert Jenkins got over for Wales enabled England to turn around 12–5 ahead. When play resumed England added a further three tries against a single touchdown by Lew Llewellyn. England's kickers had an off-day with only three successful shots at goal, two conversions and a penalty in the second half, otherwise the scoreline could have been even more embarrassing for the home side. England had recorded their first win, 27–8, in Wales in front of a worryingly low attendance, reported as 4,000.

It was in large part a Huddersfield triumph. Harold Wagstaff was again on the scoresheet with a goal and a try; his club-mate Billy Kitchin went over for two tries. Their efforts ensured that club-mate Tommy Grey ended up on the losing side. The report in the *Athletic News* praised Wagstaff: "Wagstaff by sheer skill and resource completely baffled such experienced defenders as Willie Thomas and Bert Jenkins. He was perfectly unorthodox and passed either inside or outside in a manner which made him the hero of the match ... Never have I witnessed more perfect centre threequarter back play, and the last try was a fitting termination to a game which will, I think, be regarded as Wagstaff's."

'Docker' writing in the *South Wales Argus* was mortified by the poor Welsh performance. "Wales cut an ignominious figure; they were beaten fore and aft and showed none of that pluck, resource or cleverness which characterised their display in the corresponding engagement at Ebbw Vale last season". Striving to find something positive to say he focused on the team's Monmouthshire exiles, who he thought might have been inspired by playing once again at home in front of friends and family, and who were he reckoned the only ones to enhance their reputations. Despite his disappointments, the day was not all bad and he ended his report by saying that "the display was an attractive one and shows how popular the Northern Union code might become in the Principality when played by capable exponents."

Over the first half of the 1911–12 season, Wales had lost to the touring Australians while England had shared the honours with them over a couple of matches. The teams for the meeting of England and Wales were announced and the venue confirmed as the Watersheddings at a NU committee meeting on Tuesday 9 January 1912. Despite a spell of bad weather, the match went ahead as planned on Saturday 20 January, a couple of weeks after the Australians had finished as victors over the NU in the three-match test series.

Saturday 20 January 1912: England 31 Wales 5
Oldham, 8,000

Eleven players who had played in the Australian Test series figured in the match – eight for England and just three for Wales. Only one Oldham player was selected for the match. He was Evan Davies and he had enjoyed a meteoric rise since leaving Llanelli six weeks earlier. Even more remarkable was his successful transition from winger to centre along the way. Included in the Welsh XIII were two players – 'Chick' Jenkins and Lew Llewellyn – who were the last representatives directly from the Ebbw Vale club. It proved to be their last appearances for Wales. Half of the selected Welsh pack dropped out through injury; Ben Gronow, Salford's Joe Pugsley and DB Davies were replaced by Charlie Rees, Frank Shugars and George Thomas. England's only late change saw Jimmy Hilton replace James Lomas at stand-off.

On a day of many postponements, the match went ahead on a sodden pitch, the result of recent wintry weather. There was also a major local counter-attraction; Bolton Wanderers were playing Oldham Athletic at Boundary Park which helped keep the attendance down to a modest 8,000. The late changes to the Welsh pack had left it significantly outweighed and that would prove decisive. England adapted more readily to the heavy conditions and had the Welsh almost continually defending for the whole of the first half. Poor Welsh defence made matters worse and England turned round 22–0 ahead. Although the scoring in the second half was just 9–5 in the home side's favour, the final result, a defeat by nine tries to one, the latter only coming in the closing minutes, was an embarrassment for the Welsh.

By a strange coincidence this match was held on the same day as its Rugby Union equivalent. The England XV, which was captained by Bob Dibble, who was listed as playing for Newport, won 8–0 at Twickenham in front of a 20,000 crowd. Dibble, however, was usually associated with his home town club, Bridgwater Albion. That small Somerset town also had the honour of supplying England's NU captain, Tom Woods, now of Rochdale Hornets.

At the start of March 1912, a million miners had gone on strike in support of their demand for a minimum wage. Coal shortages very soon severely disrupted rail services and with the Government slow to intervene, there was every prospect of the dispute dragging on. Unwilling to gamble on the outcome, the NU decided to end the uncertainties surrounding the journey to Wales and postpone the return match which was scheduled for Ebbw Vale on Saturday 30 March 1912. It was a wise decision. The miners did not return to work until early April and with the season drawing to a close the international would not be rearranged.

The chances of flourishing in isolation were always slim and the biggest surprise was that it took until two days before the 1912–13 season was due to get underway before Ebbw Vale resigned from the NRL. The landlord repossessed their ground and the NU's last Welsh venue for international matches was lost. While new options would take time to develop, the Welsh XIII offered an ongoing connection to South Wales if the NU could make appropriate plans.

Plymouth

With the club game dead in South Wales, the NU shifted its focus to the western counties of England where its supporters were trying to promote the game. To provide some much-needed publicity, the NU agreed to the staging of the England versus Wales match in Plymouth on Saturday 15 February 1913. The chosen venue was the cricket ground at South Devon Place, which had been shared with the Plymouth Rugby Union club. When that club had lost the tenancy and disbanded at the start of the season the ground had passed to a syndicate which intended to establish the NU game in the heart of England's champion rugby union county. The local rugby game had been thrown into disarray by an RFU inquiry which had found cases of players claiming and receiving excessive expenses. This had resulted in many members of the Devon County side being suspended.

The teams for the first international rugby match ever to be played in Devon made their way from Leeds and Manchester via London to assemble in Plymouth early on Friday evening. It had been a journey for some of nearly 400 miles and Ben Gronow was taken ill along the way. He was ordered to rest and his place in the Welsh team was filled by Jack Chilcott. With both Devon Albion and Plymouth Argyle playing away a good crowd was anticipated. A few might well have been attracted to check on the progress of the three west-countrymen on view – the Bridgwater duo, Ernest Jones and Tommy Woods, for England and Bernard Fredericks, once of Devon Albion, for Wales.

Saturday 15 February 1913: England 40 Wales 16
Plymouth, 7,500

In fine conditions, the teams laid on a "capital game of football" for a crowd which the *Western Daily Mail* reporter estimated was "approaching ten thousand". According to the

Manchester Courier "attack seemed to be the sole object and defence did not count for a great deal." The better of what defence there was, was provided by England and they had, in Stanley Moorhouse and Harold Wagstaff, a match-winning attacking combination. England put 37 points on the scoreboard while Wales were scoring their first five by which time the result was academic. Towards the latter part of the second half the Welsh found some better form and created three tries, but by then England were well on the way to a comfortable 40–16 win.

According to an excerpt from the diary of John Counsell published in *Rugby League Journal*, the score on the field had a direct impact on the players' remuneration; the winners received £3 each while the losers got only half that amount. While perhaps not as large as hoped, the attendance was respectable, producing receipts of £250.

After the match, a dinner was held at the Plymouth and Western Counties Liberal Club at which the main figures in the game could meet and discuss future plans for a western league under NU auspices. The players and officials made their return journey to the north early on Sunday morning.

The discussions were, however, all too late. Slow progress had sapped the rebel resolve; the league plan failed to materialise and the Plymouth NU club disbanded the following month. South Devon Place was ordered to remain closed so far as rugby union was concerned. When it appeared that the ground would be lost to housing, the Astor family stepped to in save it and today it forms of Astor Park.

Fees continue to rise

Wigan's representatives travelled to Swansea to watch the town club's young, uncapped half-backs, Sid Jerram and George 'Dodger' Owens, play against Devonport Services. They liked what they saw. Once the banks were open on the morning of Monday 29 September 1913, the two young men went to the Bush Hotel, where in the presence of a solicitor they waited to receive £180 in gold sovereigns plus guarantees of a job paying £2 per week and playing terms of £2.50 for a win, £2 for a draw and £2 unemployment pay if necessary. They took the money and signed the forms, after which the pair left for Wigan a couple of days later.

Forwards were a bit cheaper. In the summer of 1913 Wigan recruited Rees Richards, who had three Welsh rugby union caps, from Aberavon for £140 down, 35/- (£1.75) per match and a job in a local coal mine. Five months later and four years after his final appearance for Wales, 25-year-old George Hayward with five Welsh caps cost Wigan even more. Hayward left Swansea having reputedly received £155 in gold sovereigns, which was claimed to be a new record fee for a forward.

Signing fees, much higher than those paid to most northerners, led to higher expectations and placed huge pressure on a Welsh player. There was a need to rapidly make the grade. The price of failure was to be effectively cast aside by both codes of rugby. Both Jerram and Owens more than repaid their fees over careers that stretched out to 1927 for Wigan and brought regular selection for Wales. Of the two forwards, Richards at least played for Wales, but neither played for Wigan after 1914.

It was almost exactly a year before England and Wales met again, this time in Lancashire at St Helens on Saturday 14 February 1914. Although only four of the Welsh XIII were dual internationals – Percy Coldrick, Willie Davies, Ben Gronow and Rees Richards – the team was considered capable of posing a serious threat to England. Many of them were young and still had much to learn, having only played NU rugby for a few months. They were all only too aware of the need, after four consecutive heavy defeats, for a strong Welsh performance if the series was to maintain some credibility.

Saturday 14 February 1914: England 16 Wales 12
St Helens, 10,000

To get the Knowsley Road ground ready for its first taste of international rugby, St Helens started work on a new stand in January. A section of it was completed in time for the match.

Players from the south-west had regularly appeared for England, but their number reached a new high in this match; the selectors chose two – Billy Hall and Alf Wood – who had appeared for Gloucestershire and two – Ernest Jones and Walter Roman – who had appeared for Somerset. The selectors' failure to choose any St Helens players for the match was blamed when the attendance fell far short of the ground's capacity.

Both teams were keen to impress the selectors who were on the lookout for the sort of players who could make their mark on the tour of Australia and New Zealand that was due to begin in a couple of months' time. It was said that those who paid their admission were served up with some brilliant play. England enjoyed most of the possession from the set-pieces and led 11–6 at half-time. However, the Welsh backs, with Johnny Rogers and Gwyn Thomas to the fore, made the most of their limited opportunities.

They certainly saw a hard, bruising battle as both teams gave their all in their bid for victory. Injuries were inevitable and Wales were probably worst affected. Rees Richards was forced off the field midway through the second half. Both a hobbling Alf Francis and Willie A Davies, who had suffered a broken nose, might also have headed for the sidelines but bravely stayed on the pitch. At the final whistle it was Alf Wood's two goals, the only two of the match, that separated the two teams and gave England a memorable victory, 16–12

Summer 1914

Eight of the Welsh team were judged good enough to be selected for the tour of Australasia that summer. They were Wigan's Gwyn Thomas, the 10-year veteran Bert Jenkins and Percy Coldrick, Huddersfield's Johnny Rogers and Jack Chilcott, Halifax's Frank Williams, Leeds's Willie 'Avon' Davies and Hull's Alf Francis. They were joined in the party by Stuart Prosser of Halifax, who had missed out on selection for that match. Ben Gronow might also have toured if a fractured shoulder suffered in late December had not ruled him out of action for nine weeks. No wonder there were high hopes for the future success of the Welsh team.

Most of the party departed for Australia on 18 April aboard the RMS Otranto. Huddersfield's Johnny Rogers and Jack Chilcott were part of the second group who departed overland on the first leg of the journey to Australia after the Championship Final. They boarded the Otranto at Toulon and left behind a European summer marked by growing international tensions.

Having completed the Ashes series in Australia, the party had moved on to the New Zealand leg of the tour. While staying in Auckland the tourists awoke on the morning of Wednesday 5 August to discover that their worst fears had become reality, Great Britain was at war. Arrangements were made to make the long journey home as soon as possible. Sailing without lights at night to avoid alerting the German raider Emden, which was on the hunt for British shipping somewhere in the Southern Ocean, the touring party had a tense voyage home. Fortunately, the ship managed to steer clear of the enemy and the tourists disembarked safely at Plymouth on Saturday 26 September.

3. The First World War

Two months into the conflict it had become increasingly clear that any expectations of a short, sharp war were a fantasy. Facing up to the new realities of wartime, the NU decided in October 1914 to cancel the County Championship and abandoned the preparations for a proposed international match. The conflict put an end to a dispiriting run of five consecutive defeats for the Welsh XIII and would in due course bring to an end a few international careers. For one man, Bert Jenkins, it ended an international presence that had seen him play in every Welsh XIII since its launch; a run of 11 consecutive appearances for Wales, eight of them against England.

A year on, as the conflict had intensified and become ever more deadly, both rugby codes found themselves much changed. Except for some matches in and around the Armed Forces, the rugby union world which had ceased playing almost immediately war declared was still practically inactive. The once professional NU had been forced to suspend all its official competitions and was effectively operating as a liberal amateur body.

All that would change as the end of 1915 drew nigh. Large numbers of troops were arriving in Britain from the rugby playing Dominions – primarily Australia, New Zealand and South Africa. Both rugby codes recognised there was a need to engage with those forces by restarting some form of representative teams.

Along the way charitable funds could be raised and the handling game could reclaim its place in the football world. There was never any real doubt about which rugby code would take the lead. The NU just did not have the contacts in the right places in the military. An unofficial group of influential rugby union officials certainly did and they sprang into action in the spring of 1916.

The North of England Military XV

Even in wartime, there was something special about a meeting of England and Wales and where the NU could not tread, others did not hesitate. Bob Oakes, the honorary secretary of the Yorkshire Rugby Union, saw the possibilities of using rugby to aid the war effort. He set about raising a team and organising matches in conjunction with the military authorities for the benefit of service charities. By restricting selection to either enlisted men or those waiting for enlistment, Oates obviously felt confident enough to include NU men without incurring the wrath of either the RFU or the WFU. His teams which were linked to various northern garrisons adopted the title of the North of England Military XV.

For his team's third and final match, Oakes arranged to play early in the close season against a Welsh XV, raised by Captain Walter Rees, the secretary of the WFU, which contained six pre-war internationals and one future one. In a show of unity, Oakes's XV included seven NRL players, three of them – Willie A Davies, Ben Gronow and Johnny Rogers – Welsh. Another of them – Charlie Seeling – was an original All Black. One of Oakes's men – JEC Partridge – was a 1903 Springbok while two – John Dobson and Andrew Hamilton – were Scottish internationals. They met the Welsh on Saturday 20 May 1916 at Anfield, the home of Liverpool AFC, in aid of the Lord Mayor's Roll of Honour Fund. The Northern Military XV beat the Welsh XV 5–4. A good wartime crowd, estimated as somewhere between 15,000 and 20,000 by the *Yorkshire Evening Post*, but given as 14,000 in the *Liverpool Daily Post*, watched the match.

Wartime losses

Thrice-capped Phillip Thomas was coming to the end of his playing career with Hull KR when he enlisted in August 1914. He was killed by shellfire during the Second Battle of Ypres in May 1915. George Thomas, who had left Newport for Warrington in August 1903, was a member of the Welsh pack that took on England in January 1912. Once war broke out, he enlisted and was killed in action on the Somme at the start of July 1916.

Two English forwards who made their debut in February 1914 – Walter Roman (Rochdale Hornets) and Fred Longstaff (Huddersfield) – would go on to enlist in their respective local regiments, the Somerset Light Infantry and the West Yorkshires, before dying as a result of wounds received on the Somme in late July.

Reinstatement

With the German forces in full retreat an Armistice finally came into effect at 11am on 11 November 1918. Amateurs and professionals had got on fine during the conflict and there were some unions which wished to bring at least some of the pre-war professionals back into the fold. The WFU was one of them and a handful of prominent professional players applied for re-instatement. Among them where two former Newport (and Pill Harriers) forwards – Percy Coldrick and Gus Merry – and two former Swansea half-backs – Sid Jerram and George Owens. Coldrick and Merry's applications were refused as both had played NU regularly during the conflict. Both Jerram and Owens had been wounded while serving in France but, contrary to expectations, that cut no ice with the WFU which rejected their applications.

Two matches were arranged between a Welsh XV and a New Zealand Services XV over the festive period. On both occasions the Welsh XV included both amateurs and professionals. For the Boxing Day clash at Swansea's St Helen's ground, Willie A Davies (Leeds), Sid Jerram (Wigan) and Percy Coldrick (Wigan) were included. Coldrick retained his place alongside Bobbie Lloyd (Halifax) for the second match at the Arms Park on New Year's Day. Jim Bacon, who played in both, is often listed as a Leeds player, but he did not make his official debut until 25 January 1919. He had, however, played as a trialist under a pseudonym in mid-December, but had chosen to return to Cross Keys at that time.

In January 1919, as the WFU reasserted its authority, all those who had played in the NU were barred from any involvement in Welsh rugby union. While the WFU might have maintained some sympathies for reinstatement, it accepted that it was impossible to achieve while the RFU was intransigently opposed. All the Welsh professionals who had played in the matches against the New Zealand Services XV – Coldrick, Davies, Jerram, Lloyd and Owens – played a major part in getting their NU clubs and the Welsh XIII up and running again.

4. An emerging power

Official NU competitions got underway again in mid-January 1919 as the influenza epidemic continued to cause havoc in the country's towns and cities. As the clubs rushed to put the strongest possible teams back on the field there was no doubt that many of their returning players were past their best. Many of those younger players who had come through the years of conflict had been starved of the necessary quality game-time to reach the standard required to plug the gaps. Quality players were in short supply and the NRL's clubs would once again have to look outside the north of England to find suitable recruits. The Welsh recruits would soon be ready to try and make Wales a force once more.

Once the clubs were up and running again, international rugby was able to return. It was driven by an invitation to tour from the NSW Rugby League which was accepted by the NU committee in March 1919. That decision galvanised the NU, but not perhaps always as hoped. After their wartime hiatus, it was imperative that home international matches were restarted and it initially seemed that would happen. It was planned to hold an England versus a reborn Other Nationalities match at Workington on Saturday 7 February 1920. That match, however, was withdrawn from the fixture list by the NU committee on 16 December in favour of two trial matches in readiness for the upcoming Australasian tour.

Play restarts

Nearly seven years had elapsed by the time the NU got round to organising the first post-war meeting of England and Wales at Headingley on Wednesday 19 January 1921. Four members of the Welsh side had survived the carnage to provide some continuity – Jack Beames of Halifax and three from Huddersfield, Ben Gronow, Johnny Rogers and Gwyn Thomas. England's own continuity should have been provided by Billy Batten, Douglas Clark and Harold Wagstaff, but the latter was nursing an injury and had to stand down in favour of Albert Akroyd.

Delayed by the conflict and the tardiness of the NU in getting the international back onto the fixture list, Jonty Parkin was already in his mid-20s when chosen to make his England debut. The tactical acumen and leadership qualities he showed with Wakefield Trinity became more pronounced on the international stage and he would go on to become England's half-back general and captain of choice throughout the 1920s.

The afternoon was enlivened by the presence of a number of famous boxers who were in the city for a tournament. Georges Carpentier, the famous French heavyweight, was introduced to the players while Jimmy Wilde, the world flyweight champion, got the first half underway and Joe Beckett, the British heavyweight champion, the second. Their presence lifted a crowd of 13,000.

Wednesday 19 January 1921: England 35 Wales 9
Leeds, 13,000

Early in the match, Wales's Harold Whitney was hurt in a collision with Rothwell Marlor and had to be stretchered off. Despite being a man down, the depleted Welsh pack did well to hold the English six. Both sides attacked strongly. England registered tries by Herman Hilton and Jonty Parkin while Brinley Williams grabbed one for Wales. Ben Gronow and Billy Rhodes had matched each other with two goals apiece to leave England ahead 10–7 at the break.

Brinley Williams was the best of a Welsh back division that was badly outclassed in the second half. Harold Whitney gamely returned to the field to level up the numbers, but he could do little to change the course of the match. England added five converted tries to their total while Wales could only manage a penalty goal from Ben Gronow.

Such a one-sided victory, 35–9, was hardly the result to give the series impetus going forward. The following day the *Hull Daily Mail* reporter reflected that "some of the spectators of the match must have wondered why, in the face of the disparity in skill and vigour, it should be thought necessary to go to Wales for football players. The native Northern Union talent has always been superior in these official tests in the past, and on yesterday's showing it is immeasurably so today."

The NU committee magnanimously decided that half of the gate receipts, £818, should be given to Bradford Northern to enable the financially ailing club pay off various debts and hopefully begin to pay its way.

Other Nationalities

After the match at Headingley, the NU committee met up over dinner to pick the teams for a meeting of England and Other Nationalities that was due to take place at Workington in three weeks time. For this match, the first international ever to be held in Cumberland, nine of the Welshmen who had taken on England at Headingley were included in the Other Nationalities team along with another four Welshmen. Other Nationalities would, in fact, be all-Welsh. Proposals were made that as the title 'Other Nationalities' was a misnomer; it should be re-labelled Wales as they would wear the red shirts of Wales. The NU rejected this seemingly sensible request, and officially the match was recorded as being against Other Nationalities although both the *Athletic News* and the *Manchester Guardian* referred to England's opponents as Wales.

Only two of the Other Nationalities team had not previously played for Wales against England. Of those two, Wyndham Emery achieved that honour later in the year. The unlucky one was Wickham Powell who was said to have received a record signing on fee of £750 when he left Cardiff for Rochdale in the summer of 1920. He suffered a seemingly career-ending broken collarbone while playing for Rochdale Hornets against the touring Australians in November 1921 and his chances of becoming a dual international were effectively over, although he did make a comeback in 1924.

For more details on this match see the chapter entitled 'Off the record' later in this book.

Midweek internationals

The policy of scheduling its internationals on weekday afternoons might have meant less disruption to the first team selections for the NRL's Saturday programme, but it denied the NU the opportunity to capitalise on the interest shown in weekend rail excursions which proved so popular with Welsh rugby union fans wishing to support their teams. Their presence in the crowd greatly assisted in creating a true international match-day atmosphere.

There was a huge growth in travelling support between the wars. In January 1923 an estimated 9,000 fans travelled to Twickenham to support a very limited Welsh rugby union team. By January 1927, *The Observer* went so far as to describe the Welsh supporters arriving at Paddington *en route* for Twickenham as a "Celtic Invasion of London". Hard times did little to halt the flow. An upgraded Twickenham held a record Championship crowd of 64,000 for the visit of Wales in January 1933.

Similar huge Welsh exoduses became a feature of the union internationals at Murrayfield. The growth of Welsh travelling support was rapid. For the Scotland match in February 1928 the number making the trip north was given as 5,000. This number had increased to 13,000 in 1932 and two years later it took 27 special trains to move an estimated 15,000 Welsh supporters to Edinburgh. The attendance at Murrayfield that year was 60,000. By 1938, the railway companies were speculating that it might require 43 specials to move 20,000 Welsh fans.

If the RFL had wanted to tap into that potential Welsh interest, it had to arrange the match well in advance on a Saturday, allow plenty of time for thorough preparation on-and-off the field, and bring a touch of professional glamour to the proceedings. If high standards could be set and maintained there was reason to hope that the RFL's version could raise itself to similar heights as the rugby union internationals.

The birth of Rugby League

From the start of their tour in September 1921 there was much lobbying by the Kangaroos' management to address the issue of the rebel game's 'outdated' name. Their efforts paid off when, against a background of spreading unemployment, industrial unrest and global economic problems, the NU at its AGM held at Huddersfield's George Hotel on Wednesday 14 June 1922 voted unanimously to rename itself the Rugby Football League (RFL) in the hope that the change would give the game a wider significance in both a national and international sense.

One unintended side-effect of the change was that the team representing the NU in test matches became labelled as 'England', not Great Britain. That anomaly would persist for the next 25 years.

Hard times

Hopes of a prosperous peace proved to be short-lived. The post-war economic boom soon came to an end and an economic depression soon followed. As hard times set in, quite a few rugby union players in South Wales were open to offers to join clubs in the NRL and business was soon even brisker than it had been pre-war. The only difference this time was that the northern representatives did business with white £5 notes; the minting of gold sovereigns had ceased in 1917. Bill Samuel recounts in his book *Rugby: Body and Soul* details of Swinton's signing of 'Billo' Rees in November 1921. Young Rees, a highly promising half-back, had struck a deal with Swinton's representatives. He received £500 in white-fivers and the promise of a job in return for his signature. When he returned to the family home in the mining village of Garnant with his new-found wealth, his mother was not at all impressed by this pile of paper. Bursting into tears, she told him "They have deceived you. This is not money." She was wrong and 'Billo' was right to be happy.

Besides Rees, the second half of 1921 also saw several internationals take the road north, two of them from Llanelli, Edgar Morgan to Hull in July and Frank Evans to Swinton in August.

Edgar Morgan, a flank forward with four Welsh rugby union caps, having left Llanelli RUFC for Hull FC a couple of months before Rees went north, was considered a real catch.

In a profile published in the *Hull Daily Mail* in mid-July, it was reported that Morgan had played the NU game while in the Army and it was hoped he would therefore be able to make an impact almost immediately. Those hopes proved well founded. After only seven matches the 25-year-old Morgan was selected to play for the NU against Australia in the first Test at Headingley on 1 October 1921. His strong running play in Britain's second-row was praised and he retained his place for the second Test. The same qualities that brought Morgan international honours in Welsh rugby union – good mobility, fierce tackling and an ability to wheel a scrummage and dribble away – were what won him international honours in the NU.

Not moving

Generally, when a Welsh player signed for a rugby league club, he was expected to move north. Only the exceptional could defy that expectation. Newport's Jerry Shea was a controversial character whose time on the rugby field was curtailed by the First World War. Midway through that conflict, he decided to branch out and embarked on a career as a professional boxer. When peace returned, he continued to box professionally while pursuing international honours on the rugby field. Playing at centre, he made his debut against England on 17 January 1920. Juggling commitments was not always easy and Shea declined to travel to Paris for Wales's rugby union match on 17 February because he was booked for a boxing contest. His mercurial and sometimes wayward play had by then attracted the attention of the NU scouts. Shea certainly knew his worth and despite being in his 30th year managed to secure a record fee of £700 when he signed for Wigan on 10 December 1921. It might have been expected that sooner rather than later he would relocate to the town. He had not by the time he made his debut on Christmas Day 1921 and never lived there during the three seasons he spent at Central Park.

Over those seasons Shea continued to live and train in Newport, only travelling north for matches. After ending his career with Wigan, Shea briefly resumed his professional boxing career, and achieved a notable victory over Johnny Basham over 15 rounds at Newport on 17 November 1924.

It would be nearly two years before England and Wales met again. During that time both England and Wales had matches against the touring Australasians. England achieved the narrowest possible victory in their first post-war outing while Wales pushed the tourists all the way before losing 21–16 at Pontypridd.

The restart England versus Wales international was the first of its kind for a couple of reasons. It was the first to be held under the auspices of the renamed governing body, the Rugby Football League, and the first in which the players were paid according to an agreement made between the NU and the short-lived NU Players' Union in September 1921. In future the players would receive £7 for Test matches, but only £5 for other internationals.

By 1922–23 there were reckoned to be over 40 Welshmen playing regularly in the NRL; Rochdale Hornets alone had 10 on their register by July 1923. That was enough to provide the Welsh selectors with options in most positions, but it was still far less than the hundreds that the English selectors had to choose from.

The international held on Monday 11 December 1922 had been proposed by Charles Wreford-Brown, an Old Carthusian, a former international association footballer and future vice-president of the FA, acting on behalf of St Dunstan's Hospital for Blinded Soldiers and Sailors in Regent's Park.

England 1922–23, captained by Jonty Parkin (Courtesy *Rugby League Journal*)

England versus Wales 11 December 1922 at Herne Hill. Cartoon by Em Shaw. Players: Billy Batten, Bob Taylor, Bill Stone, George Oliver and Edgar Morgan. (Courtesy Robert Gate)

London County Athletic Ground, Herne Hill

Wreford-Brown's plans hit problems when both Stamford Bridge and Highbury were found to be unavailable and he arranged for the match to go ahead at the London County Athletic Ground at Herne Hill, better known for its cycle track. Although this was once again the home ground of London Welsh RUFC, accommodation was rudimentary with only a small covered stand. Also, the ground in Dulwich was difficult to reach by train from Victoria. For this ground, with a poor playing surface, and whose only facilities were at the nearby Half Moon Hotel, London Welsh were paying £225 per annum in rent.

When a deputation from the RFL inspected the ground the day before the match, they "expressed their disappointment at so badly-equipped a ground being provided for the match" according to the *Yorkshire Post*.

Monday 11 December 1922: England 12 Wales 7
London, 3,000

There were seven dual internationals in the Welsh XIII, five of them in the pack. There were also four players from Wigan in the Welsh team. This was lower than might have been expected as that club was probably the most assiduous and successful recruiter at the time. For the Lancashire Cup Final against Leigh three weeks earlier, Wigan's victorious team had included 11 players recruited from the Principality – all seven backs and four of the forwards. The Wigan team that day was: Jim Sullivan (Cardiff); Danny Hurcombe (Talywain), Jerry Shea (Newport), Tommy Howley (Ebbw Vale), Johnny Ring (Aberavon); George Owens (Swansea), Sid Jerram (Swansea); Wilf Hodder (Pontypool), Tom Woods (Pontypool), Bert Webster, Percy Coldrick (Newport), Harry Banks, Fred Roffey (Ebbw Vale). It says a lot about the quality of Wigan's scouting that Danny Hurcombe had been signed before he even left his junior club, Talywain, for senior Welsh rugby. Of those 11 Welsh recruits, three – Owens, Jerram and Coldrick – had been signed prior to the First World War. Banks and Webster were the only Wiganers.

Pontypool-born seaman, Tommy Woods, was both a dual international and on Wigan's books. His play for the Royal Navy and United Services had caught the attention of the RFU's selectors and he had accepted their invitation to play for England in the Calcutta Cup match on 20 March 1920. He made another four appearances for England the following season before accepting an offer to join Wigan. Although at 32 he was nearly at the veteran stage, the Welsh selectors made contact and Woods grabbed the chance to revert to the country of his birth. He made his debut packing down alongside his Wigan team-mate, Wilf Hodder.

The Welsh full-back, also from Wigan, was at the other end of the age-spectrum. Cardiff-born Jim Sullivan, then just 18, had been called up in place of the injured Gwyn Thomas to face the touring Kangaroos the previous December. One year on, the precociously talented teenager was given his first outing against England. English XIIIs would soon grow weary of the sight of Sullivan in a red jersey.

A keenly fought encounter played to a high standard was captured by a *British Pathe* film crew for use in cinema newsreels. The forward battle took up much of the match. The Welsh pack did well to hold the wholly Lancastrian six facing them and laid the basis for their side to reach half-time with a one-point lead. After the break, Brinley Williams damaged an ankle and had to leave the field. This limited the effectiveness of the Welsh backs. The two sides' attacks largely cancelled each out in the second half. Very near the close of play, Billy Stone and then Jonty Parkin crossed the line to ensure an English victory. Gold medals were presented to the winning English team by Lord Colwyn.

A meagre Monday afternoon attendance was estimated at 3,000, the majority of whom had to stand in the cold on the surrounding cycle track. They provided receipts which only covered the cost of staging the match. The RFL generously agreed to defray that cost and donated £250 to the funds of St Dunstan's Hospital.

Two months later, a return match was held in the north of England. For the first time the venue was Wigan's Central Park, which was considered by many associated with the town to be the best NU ground in Lancashire.

Wednesday 7 February 1923: England 2 Wales 13
Wigan, 12,000

This time six Wigan players, five of them backs, were picked for the expensively assembled Welsh XIII. Sullivan, Shea and Woods retained their places and were joined by Hurcombe, Jerram and Owens. It speaks volumes for Wigan's recruitment strategy that none of their players were picked for England.

On a muddy pitch, the Welsh were far more enterprising in attack. They shocked the supposed 'home' side by their endeavour and led by a converted try and a penalty goal to nil at the break. England lost Jonty Parkin due to injury shortly after the break and the task of containing the Welshmen with just 12 players proved beyond them. The Welsh crossed for two more tries. All England had to show for their efforts was a penalty goal from Billy Stone. The Welsh scorers – Danny Hurcombe, Fred Brown and Jim Sullivan – were either Wigan men or soon would be and they ensured that the visitors recorded their first victory on English soil.

Monday 1 October 1923: England 18 Wales 11
Huddersfield, 11,066

It was a sign of the decline of Huddersfield's once all-powerful 'Team of all the Talents' that its only representative on its own Fartown turf was Ben Gronow. There was a late change to both teams – Evan Davies came in for Jim Bacon and Frank Todd replaced Jonty Parkin.

After only two years in the NRL, Featherstone Rovers had their first international. Jack Hirst appeared at centre for England. Hundreds of supporters travelled from Featherstone to Fartown to cheer on their man, but he had little chance to shine as the half-backs were said to have wanted "to go it alone".

On an otherwise fine autumn day, strong wind and sun made this a definite game of two halves. England played with the elements behind them in the first half and notched up 18 unanswered points. After the break it was Wales's turn, but their reply fell seven points short.

Crossing borders

In the days before the rugby game split, both England and Wales had selected players who were equally qualified for either. It is hardly surprising that the NU and later the RFL also faced the same problem in setting a hard and fast rule on the question of national eligibility. In practice, it came down to an individual's preference and both nations attempted to convince any players with a choice to choose them. England derived the most benefit.

Frank Williams, who played for Wales NU in 1914, was Birmingham-born but Welsh-raised. He had played for Wales against England in the first-ever schools international held in Cardiff for under-14s in March 1904. Williams received £200 in gold sovereigns to leave Swansea and join Halifax in May 1913. He was one of many Welsh schoolboy caps to make their way north.

Jack Evans from Llanelli had been a stalwart Welsh forward in the late 1890s before accepting an offer to join Swinton. After a spell back in South Wales when his playing days were over, he returned to Swinton to assist with coaching in 1914. Moving north with him was his son Evan Evans, better known as Jack. Jack turned out to be a very good rugby player and made his first appearance for England in 1924–25. His younger brother, Bryn, born in Swinton, was a good player as well and made his debut for England in 1930–31.

Salford signed the Bath-born Edward C 'Teddy' Haines from Bargoed in August 1921. His play in a struggling side caught the selectors' attention and he made his debut in England's pack in April 1927. Arthur G 'Ginger' Thomas, who made his debut in the Leeds pack in the 1922–23 season, was born in Llanelli, but had moved aged five to Leeds with his parents. A nephew of Jim Watts, a Welsh forward in the first 'Golden Era', Thomas was a product of Hunslet Intermediates. Thomas spurned the approaches of the Welsh selectors, opted for England and was capped against Wales in 1930–31.

Wales did manage to 'capture' a few very useful forwards. Ten days after winning his first and only Welsh union cap against England in January 1923, a 20-year-old Bristol-born forward named Joe Thompson had left his job as a miner and was leaving Cross Keys for Yorkshire with £300 to his name. He made six appearances for Wales against the country of his birth. Aubrey Casewell might have hailed from Powys but it was as a product of the Manchester and District League that he signed for Salford as a teenager and went on to play for Wales in 1932–33. Another who stayed loyal to the land of his father's was Edwin 'Sandy' Orford, born in Pontypool but resident in Wakefield from when he was a teenager. Orford joined Dewsbury at the age of 16. He later played for Bradford Northern in 1934–35 before signing for Wakefield Trinity in 1938–39 and went on to represent Wales during the Second World War.

Propaganda in Cumbria

The RFL had planned its international programme along the same format as that of 1920–21 with the England versus Wales match at Headingley on Wednesday 15 October 1924 and England versus the Other Nationalities at Workington on Saturday 7 February. That plan was subsequently changed and the fixtures were transposed.

Lonsdale Park, once the home of the handling game in Workington, was taken over by the Workington 'Reds' association football team in 1921 and was their home until 1937. It was not an exclusive lease and during that time it was regularly hired by the RFL for county matches and also staged three internationals.

The second of the internationals brought Wales to Workington and was part of a bid to revive rugby league's fortunes in the town, which had been depressed since the loss of the old senior club, the Zebras, in autumn 1909.

Having previously lost to the Other Nationalities, only six members of the England team retained their places. Their opponents made only one team change, Edgar Morgan replacing Wigan's Fred Brown in the Welsh pack.

Saturday 7 February 1925: England 27 Wales 22
Workington, 14,000

On a bright sunny afternoon, a county rugby league record crowd of 14,000 enjoyed the feast of attacking rugby that the two sides served up. On a heavy pitch, England went on the attack right away and had three tries and two conversions on the scoreboard in the first 15 minutes. It seemed that the Welsh were facing a drubbing. However, they organised themselves and fought back. Johnny Ring scored twice to close the gap which England countered with a try by Jack Evans. Joe Thompson in turn crossed for Wales and Sullivan was successful with his first kick of the afternoon. That score was the final one of the first half, the teams turning round with England 18–11 ahead.

When the game restarted, the tries began to flow once more. Frank Evans touched down for Wales and Charlie Carr and Bob Taylor for England to put the home side ahead 24–14. But, the Welsh were not finished yet and a third try for Johnny Ring and a second for Frank Evans, converted by Jim Sullivan narrowed the gap to just two points. English anxiety was quelled when the locally-born veteran, Douglas Clark, got over for his side's seventh try of the match in the 75th minute to seal a 27–22 win. The usually reliable Jim Sullivan missed three easy conversions which effectively cost Wales the match.

Just four weeks into the new season, an international was held at Wigan on Wednesday 30 September 1925. The only changes to the published teams were Stan Langshaw for Sid Rix and Sid Jerram for Ike Fowler. Laurie Osborne had passed a late fitness check prior to the match.

Wednesday 30 September 1925: England 18 Wales 14
Wigan, 12,000

On a dull afternoon, there was a 'satisfactory' midweek attendance of 12,000. England played for all but 10 minutes of this match with only 12 men. Stan Langshaw had to leave the field with a rib injury. Frank Gallagher was withdrawn from the pack, but his absence had little effect as England's five forwards managed to hold the Welsh six and even managed to secure plenty of possession from the scrums. It took half-an-hour for the first points to be scored by England's Bill Burgess. Wales replied through a try by Dai Rees and the first half finished with the score tied at 3–3.

The teams continued to match each other, try for try, as the lead changed hands after the break. England managed to defend a narrow four-point lead for the last quarter of an hour to claim victory. In the end the win was down to the contribution of Laurie Osborne whose two conversions and a drop-goal made the difference over Jim Sullivan who could only manage a drop-goal on his home ground.

Taff Vale Park, Pontypridd

Taff Vale Park in Treforest was a well-known venue, famous for its promotion of professional athletics and cycling meetings since the turn of the century. It claimed a capacity of around 35,000 even though its seating was rather limited. In 1911 it had become the home of Pontypridd's Southern League association football team, the Pontypridd 'Dragons'. When the Welsh XIII had first hired Taff Vale Park for the visit of the Australasians in December 1921, they had drawn an encouraging crowd of 13,000. Besides being situated at the confluence of the industrial Rhondda and Taff river valleys, Pontypridd was well-served by railway connections.

British politics was polarising, especially in the industrial districts as labour and capital squared off for what some of the militants from both sides hoped would be the final showdown. The outlook was certainly stormy as the teams journeyed south to meet in the Principality for the first time in 13 years. Jim Sullivan took over as Welsh captain for the match which was arranged for the afternoon of Monday 12 April 1926.

Both teams made changes from their match in Wigan, Wales made seven changes, including both half-backs and three in the pack. England made five, mainly in the backs and half-backs. The English XIII were considered favourites after easily accounting for Other Nationalities in a promotional clash at Whitehaven two months earlier.

Monday 12 April 1926: Wales 22 England 30
Pontypridd, 23,000

Jim Bacon was late replacement for Johnny Ring in the Welsh line-up. The original clubs of the members of the Welsh XIII were, Jim Sullivan (Cardiff); Frank Evans (Llanelli), Mel Rosser (Penarth), Joe Jones (Swansea), Jim Bacon (Cross Keys); Ike Fowler (Llanelli), 'Billo' Rees (Glanamman); Wilf Hodder (Pontypool), Edgar Morgan (Llanelli), Fred Roffey (Ebbw Vale), Joe Thompson (Cross Keys), Dai Rees (Llanelli) and Bryn Phillips (Aberavon).

Nine of them had been capped by the WRU before moving north. Four had been awarded just one cap while the most capped with five was Bryn Phillips. He had been a Glamorgan Police constable who had earned five caps in the Welsh rugby union pack in 1925 and 1926. The last of those had come against England at the Arms Park on 16 January 1926. Having resigned from the force, the 25-year-old signed for Huddersfield for a fee of £600 and scored the opening try for his new club on his debut on 6 February. Ten weeks later he was in Pontypridd making his debut for the Welsh XIII.

The match got underway at five o'clock. The huge crowd was said to be enthralled by the fast open play. For the *Yorkshire Post* reporter, it was perhaps too open; in his opinion the match was "If anything, too much on the exhibition side". With attack taking priority over defence, there were eight tries in the first half, five of them to England. Trailing 19–13 when play resumed after the break, the Welsh had also lost the services of Joe Jones while Dai Rees was severely hampered by a leg injury which made the contest rather one-sided. England capitalised; three quick tries from Bill Burgess, Billy Bentham and Charlie Carr gave them in an unassailable lead. A beleaguered Welsh side never stopped trying and as England relaxed, Frank Evans and Ike Fowler grabbed a couple of consolation tries. If Jim Sullivan had had a better day with the boot the final score might have been closer than 30–22.

The *Yorkshire Post* report reckoned that "every rugby stronghold in the Principality was represented at the match" which attracted an attendance of 23,000, the highest ever for an England-Wales international and a record at the time for a rugby league match in south Wales. It was hoped that some of the enthusiasm shown at the international match would rub off on the new Pontypridd RLFC which was formed in mid-May 1926 by a group of local businessmen to take over the defunct Dragons' lease on Taff Vale Park. This new club, which was entirely self-funded, had to be put together in just three months. Pontypridd's application to join the NRL, which received unanimous support on 10 June 1926, raised the league's membership to 29 clubs.

Wales versus England 12 April 1926 (Courtesy Robert Gate)

Hard times in the strike-bound valleys

The inter-war years were an unhappy time for the Welsh RU's national team. Inconsistent selection and captaincy choices produced some poorly balanced teams which in turn led to too many defeats, some of them heavy. Some of the associated problems could be attributed to the dismal economic situation in the coal and steel producing areas where unemployment reached almost catastrophic levels. Many good players, in the valleys especially, were only too willing to listen to the offers that were forthcoming from representatives of rugby league clubs.

Many sports suffered in the aftermath of the 1926 General Strike. Arguably, rugby league's Pontypridd club suffered more than most, being launched at undoubtedly the worst possible time. Although the TUC called off the May strike action after 10 days, the continuing miners' dispute lasted until the end of November. By then the strike was collapsing and the miners returned to work facing longer hours and lower wages. Unemployment in general, and in the mining districts in particular, rose sharply and the future for many young men looked bleak.

There was no doubt the prolonged miners' strike dealt a profound economic blow to the south Wales valleys. Strike-bound, the impoverished inhabitants struggled to maintain even a basic standard of living. Leaving might be a wrench, but it offered a lifeline. Many of the young people sought new opportunities in England, some of them in the northern counties where a job and a rugby league career often went hand in hand.

Among the capped players who decided to go north that dreadful autumn were five forwards – Emlyn Watkins and Dan Pascoe, both to Leeds, Dai L Jones to Wigan, Syd Hinam to Rochdale Hornets and David M Jenkins to Hunslet. Quite a few others, as yet uncapped, would make the same journey.

33

Welsh talent exhausted?

It was the worst possible timing for the New Zealand rugby league team, who were making their first tour of Britain for nearly 20 years as the miners battled on through the autumn. To make matters worse, the Kiwi party was torn apart by internal feuds and were not expected to provide strong opposition, especially in midweek. The New Zealand management was invited to attend a meeting of the RL Council in late November where moves, ultimately successful, by the NRL's wealthiest clubs to lift the ban on the signing of colonial rugby players were agreed. In a dispatch home one of the Kiwi managers, Norman Mair, wrote that "it is apparent that the feeling amongst many of the League clubs is to even raise the ban on rugby league players in Australia and New Zealand. The English clubs are ever on the lookout for classy backs, and now that Wales has been exhausted their field for players must naturally turn towards Australia and New Zealand."

A couple of weeks later Mair had the opportunity to see for himself the quality of the NRL's Welsh recruits. New Zealand took on a supposedly below strength Welsh team containing four Pontypridd players at Taff Vale Park on Saturday 4 December. The Welsh proved far too good, overwhelming the Kiwis 34–8. Despite the great hardship in the mining districts, the attendance, 18,000, producing receipts of £700, was remarkably good in the circumstances.

The next England versus Wales match was tucked into the gap between the Challenge Cup semi-finals and the semi-finals of the NRL Championship on Wednesday 6 April 1927. Broughton Rangers hosted the match once again, but this time at a different venue. The Rangers had moved home in 1913 to The Cliff in Higher Broughton, a short tram ride northwards along Lower Broughton Road from where Wheater's Field had once stood.

Pontypridd supplied three members of the Welsh pack – Albert Green, George Oliver, once of Hull, and Ponty Davies. Alf Frodsham won his first England cap at the expense of the injured Jack Evans.

Wednesday 6 April 1927: England 11 Wales 8
Broughton, 6,000

A thrilling, highly enjoyable match at The Cliff was watched by a disappointing crowd of 6,000. Despite being well beaten in the scrums – they secured possession from only one in every four – the Welsh backs kept their team in the hunt. A low-scoring first half finished with Wales leading 5–3, thanks to a try by Johnny Ring, converted by Jim Sullivan against Charlie Carr's try for England. Each nation scored a try after the restart, but the crucial moment came in the 65th minute, when England's star winger Alf Ellaby crossed for a try to secure the home side's victory.

Hard times in the valleys had hit Pontypridd's gates badly and for the visit of Oldham on Saturday 22 October 1927, only £24 was taken. It proved to be Pontypridd's final match; the club's resignation was accepted four days later at a meeting of the NRL management committee in Manchester. The previous month, Taff Vale Park, where the layout made it suitable for greyhound racing, was bought by a group of promoters with the backing of the Greyhound Racing Association (GRA). Rugby league had no place in their plans.

Although the NRL's sole Welsh club was no longer operational, their hooker, Les White, was chosen for the Welsh team two months later. The 22-year-old White kept his place by signing for Hunslet in June, where he succeeded his fellow country-man Charlie Sage.

Ahead of the match at Central Park on Wednesday 11 January 1928, injuries ruled out Jim Brough and Charlie Carr. They were replaced in the England line-up by Tommy Dingsdale and Joe Oliver.

Wednesday 11 January 1928: England 20 Wales 12
Wigan, 12,000

On a sunny winter's day, this match marked the start in many ways of the long road to a place on the summer tour of Australia and New Zealand. It was a fluctuating contest with the advantage swapping sides throughout the match.

Wales opened the scoring with a Jim Sullivan penalty goal after six minutes play. The lead reverted to England thanks to an Ellaby try before a Jack Gore touchdown, converted by Jim Sullivan put Wales back in front 7–3 at the interval. Two equally matched sides struggled to put points on the board after the break.

Finally, a Joe Oliver try broke the deadlock to narrow the Welsh lead to a single point. The Welshmen responded with a try from Gwynne Parker, converted by Sullivan, which was partially matched by a try from Ben Halfpenny to leave Wales ahead 12–9.

The match then entered a dramatic and unexpected last 10 minutes which saw England create two tries for Alf Ellaby, one converted by Tommy Dinsdale, and a further try for Tom Holliday. That rush of 11 points not only secured the win, but made it appear much more comfortable than it had been.

Welsh White City, Cardiff

As one opportunity closed in Pontypridd, another, with the involvement of the same greyhound promoter, the GRA, appeared to open, offering even greater opportunities. Modern greyhound racing using an electric hare had only started in Britain in June 1926, but since then the number of syndicates running its operations had mushroomed.

In Cardiff the GRA was using its profits to develop a new, spacious and well-appointed stadium near to Ninian Park on Sloper Road in Grangetown. Its construction was similar to that of the GRA's headquarters in west London and would lead it to be popularly known as the Welsh White City.

One week after the Pontypridd club closed down the GRA proposed to establish a rugby league team at the Cardiff track. Following a meeting with a deputation, the NRL held a SGM on 21 December 1927 which agreed to accept another instant member with only one vote against. Although the dogs took to the White City track on Easter Saturday 1928, doubts about the future rugby league club were being aired the following month.

In June it was confirmed that the owners had no intention of their club taking its place in the NRL. By then, the promoters had other issues to deal with; they were funding the remodelling of the stadium for a speedway team and a rival greyhound syndicate had just opened in direct competition at the Arms Park.

Although there was little chance of a club ever being based there, the White City Stadium's managers were happy to hire out the venue and give the RFL its first opportunity to showcase the game's attributes in the largest Welsh city on the afternoon of 14 November 1928.

Wednesday 14 November 1928: Wales 15 England 39
Cardiff, 15,000

England planned to field 11 members of the summer touring party, but that number was reduced to 10 when a knee injury forced Featherstone Rovers' Tommy Askin, one of the successes of the tour, to withdraw. He was replaced by Billy Dingsdale. Wales included just four tourists. A good crowd looked on as the two sides tested each other out. Once again, the Welsh struggled in the scrums, but made up for it by working hard in the loose where they combined well with their lively back division.

Two great wingers, Alf Ellaby and Johnny Ring, ran in tries to complement tries from Alf Frodsham and David M Jenkins. A Jim Sullivan penalty goal and a conversion from Jonty Parkin left the scores tied at 8–8. The Welsh completed their first half scoring with a try from Dai Maidment, converted by Sullivan, before Ellaby got over for his second score. Finally, Jim Sullivan and Jim Brough kicked penalty goals to leave Wales ahead 15–13 at the break.

When play restarted, it seemed like a different match. The England backs seized the initiative and the Welsh seemed unable to respond. England's attack slipped into gear and created six tries, four of which were converted. Wales were unable to add a single point to their half-time score. It had not looked so easy at the interval, but England won comfortably in Cardiff, 39–15.

Even the normally sceptical 'Old Stager' writing in the *Western Mail* had to praise the English performance. "The blend and understanding of England's attacking line ... reached a stage which has rarely been approached in Rugby or Rugby League football and is doubtless the outcome of the continuous association of the players concerned while they were on the Australasian tour." High praise indeed.

In 1929–30, with the Kangaroos touring, a match between Wales and Australia was originally planned to be played at Cardiff's White City on 18 January. When it was discovered that this would clash with the Wales versus England match at the Arms Park the fixture was switched to the Empire Stadium at Wembley. The White City's directors lost interest in rugby league as their fortunes waned; the speedway team rode its final season in 1930, but did return briefly a few years later.

The stadium owners' fortunes dipped further after the Wall Street crash in the autumn of 1929 ushered in a worldwide economic slump. The depression, as the slump was known, hit Great Britain hard, pushing the number of people unemployed over three million at times between 1929 and 1933. It was particularly severe on those towns and villages that were reliant on a single industry such as coal mining or iron and steel. As a result, parts of South Wales such as the Rhondda and the valleys further east suffered terribly.

The depression rapidly pushed thousands onto the 'bread-line' with the result that it meant the end of greyhound racing in Pontypridd in 1932. At the White City in Cardiff greyhound crowds were also smaller than those at the centrally located Arms Park. By the end of 1936 the greyhound meetings had ended there and the following year the stadium was closed.

It was over two years before England and Wales met again. This time the venue was Huddersfield's Fartown ground on the afternoon of 18 March 1931. England retained only six of the team that had just managed to defeat the Other Nationalities six months earlier. Wales had to make a number of changes to their selected team. Gwynne Davies (Wigan), Billy Williams (Salford) and Llewellyn Williams (Oldham) withdrew and following a re-organisation among the backs, they were replaced by Gwyn Parker, Tommy Flynn and Dai Rees.

Wednesday 18 March 1931: England 23 Wales 18
Huddersfield, 6,000

Wales were the better side for the first hour of the match. They led 10–7 at the interval and extended that further with a try from Joe Thompson. The Englishmen had left it late, but at last stirred themselves; tries from Alf Ellaby and Tommy Banks with a conversion by Jack Walkington gave them a two point lead.

Gus Risman's decision to take the professional rugby route had attracted little attention at the time, but two years on he had become an accomplished member of Salford's back division, usually at full-back. Making his international debut as a centre, Risman scored a spectacular individual try to put his side back in front, 18–15 late in the second half. It did not prove to be a big enough lead. Continual English pressure produced tries for Ellaby and Dingsdale and a fourth conversion from Walkington to grab the spoils in the last 10 minutes.

Sadly, the casual approach of both teams in the first half led the *Yorkshire Post* to air once more the criticism that 'friendly' matches failed to merit the label of an international contest: "There is not the sternness in attack or defence that there might be in these games to make them really worthwhile; chiefly they are looked upon to provide a demonstration on exhibition lines of the finer points of the game." The writer obviously hoped that the authorities might take notice.

With a tour of Australia and New Zealand looming large on the RFL's agenda, selections for the next match were placed in the hands of the tour sub-committee. The formerly unemployed captain of Abertillery, Trevor Thomas, was one of seven new caps in the Welsh XIII. He packed down alongside his club-mate, Reg Hathway, at Salford on the afternoon of 27 January 1932. Thomas added his first Welsh rugby league cap to the four Welsh union caps he had collected before signing for Oldham the previous November, just nine matches earlier.

Both Wales's first choice stand-off, Halifax's Ivor Davies and the reserve, Huddersfield's Gwyn Richards, ruled themselves out of the match. The selectors decided to fill the vacancy with Huddersfield's Idris Towill, rather than someone like Billo Rees or Evan Williams of Leeds who regularly occupied that position. Towill, who normally played centre, took the blame for the inability of the Welsh threequarters to really get moving.

Wednesday 27 January 1932: England 19 Wales 2
Salford, 8,000

Although the ground-staff had done a great job in getting the pitch, which had a reputation as a mud-bath, into a good condition the match was marred by poor visibility.

Even in the murk the lack of combination among the Welsh backs was clear to see and contrasted poorly with some flashes of brilliance from their opposite numbers. In the second half, the tour sub-committee intervened, swapping Stan Brogden and Ernest Pollard to check on their versatility. Wales only score – a first half penalty goal from Jim Sullivan – left them trailing 6–2 at the interval. When play resumed England added three more tries to leave Wales badly beaten.

At the start of his visit to Britain to finalise arrangements for the upcoming Kangaroo tour, the Australian rugby league administrator and journalist, Harry Sunderland, recognising the fixture's worth, had induced *British Movietone* to film the match for future showing as part of his expansion efforts for the sport. The *Yorkshire Post* on 3 February 1932 carried a report of an informal luncheon the indefatigable Sunderland had organised for northern sportswriters and the RFL's designated tour managers in Manchester the previous day. A small part of the film, which was being shown on Shaftesbury Avenue to boost interest in the game in London, was shown to the pressmen. Sunderland was at pains to point out to them that "such passing as was provided is very seldom seen in the rugby union game."

The 1932 tour party had returned home with news that the Australians had made a change to the laws. Instead of a 25-yard drop-out when the defending side made the ball dead, the Australians had required the defending side to drop out from the goal-line. This change denied the defending side the 'gift' of 25 yards when restarting play. It had obviously found favour among the tour party's management because the RFL was convinced to give the new law a trial at the upcoming international match.

Wednesday 30 Nov 1932: England 14 Wales 13
Leeds, 4,000

There were only 4,000 spectators present at a rain-soaked sad-looking, three-sided Headingley on Wednesday 30 November 1932. Large-scale building work was underway on the north side of the field to replace the old North Stand which had been gutted by fire on Good Friday.

England included nine members of the touring party that had spent the summer in the Antipodes, seven more than the Welsh, and were made clear favourites. Wales included Dai M Jenkins, who although not enjoying a summer in the Antipodes, had completed a successful transfer across the River Aire for what was then reputed to be a record fee for a forward of £450.

The weather, however, made handling difficult and forward play dominated the afternoon. Initially, Wales made the pre-match predictions look foolish as they controlled the ball better, collecting two tries from Les White and Jack Morley which with a conversion from Jim Sullivan built an 8–0 half time lead.

Unfortunately for the Welsh, their lighter pack was eventually overpowered by the English-six. Even as the dynamic changed, Wales added a further try by Mel Rosser, converted by Sullivan, to prolong their lead. On the back of that forward power, however, England created four tries, only one of which was converted by Martin Hodgson, but it was the latter two points that sealed England's victory.

This would turn out to be Alf Ellaby's final appearance against the Welsh XIII and they were undoubtedly pleased to see the back of him. Although he had failed to get on the scoresheet at Headingley, Ellaby stood down with the remarkable record of 10 tries from his previous five appearances against the men from the Principality.

Most reactions to the trial of the law change were favourable and the RFL amended its laws accordingly at the AGM in 1933.

In 1933–34, with both nations having matches against the touring Australians, there was no match between them.

First get a cap?

In his book *Salford RLFC: 100 Greats* Graham Morris includes a couple of personal accounts of the sort of pressure that could be brought to bear on a player who was faced with the choice between a contract and a cap in the Depression. With the number of unemployed in Britain approaching three million, mass poverty beckoned. More than half the miners in the Rhondda were out of work. Many Welsh union players might have lived in the hope of being offered a big fee by a northern club, but a few knew it would place in them in a quandary if the WFU's selectors had not recognised their talents before a scout came knocking. Dare they delay signing a professional form until after that precious first cap came along?

Having been a reserve the previous season it seemed likely that Cardiff's stand-off, Emlyn Jenkins, could get his first Welsh union cap in 1931. Salford's ambitious, driven, manager, Lance Todd, was keen to add him to the club's roster and feared that Jenkins' desire for a cap might lead him to delay signing. Negotiations were proceeding ahead of the final trial in December 1930 and the time for decision was at hand. When Todd heard that Maesteg's Windsor Lewis was likely to step down and Jenkins would be called up to take his place in the trial he acted quickly. Todd did not pass on that information and no one officially seems to have informed Jenkins. Taking advantage of the situation Todd convinced Jenkins where his future lay and hurried him onto a Manchester-bound train as soon as possible. By the time he heard the news about the trial Jenkins was a Salford player, making his debut five days after his 20th birthday, 1 December. Jenkins never forgot what happened. As he later told a reporter "You can call it cleverness on Todd's part, but it always stuck in my throat".

Lance Todd was similarly determined to secure the services of Cross Keys scrum-half Billy Watkins. Having had a test trial in 1929, Watkins still harboured hopes of a call from the Welsh selectors and a future Welsh cap when Todd came to see him. Trying to keep his options open, he did no more than promise the forceful Todd that if and when he did decide to go north, it would be to Salford. Family pressure was mounting on Watkins and Todd's approach was becoming tougher. It was time for tough choices to be made and Todd posed the question "What if you break your leg again? I won't want you and nobody else will!" Realising the risks he was running, Watkins agreed to shelve his dreams and join Salford in June 1931. They may not have achieved international honours in union, but both Billy Watkins and Emlyn Jenkins were rewarded with Welsh rugby league caps in 1932.

For quite a few of those who achieved their aim, to play for the Welsh XV and then take up the offer from a northern club, there was a final slight to bear. Their names might have been written into the record books, their family and friends would feel proud, but there was no actual cap forthcoming. The Welsh Union could not resist the urge to withhold the cap itself. That slight would not be put right until the WRU declared an amnesty in 1975 by which time, sadly, quite a few of those who were owed a cap had passed away.

Was it worth it?

They may have been labelled mercenaries by their detractors, but those who took the opportunity recognised the potential both for them and their family. So, were the years of ostracism and exile that many players endured worth it? While it is impossible to provide a definitive answer to that question, it is interesting to look at some of the ways that players put the money to life-changing use.

For some, the fee funded an immediate goal – to be bought out of the Army for Tommy 'Guardsman' Rees, Frank Whitcombe, James Croston and Ted Sadler, or to get out of the mines for Dai Rees and Barney Hudson.

After signing Jim Sullivan, Wigan returned to South Wales in search of more talent the following summer, finally paying what was said to be a new record fee of £800 to secure Aberavon's international winger, Johnny Ring, on 23 August 1922. According to team-mates,

Johnny Ring used part of his fee to engage a surgeon to operate on his sister who had a disability.

For young men without independent means, it could fund loftier ambitions. Iorwerth Isaac, who had resigned from the Glamorgan Police to join Leeds in 1933, accepted a fee and a college place where he successfully studied to become a teacher. Jack Morley, who left Newport for Wigan in 1932, shrewdly used his fee to build a new career. An orphan, Morley moved on from working as a clerk in a brewery to study dentistry at Liverpool University. On his return to Wales, he worked as a school dentist.

For the fortunate few who switched successfully and went on to enjoy long careers there was always the benefit to look forward to. Even in the hard times between the wars some players could receive significant sums that set them up for life after the game. Ben Gronow received £490 in 1924, Jim Sullivan received £475 in 1931 and Dai Rees £420 the following year.

A northern finishing school

There were signs as the 1930s wore on that the northern clubs were willing to sign players with youthful potential rather than seeking readymade capped players. It was obviously a riskier approach, but certain clubs proved able to spot and nurture talent.

Weighing little more than 10 stones, Alan Edwards, a 19-year-old wing threequarter, was spotted by Lance Todd while playing for Aberavon. He signed for Salford in August 1935 and made two appearances for Wales in his first season, the second against England in February. Before he was 20, Edwards had become the youngest tourist so far when he set off for Australasia in April 1936 and would go on to become the regular winger for Wales.

He had plenty of youthful competition. Dai Rees brought the 19-year-old wing threequarter Des Case to Bradford in September 1937. Case, who had first appeared in the Cross Keys' first team six months earlier, would play for Wales on the opposite wing to Edwards against England in November 1938.

There was an even younger winger waiting in the wings. Reginald Lloyd was thought to be only 16 when he left Neath for Keighley in August 1936. At the end of a remarkable debut season, Lloyd had the good fortune to appear at Wembley which led to him being dubbed the youngest player ever to appear in a Cup Final. Nearly 40 years would pass before the truth emerged, he had in fact been 18 when he signed for Keighley and his claim to fame was false. Whatever his age, Lloyd's hopes of international honours were blocked by the youngsters in front of him and then by the outbreak of the Second World War. He was not capped until peace returned.

Last but by no means least on this youthful list that made the grade is Roy Francis. Francis was just 17 when he packed his bags and made his way to Wigan from Brynmawr in November 1936. His potential was obvious but his first team chances at talent-laden Wigan were few and it was a case of wait for one of the established wingers to falter. Over his two years at Wigan Francis would make just 12 appearances. A fresh start had its advantages and he moved on to Barrow in January 1939, a few days short of his 20th birthday. At Barrow he grabbed the opportunity to show he really was one for the future before war intervened. Like Reg Lloyd, Francis would have to wait until the impending war was over before the got his first Welsh cap.

5. The International Championship is launched

The Ligue Francaise de Rugby à XIII was officially constituted on 6 April 1934. Steps were taken immediately for an official French national team to take on England. That match went ahead on 15 April 1934 at the Stade Buffalo in Paris in front of 20,000 spectators. Joe Lewthwaite, the chairman of the RL Council, and the secretary, John Wilson, attended a meeting of the French League at Toulouse on 21 August 1934. Besides planning the domestic programme, the meeting also considered representative matches and agreed to establish the International Tournament Championship with teams from England, France and Wales. With a championship at stake there was at last something tangible to play for.

The Championship's inaugural match, between France and Wales, took place at Bordeaux on New Years' Day 1935. The new-look French team thrilled the home crowd with a winning debut on the international stage.

After a single season based at the GRA's White City Stadium in west London, London Highfield had decided to move on and with the assistance of the RFL settled at the Stanley Stadium, a greyhound and speedway venue on Prescott Road in Liverpool. Further assistance was forthcoming when, as Stanley's inaugural season was winding down, the RFL staged the England versus Wales match there on the afternoon of 10 April 1935. After more than 20 'friendlies', England and Wales would meet in their first ever officially competitive match.

Billy Belshaw was a late replacement for Castleford's Arthur Atkinson and Les Adams was recalled after four years absence in place of Widnes's Tommy McCue in the England team. Just when it seemed no one else would ever get a look in, injury forced Jim Sullivan, an ever-present in the Welsh XIII since 1921, to sit out this match. From quite a few very good Welsh full-backs, the selectors chose Huddersfield's Tommy Scourfield to fill in for the great man. Wigan's Jack Morley was also forced to withdraw; his place was taken by Islwyn Davies. With those two late changes, it made eight new caps in the Welsh XIII.

Having lost the opening match, Wales had no chance of the title. England, however, could finish as champions, but only if they beat Wales by at least eight points.

Wednesday 10 April 1935: England 24 Wales 11
Liverpool, 7,100

Unfortunately, gale force winds deterred many travelling fans, but fortunately the stadium had enough cover to shelter the 7,100 hardy souls who paid to watch. England dominated play from the start, taking possession from three out of every four scrums, and had established a lead of 18–5 as the interval approached. Then, just ahead of the whistle, Barney Hudson suffered a dislocated shoulder and England were a man down. Harry Beverley was pulled out of the pack to replace Hudson and as England re-organised Ossie Griffiths got a try, converted by Izzy Davies.

Two tries from Nat Silcock gave England a commanding 24–5 lead early in the second half. Further problems arose to threaten that lead when Stan Smith suffered a bad knee injury and had to retire. England had to play the last 15 minutes with 11 men. Inevitably, space opened up allowing Len Orchard and Gwynne Davies to score for Wales to make the final score 24–11.

The crowd enjoyed seeing England grab the inaugural title on points' difference. At the first time of asking Wales ended up with the wooden spoon. Liverpool Stanley had also performed well and finished a creditable 15th in the table at the end of its first season on Merseyside.

With France involved there appears to have been a change of heart at the NRL regarding the playing of internationals on Saturdays, because from 1935–36 onwards, the International Championship matches were played on weekends.

Same old union

In 1935 the WFU fell in with the global consensus and renamed itself the Welsh Rugby Union (WRU). Under the renamed union, the Welsh XV regained their version of the International Championship, winning two and drawing one of their three matches. For the spectators play was becoming even less of a spectacle. With tight defences dominating play, those games could hardly be described as exciting – the Welsh XV scored just 16 points in its three matches. This was the lowest title-winning aggregate since 1894. Showing their mastery of the prevailing style, the Welsh XV conceded just three points.

There was no such stultifying defensive mindset in rugby league. The Welsh XIII opened their campaign by running in 11 tries in a 41–7 thrashing of France at Llanelli in November 1935. Four months later their meeting with England in the City of Kingston-upon-Hull would decide the destination of the championship. Salford's Tom Kenny was a late replacement for Arthur Atkinson and Wakefield's Bill Horton took the place of an unwell Harry Woods. Norman Fender took over from the selected Iorwerth Isaac of Leeds in the Welsh team. It was a historic afternoon for the Risca-born George Bennett. Having already played against France, Bennett became the first black player to appear for Wales against England.

Saturday 1 February 1936: England 14 Wales 17
Hull, 17,000

There was tremendous interest in and around the city and Rovers' Craven Park welcomed a very good crowd of 17,000. A cold and wet January had left large parts of the pitch covered in ankle-deep mud. It was a day for the forwards and their stamina proved to be a key factor in their team's success or failure. A major match just three days earlier would have had a major bearing on the outcome. The RFL had held the first tour trial at Salford on the previous Wednesday; five of England's pack had been involved, but only two of the Welsh six. That imbalance did not reflect Welsh forward strength – it had been a long time since Wales had fielded a pack as good as the one that took the field at Craven Park. That pack, ably led by dual international Hal Jones, handled the ankle-deep mud better, outlasting their opposite numbers to lay a great platform for their half-backs, George Bennett and Billy Watkins, to control the game.

Despite the poor conditions both sides started out trying to play some fast and clever rugby. It was Jim Sullivan who got the scoreboard moving with a penalty goal in the first minute to give Wales an immediate lead. Although England held the advantage in the first half scrums 19–12, and twice took the lead through tries by Barney Hudson and Joe Oliver the Welsh hit back each time with tries by George Bennett and Dennis Madden. When the half-time whistle sounded, Wales were ahead 14–12. As the pitch worsened, the second half became a grim struggle in the mud. The Welsh pack rose to the challenge better than their opposite numbers and gave their-half backs greater room for manoeuvre. George Bennett, whose strong and clever play throughout the match drew compliments, seized his chance to grab the only try of the half. Martin Hodgson replied with a penalty goal for England.

With Wales hanging on for victory, an England break put Tom Kenny over the line, but the final pass was judged forward and England's last chance to save the match had gone.

The Welsh victory by three tries to two was their first over England for 13 years and it clinched the International Championship. At the end of the month England avoided the wooden spoon with a victory in Paris.

With a surfeit of talent chasing the stand-off shirt, the Welsh selectors did not turn to George Bennett again, but he had led the way for many more black players to represent their country over the next 60 years.

Saturday 7 Nov 1936: Wales 3 England 2
Pontypridd, 12,000

After the collapse of the Pontypridd and District League, Taff Vale Park no longer figured in the RFL's plans. By 1936, the stadium was council owned and at the start of that year the town clerk wrote to the RFL requesting that it be used for an England versus Wales international. His request was granted, and the defending champions and England duly arrived in the town on Friday 6 November ready to do battle the following day at Taff Vale Park once more.

For England, Barney Hudson was unable to start. His place went to Stan Pepperell. Harry Woods dropped out to be replaced by Alec Higgins. Wales were unchanged. Rain, which fell almost all morning, almost caused the match to be called off. However, it went ahead in front of a respectable crowd of 12,000.

Stars from the England versus Wales matches between the Wars: Billy Cunliffe (Courtesy Gary Slater), Jonty Parkin (Courtesy *Rugby League Journal*) and Harold Wagstaff (Courtesy Robert Gate)

In such dire conditions it was never going to be a high-scoring game, but both teams gave an excellent display of wet weather rugby league. In the whole of the first 40 minutes there were just two scores – a try for Wales by Alan Edwards and in reply a penalty goal from Martin Hodgson. An ankle injury forced England's Billy Stott to sit out the second half. Once again, Harry Beverley was pulled out of the pack to cover for an injured winger. Those reporters present thought England's performance actually improved in the second half, but there were no further scores to show for it and Wales hung on to win 3–2. A month later, Wales won in Paris to retain the International Championship title.

Wales selected a young stand-off, Oliver Morris, for the opening match of the 1937–38 tournament. Morris had been keen for a while to secure a professional contract, but alas his talent was overlooked because he was thought to be too frail – at less than 10 stones – to withstand the rigours of the NRL. Finally, Hunslet took the chance and Morris accepted their £400 offer.

Wary of the Anglo-Saxon moneymen, legend has it that Oliver's father demanded his fee in cash and Hunslet's deputation had to remain in Pontypridd until the banks opened. Morris had only made his debut for Hunslet on 20 November and with only a further 10 appearances to his name was called up to make his debut for Wales in Bradford.

There was real hope in Bradford that the City's 30-year wait for a ground capable of hosting international rugby was about to end. Thanks to the vision of the City Council the site of a disused quarry was transformed into Odsal Stadium. Bradford Northern became the long-term tenant when it opened for business at the start of September 1934. The potential of the huge bowl was obvious, but much work was still needed to complete even a basic stadium. It had been planned to hold an England versus France match there, but when the pitch was inspected on Friday 9 April 1937 it was deemed to be waterlogged and unfit for play. This forced the match to be switched to Thrum Hall in Halifax. Having made improvements to the drainage system, Odsal Stadium was given a second chance by the RFL, this time to stage the meeting of England and Wales on 29 January 1938.

Spectator provision for the first international to be played in the city was still fairly basic and the Stadium was less than half-full for the match.

Saturday 29 January 1938: England 6 Wales 7
Bradford, 8,637

Rain had left the ground heavy and the players faced even more problems with a gale force wind blowing down the pitch. Sadly, it meant the play was riddled with handling errors. Although scrum possession went 41–28 to England, the Welsh adapted themselves better to the conditions.

Wales chose to start with the gale at their backs. Within minutes Oliver Morris's whirlwind start in rugby league got even better. He put in a high cross field kick, Cliff Evans followed up and scored out wide. Jim Sullivan did well to convert and Wales were 5–0 up after just six minutes. Barney Hudson led England's fightback with a spectacular try, but the deficit mounted again just before half-time when Jim Sullivan landed a penalty goal.

With the gale at their backs in the second half England struggled. It took until four minutes from time for England to create a score, Jimmy Cumberbatch was the try-scorer, to crown a special day for him. He had become the first black man to represent England against Wales.

44

In the conditions the match had served up few thrills but the Welshmen were very happy with their victory nonetheless.

Three months' later, the Welsh beat France in Llanelli to complete a hat-trick of International Championship titles.

Stebonheath Park, Llanelli

Stebonheath Park, the home of Llanelli AFC, had almost been bought by the RFL in the late-1920s. The asking price was, however, considered to be too high and the purchase of what could have been a home for rugby league in South Wales fell through.

Since then, Llanelli AFC had enjoyed a few ambitious years during which they had been a leading contender for a place in the Football League's Division Three (South).

To support the club's ambitions, the ground, which lay close to the town centre, had been enhanced with a large wooden grandstand, a covered end terrace and a large open popular side. To help fund their ambitions, the ground had been adapted to become a venue for greyhound racing. Election to the Football League proved beyond the club's resources and the ensuing financial problems forced it to drop down the 'pyramid' into the First Division of the Welsh League.

Staging rugby league matches provided a welcome source of revenue. Prior to England venturing out to west Wales, Stebonheath Park had twice hosted the French team in front of very good crowds. After the meeting with France at the start of April 1938 'Nomad' writing in the *Llanelly Mercury* had observed that "In some ways the display made one feel that the amateur code was an old man's game."

Saturday 5 November 1938: Wales 17 England 9
Llanelli, 15,000

The Championship opener, Wales versus England, took place on Saturday 5 November 1938. Despite a rainy morning which turned into a misty afternoon there was a good crowd of 15,000. As the following Thursday's issue of the *Llanelly Mercury* noted that "besides the contingent from Lancashire and Yorkshire, many people travelled from the different parts of Wales to see former Welsh club players who are now 'stars' of the Rugby League". If the response had been localised then the attendance would undoubtedly have suffered as there was only one player from west Wales in the team, Llanelli's Emlyn Hughes. All his team-mates were originally from the other side of the Vale of Neath.

Facing an England side whose pack – containing three new caps – failed to function as a unit, Wales was able to dictate play in the first half. Their youthful wingers, Des Case and Alan Edwards scored tries to which Jim Sullivan added two conversions and a penalty goal to put his side up 12–0 at the interval.

Despite playing a man short in the second half, Harold Thomas having suffered a leg injury, Wales, through Risman, added a try and a drop-goal which were incredibly valuable when England made a late rally. Some reporters thought that if the home side had been at full strength, then Wales's fourth consecutive win over England could have been by a much greater margin. It had been a fast, exciting match and Wales fully deserved their 17–9 victory.

England's disappointing performance drew much criticism. Despite having a man-advantage for half the match and taking the scrums 36–24, they had still contrived to lose which was deemed unacceptable by most critics. The report in Monday's *Yorkshire Post* had an astute assessment of the new dynamic in these matches: "The Welshmen in the Rugby League find rare inspiration when they play in their own country these days." Sadly, there would not be a chance to see that home inspiration lift a Welsh XIII for seven long years.

A Welsh defeat at Bordeaux the following spring ended the Welshmen's grip on the title which went to France for the first time. A young and strong Welsh team would undoubtedly have bounced back, especially once the latest influx of new blood, that was in the process of being recruited, was assimilated.

What might have been

The winter of 1939 proved harsh for Welsh rugby union. Cardiff lost their star winger, Arthur Bassett in January 1939 when he accepted a huge fee of £1,000 to join Halifax. Having made his debut for Wales against England at Twickenham that same month Leeds stepped in opening negotiations with Swansea's David Idwal Davies. One week later he had signed for Leeds for a fee of £700 to become the 17th Welsh rugby union international to be directly signed by the club since the First World War. Even though tensions continued to mount in Europe, the NRL's wealthier clubs maintained their pursuit of the leading members of the Welsh XV. The following month Wigan signed Cardiff's highly regarded forward, Eddie Watkins. Salford recruited Aberavon's winger Sydney Williams in May.

It might have been expected that the Government's preparations for war, such as the recent re-introduction of conscription, would make clubs rethink their team-building efforts. Over an overcast and often wet summer, more and more measures came into force and there was a lull in signings. During that time, air-raid shelters were constructed, gas masks and identity cards issued, barrage balloons readied and military training stepped up.

And yet in August, as practice matches got underway ahead of the new season Salford signed Emrys Evans, a forward from Llanelli, and Bradford Northern secured Swansea's mercurial stand-off Billy Davies. Not all Welshmen had to be recruited from South Wales. After the Lazenby Cup match on Saturday 19 August, Leeds inquired about Hunslet's diminutive 23-year-old Welsh stand-off, Oliver Morris, who had requested a transfer. Negotiations proceeded rapidly, a record fee of £1,000 was agreed with a further £500 being payable if there was no war within two months. Within the week Morris was a Leeds player and peace did not last beyond that month.

By the time war broke out, 69 Welsh rugby union internationals had 'gone north' since the last conflict. Leeds had signed roughly a quarter of them. Their total was the highest in the NRL and more than double that of Wigan, their nearest rival. It is extremely difficult to quantify just how many others went north before achieving international recognition.

BBC radio

BBC radio regularly provided a commentary of the second half of rugby league internationals on its North regional service. For those who were unable to attend, the BBC Northern service was a welcome alternative. Hubert Bateman provided the commentary from Odsal in January 1938. Lance Todd provided the commentary in November 1938 and continued to do so in the early war years, prior to his untimely death in a blackout road accident on 14 November 1942. Parts of the broadcasts were later relayed to Wales on the Forces network. The second half broadcasts continued after the war.

46

6. A different war

Unlike the First World War, with the start of a new conflict on 3 September 1939, both codes of rugby and other sports were, after a short break, officially encouraged to carry on. International and club matches in both codes of rugby would continue with the full support of the military authorities so long as their grounds were not requisitioned or too many of their players conscripted. This gave rise to the practical, but slightly surreal instructions in the early years of the war when Luftwaffe raids were a real threat to life and limb being included in match programmes telling spectators what to do in the event of an air raid.

With the country in grave danger, conscription, for which legislation had already been passed was widened to cover all men aged 18 to 41. Although the call-up moved slowly as the Armed Forces struggled to cope with the influx of men, the way was clear for the two rugby games once again to co-operate closely on the field in the national interest.

Barriers down

Just over two months into the conflict, on 12 November, the RFU passed a resolution allowing rugby league players in the Armed Forces who had had no association with rugby league since their enlistment to participate in union matches between clubs and service teams for the duration of the war. That resolution accepted that

a. A Rugby XV may play against a Service XV containing players who have played rugby league football.

b. A rugby union XV may include rugby league players belonging to His Majesty's Forces when playing matches against Service teams.

c. A rugby union XV may include rugby league players belonging to the Forces when playing against another rugby union club.

As in the previous conflict the WRU followed the RFU's lead, whereas the Scottish Rugby Union insisted the ban on rugby league players taking part in any match against a team under its jurisdiction must remain in force.

The rugby union services' teams

It took a little time before the home rugby unions took full advantage of the new possibilities. Under the auspices of an inter-services committee a series of international matches was launched in March 1942. Services teams representing England, Scotland and Wales were to meet each other with the receipts being used for war-time charitable causes. As a result of a German air raid at the start of January 1941, Cardiff Arms Park had been badly damaged and rendered unusable. St Helen's Field was requisitioned by the Air Raid Precautions (ARP) service, but it was able to remain open as a sports venue and all the Welsh services' home matches were played there.

League players were eligible to take part and Wales made the most of the opportunity selecting 16 of them over the remaining four seasons of the conflict. It meant those players, listed below, were in high demand from both rugby codes as the Welsh services scheduled home and away fixtures against England each season. They were, in alphabetical order, Alban Davies (Huddersfield), Billy Davies (Bradford N), D. Idwal Davies (Leeds), Alan

Edwards (Salford), Cliff Evans (Leeds), Emrys Evans (Salford), Trevor Foster (Bradford N), Randell Lewis (Swinton), Ike Owens (Leeds), Doug Phillips (Oldham), Jim Regan (Huddersfield), Gus Risman (Salford), Syd Williams (Salford), Harold Thomas (Salford), Eddie Watkins (Wigan) and Gwyn Williams (Wigan).

In 1941–42, Gus Risman had the unique honour of simultaneously captaining the Welsh XIII and the newly established Welsh rugby union services team. If Risman was unavailable, the captaincy of the Welsh rugby union services team passed to Bradford Northern's Billy Davies. This occurred in November 1943 and April 1944. Risman regained the captaincy of the union team in 1944. For the victory over England at Swansea in November 1941, Risman was one of eight rugby league players in the Welsh XV.

Conflicts over the selection of players were inevitable especially when a rugby league international match coincided with a union Scotland versus England services' international. Roy Francis was serving in the Army Physical Training Corps when his performances for Dewsbury caught the Welsh rugby league selectors' attention. They offered him the chance to make his debut at Wigan on 27 February 1943. His happiness rapidly turned to confusion when the Army stepped in and chose him to play alongside Ernest Ward, Johnny Lawrenson and Ted Sadler for England in Edinburgh that same day. The Army's interests inevitably won out and so instead of appearing for Wales in Wigan, Francis had the novel experience of turning out for the English services against the Scottish services. He appeared for the English services on six more occasions, three of them in opposition to the Welsh services team.

Rugby league's wartime internationals

With the approval of the Home Office, the RFL continued to arrange meetings of England and Wales provided in the early days that spectator numbers were limited and unnecessary travel avoided. The RFL decided it would continue to award caps for those who appeared in the matches which were mostly played in aid of the British Red Cross Society.

The first went ahead on 23 December 1939 at Odsal Stadium. With not a single War Emergency League match scheduled in Lancashire or Yorkshire, a big crowd was anticipated. Just in case, with only four days to go, the Home Office agreed to increase the crowd limit to 30,000, nearly half the Stadium's capacity, but only for the international matches. Although that limit was not to be tested it showed there was still a healthy interest in international rugby league. The RFL had suspended all professional contracts in mid-September. Subsequent player remuneration was effectively amateur; match fees for the international being set at £1, expenses were 10 shillings (£0.50) with fares on top. There was one change to the advertised teams, Francis Gregory replaced the injured Laurie Thacker (Hull).

Although it was said some Welsh players had returned home, to await seemingly inevitable conscription, a strong Welsh XIII gathered in Bradford. Jim Sullivan led the Welsh team once again and let them know what was expected as they prepared to run out: "I want every last ounce of effort from you. When this match is over, I want to see your tongues hanging out." His team responded to his call.

Saturday 23 December 1939: England 3 Wales 16
Bradford, 15,257

With the English backs being younger and less experienced, Wales were made slight favourites. Prior to kick-off, the players were presented to Lord Harewood. Surprisingly for

Odsal in those days, the pitch was reported to be in perfect condition. England took the game to Wales from the start, but could not put any points on the board. Wales forced their way back into contention and led at the break by three Jim Sullivan penalty goals to a try by Eric Batten.

Wales dominated the second half, but it was not until the final 20 minutes that they managed to turn pressure into points. They scored two converted tries, one of which came from Northern's recent convert Billy Davies, without reply, to convincingly beat a poor England side 16–3. What also mattered was that approximately £600 had been raised for the Red Cross.

Saturday 9 November 1940: England 8 Wales 5
Oldham, 5,000

Essential war work kept Jim Sullivan out of this match and his place went to his Wigan understudy, Joe Jones. The Welsh captaincy passed to Gus Risman. When Salford's Harold Thomas was unable to obtain leave, Sandy Orford was chosen to take his place in the Welsh pack.

Since the summer, Britain had been on the receiving end of a huge German air assault that sought to bring the nation to its knees. The Battle of Britain might have been brought to a successful conclusion, thwarting the Luftwaffe's original strategic plan, but the mass air attacks continued in a different form. The Germans hoped an aerial assault would destroy Britain's war industries and force the country to surrender. By November, most of the German raids struck at night, but there were occasional daylight raids. One of these caused the air raid sirens to blare and interrupt play. According to the Welsh forward, Trevor Foster, the players took shelter under the stand for about 20 minutes until the all-clear sounded.

This match developed into a forward battle. A try by Foster and a goal from Joe Jones were matched by only a Jack Moore try for England which put Wales in front 5–3 at the break. In the second half England took the lead through a Jack Waring try, converted by Billy Belshaw. Syd Williams almost brought the scores level with the last play of the match before he was bundled into touch. A thrilling match ended 8–5 to England.

Saturday 18 October 1941: England 9 Wales 9
Bradford, 4,339

Bad weather kept the attendance down to a meagre 4,339. The press described it as a poor match played in bad conditions. Almost immediately after the kick-off, Wales were penalised and Billy Belshaw gave England a two-point lead. In reply, Wales set up a try for Alan Edwards, converted by Gus Risman, who subsequently was successful with a penalty kick to put the men in red 7–2 up at the break. England rallied in the second half with a Johnny Lawrenson try, converted by Belshaw, and a penalty goal from Belshaw. Risman also kicked a penalty goal to level the scores and secure a draw at the final whistle.

With Gus Risman serving overseas, a new captain was needed. The new man chosen to lead the Welsh XIII in 1942–43 was Trevor Foster of Bradford Northern, then at the height of his powers.

By 1942, only three NRL clubs in central Lancashire were still active – Oldham, St Helens and Wigan. All the other eight had suspended activities primarily due to their grounds being needed in various ways to support the war effort. It was a difficult time for the game in the area and the RFL offered some support by organising an international match at Central Park. Situated in the centre of town, Central Park was showing signs of wartime wear and tear by February 1943. An anti-aircraft battery on Spion Kop looked down on a worn pitch used as a drill ground by a variety of military training units based there. There was only one NRL fixture in the region that day – St Helens at Oldham – which helped deliver a bumper crowd. Central Park reliably delivered excellent crowds for the remainder of the conflict.

Wartime threw up some interesting anomalies for the game's records. With some clubs having closed down their players were left idle. Neither the RFL nor the players involved liked that idea so the latter were allowed to guest for other clubs. The team lists for this international and those throughout the war showed the player and his registered club, but he might well have attracted the selectors' attention by the form he was showing regularly with another one. For this season Billy Belshaw was regularly turning out for Huddersfield, George Aspinall for Wigan and Alan Edwards for Dewsbury.

Huddersfield's WT Davies moved up to fill the gap at stand-off left by the withdrawal of WTH Davies. That left a vacancy at full-back in Welsh team. There was some suggestion that the 40-year-old Jim Sullivan should be recalled but the selectors preferred Joe Jones.

Saturday 27 February 1943: England 15 Wales 9
Wigan, 17,000

After more than three years of conflict, the toll the war was taking on all aspects of life was clearly visible as the players took the field. Their shirts were worn, missing numbers in some cases and their stockings were an irregular mixture. Only their pride in representing their countries was unchanged.

From the kick-off, England showed superior teamwork and proved more adept at taking their chances. A Billy Belshaw penalty put England in front after 10 minutes. Tries from George Aspinall and Martin Ryan followed, neither being converted. Wales's only response was a penalty goal from Alban Davies to leave his side trailing 8–2 after the first 40 minutes. At the start of the second half Davies and Belshaw traded penalties. The equality in scoring continued; a try by Ken Jubb and another goal from Belshaw was answered by a try from Joe Jones and another Davies goal. When the final whistle sounded England had won 15-9.

Saturday 26 February 1944: England 9 Wales 9
Wigan, 16,028

Twelve years on and now at the veteran stage, Jack Walkington was recalled in place of the injured Billy Belshaw as England's full-back. Then, with only an hour to go before kick-off, there was another change to the England line-up when James Croston dropped out. Bryn Knowelden, England's reserve back, had signed for the re-activated Barrow club at the start of the season. Suddenly, and with only 14 first-team appearances to his name, Knowelden found himself representing his country against Wales.

Once play got underway, the Welsh forwards with Con Murphy, Dai Prosser and Trevor Foster to the fore, had the better of the English pack in the loose. Given the opportunities, the Welsh backs showed themselves more dangerous than their opponents. Alan Edwards and Joe Jones crossed for tries to open an early lead. Later, Bryn Knowelden capitalised on a fumble by Joe Jones to cap a memorable international debut with a try which Ken Gee converted to leave Wales with a two tries to one advantage but only a one point lead on the scoreboard at the break.

Sound defence by both sides marked the second half play. Against the run of play, Stanley Pepperell's two drop-goals gave England the lead and they began to look like the winners. Wales, however, worked a third try to secure the draw they deserved. But, that third try was contentious. Bursting onto a Risman pass, Alan Edwards raced along the touch line and the touch judge momentarily raised his flag. Immediately the English cover gave up the chase. Unfortunately, the referee did not notice the touch judge's flag and Edwards's try was given. Wales's inability to produce a goalkicker on the day cost them dearly and the match ended all square.

Saturday 10 March 1945: England 18 Wales 8
Wigan, 23,500

Gus Risman regained the captaincy of the Welsh XIII. More changes were needed as Trevor Foster and Emlyn Walters were posted overseas. Fred Hughes came in to replace Frank Whitcombe, Stan Powell for Syd Williams and Jack Bowen for Trevor Foster. On the Friday before the game, Dai Jenkins was forced to withdraw due to illness. It was left to the RFL general secretary, John Wilson, to find a replacement. Dewsbury's Harry Royal was the first choice, but he was billeted in the south of England and unavailable. Next in line was Mel de Lloyd. He was also serving in the south, but was able to get leave and travelled to Wigan. Just three years earlier de Lloyd had been suspended indefinitely while guesting for Keighley after striking a match official. Two years later, he had been fully rehabilitated and now was to be capped for Wales.

Barrow supplied five players – three for England and two for Wales. One of them, Willie Horne, was to make his England debut. Two days before the match Horne received a telephone call during evening training at Barrow's Craven Park. The caller was his prospective half-back partner Tommy Bradshaw who was keen to try and get some understanding prior to the match. He asked Horne to take an earlier train to Wigan where he would be waiting at the barrier to invite him round to his house for a sandwich, a cuppa and a bit of tactical planning.

As the nation prepared to celebrate an end to the war, a large crowd assembled at Central Park. All 2,000 stand seats were sold out in advance, 500 of them to enthusiasts from the Barrow district eager to cheer on their club's representatives. According to 'Observer' in Monday's *Daily Dispatch* there was a surprise for the locals when "in the early hours of Saturday morning about 1,000 Welshmen, some wearing leeks and carrying national flags, arrived in Wigan" having travelled through the night.

Billy Belshaw opened the scoring with a penalty goal which was equalised by Stan Powell. England soon gained an advantage in the scrums and this allowed Willie Horne to set up some bright and entertaining play, to give his backs plenty of scope on attack. Tries followed from Eric Batten twice and Willie Horne, two of them converted by Ernest Ward. An unconverted try by Alan Edwards was the only other score Wales could fashion in the first half to leave them trailing 15–5 at the break.

Although weakened by the absence of Dai Jenkins, Wales came out for the second half determined to address the deficit and succeeded after just four minutes as Edwards touched down. The Welsh continued to apply strong pressure on the English defence, but indifferent finishing meant they added no more points. Finally, Eric Batten crossed to complete his hat-trick and make the final score 18–8 to England. The gate receipts of £1,880 were the highest ever for an England versus Wales match in the north of England.

The human cost of victory

Dai Evans who had played against England at Pontypridd in November 1936 was lost when HMS Hood was sunk during the Battle of the Denmark Strait in May 1941.

Thrice-capped Oliver Morris, serving with the Welch Regiment, was killed during the fighting around Rimini in September 1944.

Jack Moore of Bradford Northern who had earned his first and only cap against Wales in November 1940 was lost at sea when HMS Electra sank off Java in May 1941.

While serving as an air-gunner with the RAF, Castleford's Les Adams was posted as missing presumed dead when his flight over Burma (now Myanmar) failed to return in January 1945.

Barriers up

The defeat of Nazi Germany followed by the surrender of Japan brought the Second World War to a rapid end. For the British people the end of the conflict offered the chance to break free from wartime restrictions and enjoy a freer life. Somewhat perversely, immediately that happened the RFU and the WRU moved to restore the old battle lines between them and rugby league. Despite the good relationships in wartime between the players, once peace came, the freedom of players outside the services returned to the restricted pre-war position. Rugby league players were back to being outcasts once more.

7. Brave new world

As the war ended there was some startling news coming from Wales and France.

St Helen's Field, Swansea

Not long after the start of the war, Swansea RUFC had suspended operations and surrendered its lease on St Helen's Field to the Swansea Corporation. It was a prestigious and historic cricket and rugby ground which had been a regular international venue since the Welsh XV first got underway. Rugby matches were held on the cricket outfield which meant that some sections of the crowd for a rugby match were quite far away from the action. Large crowds could be accommodated, although the record near 50,000 for the visit of Scotland in February 1921 had caused major problems. In February 1945, the RFL seized the opportunity, opening negotiations with the Corporation to hire the ground for an international match.

Vive la France

Four years of suppression by the Vichy regime had not diminished the appetite for rugby league in the south of France and word was soon received that the domestic competitions were being restarted. Also, the French national team would return in time to take its place in the post-war International Championship. Sunday 6 January 1946 marked the official re-launch of French Rugby League. On that day a RFL XIII – including five Welshmen – beat a French RL XIII 19–6 at the Parc des Princes in Paris. On the Friday prior to that, a six-man delegation from the RL Council met their French counterparts in Paris. It was the first meeting between the two bodies for six years.

Back into action

Once the end of the war in Europe had been declared and VE Day celebrated on Tuesday 8 May, the NRL met three weeks later and decided to restart the official league competition in three months time. This was not without difficulty as this was austerity Britain – there was rationing and money was in short supply. Undeterred, the game restarted with depleted teams and rundown grounds, but it still enlivened life in what was a very monochrome post-war England. Fortunately, there was a huge pent-up hunger for sport and crowds flocked to all the big events.

It was remarkable that just three months after the celebrations of VJ Day on 15 August 1945, the International Championship was back underway and the Welsh XIII was to be seen once again in west Wales. Freedom might be in the air, but the demands of wartime had not all been lifted. Trevor Foster was still serving in the Middle East and Ted Ward had only just returned to Wigan after recovering from a motorbike accident. Losing those two players was a major blow, but the Welsh selectors were still able to base their team around a strong core of experienced pre-war caps – Arthur Bassett, Alan Edwards, Dai Jenkins, Con Murphy, Gus Risman and Frank Whitcombe – to take on the English.

Having had little involvement with rugby league during the conflict due to his duties with Derbyshire Constabulary and travel difficulties, Arthur Bassett had kept in reasonable shape by taking advantage of those wartime freedoms. He had played as regularly as possible with Nottingham RUFC. With the conflict over Bassett had rejoined Halifax and was keen to wear the red shirt once more.

The experience of Con Murphy and Frank Whitcombe in the pack would be invaluable to one player making his international debut that day. Doug Phillips was still a serving soldier and the Army's demands on his time meant he could be described as very inexperienced in the ways of rugby league. He had only been able to play in one wartime and four peacetime matches since signing for Oldham.

A Services Rugby Union party had been dispatched on a continental tour. Included in the party were five players who were wanted at Swansea – Gus Risman, Emrys Evans and Doug Phillips by Wales and Ernest Ward and Albert Johnson by England. Due to fog, it was thought their return might be delayed, but they managed to make it to Swansea the night before, just in time to play in the match. There was a final hitch. Family circumstances prevented Emrys Evans from playing and he was replaced by his club-mate Dai Davies. Tommy Taylor replaced St Helens' Norman Thompson in the England pack.

The Championship's opening match on Saturday 24 November provided an unexpected chance for three of the team – 'Billy' Davies, Fred Hughes and Doug Phillips – to tread on St Helen's turf, once their home ground, once more. For some of the players who had not visited Swansea before what they saw would have shocked them. Enemy bombing and the subsequent fires had destroyed most of the town centre, but St Helen's Field itself had survived unscathed.

Saturday 24 November 1945: Wales 11 England 3
Swansea, 30,000

Many of the players on both sides were well known to the locals from their performances in wartime rugby union. That, and a contingent of United States servicemen, helped swell the crowd to a new record high of 30,000. Play began evenly, an unconverted Ike Owens try being matched by a similar one from Bob Nicholson. There were no further points until the half-hour mark when Gareth Price touched down and Gus Risman converted to give Wales a five point lead that they held at the break.

England were severely handicapped in the second half. Fred Higgins did not return to the field after the break. Albert Johnson was also injured and had to spend 15 minutes on the sidelines. Under-strength, England spent most of the half defending, which they did surprisingly well. Gareth Price, who the press rated the most brilliant back on the field, registered the second half's only points with a try that followed a fine Welsh passing movement. In a match notable for its keen tackling, the Welsh XIII delighted their supporters with a stylish win. Victory was the perfect way for Gus Risman to wind down the curtain on his Welsh career. It was not the end of international rugby for him, however. He would be called upon to lead Great Britain 'down-under' at the end of the season.

At a civic reception that evening Richard Lockwood, the RFL chairman, expressed the hope that this would be the forerunner of many more such matches in Wales and was pleasantly surprised to find that the Mayor of Swansea agreed. A formal agreement was soon reached and a total of 10 internationals would be held in Swansea over the next five seasons at a cost of £250 per match.

Only six members of the Welsh team that won at Swansea travelled to Bordeaux for the final match against France on Sunday 24 March. England had already beaten the French and now in turn the French beat the Welsh. As each nation had won one match the Championship had to be decided on points scoring average; England finished top, France second and Wales third.

One of those who missed the trip to France was Doug Phillips who was still required for duty in the Army XV. He was playing for them against the RAF at Twickenham that same weekend. The 26-year-old Phillips had managed only three more appearances for Oldham since the victory at Swansea, but that did not matter. The selectors had seen enough and were convinced that his formidable presence was needed in the tour party bound for Australasia.

The 'Indomitables'

In response to an invitation from Australia the RFL announced its intention to tour Australia and New Zealand on 24 October 1945. Acceptance was the easy part as the tour remained in doubt until the end of March 1946 when it was confirmed that the tour party would sail for Freemantle aboard the aircraft carrier HMS Indomitable on Wednesday 4 April. That tour would forever be linked to that mighty ship and the party known as 'The Indomitables'. Despite the party containing a record 11 Welshmen the team was still referred to as England as it made its way through Australia and New Zealand.

In his account of the tour, Eddie Waring mentions that of those 11 Welshmen only two spoke Welsh. When it came to the hard-fought match against Newcastle in mid-June the British team fielded Welsh half-backs. Rugby league folklore abounds with tales of half-back pairings trying to use Welsh to their advantage against opponents who only spoke English and they obviously tried in this match. The pair called a move in Welsh, but it failed. They tried a second time and it failed again. Believing their luck must change they decided to go for third time lucky. Before they could try again a voice boomed out from among the opposition's ranks. "Don't bother boys, I come from Swansea too!" shouted Madge, the Newcastle captain. It turned out he was from Garnant, the same as Ted Ward, one of the tourists, and the ploy was abandoned. Obviously, not all league playing Welshmen had gone north.

New blood needed

Although rugby of both codes had continued throughout the conflict, youth development had been affected badly in all parts of the country. Professional teambuilding had been practically impossible for the duration of the conflict. The fortunes of war may have brought Ike Owens and 'Dickie' Williams to Headingley and Doug Phillips to Watersheddings, but there had been few others over the six years of conflict.

As the game raced back to normality in the summer of 1946, it appeared that the Welsh presence was likely to be as strong as ever in the strongest NRL teams. Much of that was the result of a signing spree as the NRL's clubs rushed to bring their teams back up to pre-war standards and for that they thought Welsh talent would be the best choice.

The NRL's thinking was made clear by Eddie Waring in his contribution to a tour souvenir published by Sydney's *Sunday Telegraph* on 16 June 1946. In it he explained to his Australian readership that "When we are short of classy backs we send agents to South Wales, noted training ground of rugby union's nippy halves and centres, where, without trouble, one can find 'readymade' potential internationals. And we are always prepared to pay big money for them". If necessary, the latter part was certainly true and it seemed that the old days were not over yet as the NRL recruiters made their approaches.

Over that first post-war season, a Welsh XV had taken part in a series of Victory Internationals for which caps were not awarded. Some talented young players were identified by NRL scouts and among them were a number who would very shortly 'go north'; Tyssul Griffiths went to Hunslet, Elwyn Gwyther to Belle Vue Rangers (the former Broughton Rangers) and Les Thomas to Oldham in the summer of 1946. One full-back and two forwards was not quite what Waring had in mind and his view of the depth of the Welsh talent pool would soon appear somewhat outdated.

France had proposed successfully that the Championship's fixture schedule be reorganised to allow the teams to meet each other home and away. England and Wales would therefore meet twice a season. Also, while the tourists were away, Swinton were notified that Station Road would be hosting the International Championship's opening match, England versus Wales, on 12 October 1946. After the previous year's defeat at Swansea, the selectors made seven changes to the England team. Joe Egan was the only member of the pack to retain his place. Gus Risman's omission from the Welsh team was a surprise to many. Barrow's Roy Francis, after playing so often in wartime rugby union internationals for England, finally got the chance to don the red jersey of Wales against the Anglo-Saxons.

There were two changes to the published teams. Reg Lloyd was called up to replace Arthur Bassett in midweek, but it was not until Saturday morning that Eric Batten cried off and had to be replaced by his club-mate Jack Kitching

Saturday 12 October 1946: England 10 Wales 13
Swinton, 20,213

So just three weeks after the 'Indomitables' arrived home, 10 of them turned out for England: Ernest Ward, Jack Kitching, Albert Johnson, Willie Horne, Tommy McCue, Ken Gee, Joe Egan, Les White, George Curran and Harry Murphy. Seven played for Wales: Gus Risman, Bill Davies, Dai Jenkins, Frank Whitcombe, Doug Phillips, Ike Owens, and Trevor Foster. Some reporters commented that many of those tourists on the day looked unfit.

A try by Les White opened the scoring, but Bill (WT) Davies, with a try which he converted himself, put the lead back into Welsh hands before half-time. Lawrenson levelled the scores with a penalty goal early in the second half. However, it was the Welsh who seized the initiative with tries by Reg Lloyd and Roy Francis and a conversion from Bill Davies that gave them a solid lead. They needed it in the closing stages. England threw everything at the Welsh line in the last 10 minutes, but could only register a try from Alec Dockar, converted by Johnny Lawrenson. In a match that did not live up to expectations, the Welsh did enough to deserve their 13–10 win.

None of Swinton's existing contingent had found a place in the Welsh line-up which some of their supporters saw as an indictment of the quality of the club's recruitment policy. Swinton's management was already taking steps to rectify that situation. Their latest Welsh recruit, WE 'Billy' Williams, formerly of Newport, another who had appeared for Wales in a Victory International, was sitting watching in the stand. Newport provided two more recruits for Swinton later that season – a full-back, Ralph Morgan, and a hooker, Frank Osmond. Both went on to represent Wales at rugby league.

Wales versus England at Swansea 16 November 1946 at Swansea. (Courtesy Robert Gate)

England made a number of changes for the rematch at Swansea the following month. Martin Ryan was recalled after three years, this time at full-back. Ernest Ward replaced Ernie Ashcroft in the centre, Eric Batten regained his place on the wing at the expense of Jack Kitching and Tommy Bradshaw took over from Tommy McCue at scrum-half. Bradford Northern had the honour of supplying both captains – Northern's vice-captain Trevor Foster leading Wales and his club captain Ernest Ward leading England. They were the most prominent of the five players Northern supplied to the match.

Saturday 16 November 1946: Wales 5 England 19
Swansea, 20,500

Practically from the kick-off England were on the attack. England's overwhelming scrum superiority, courtesy of Joe Egan, meant they had possession for threequarters of the match and this allowed their backs to shine. The left-wing pairing of Albert Johnson and Johnny Lawrenson had a field day. Lawrenson had his first try after 10 minutes and his second five minutes after that. Albert Johnson got his first two minutes later and his second eight minutes after that. With 25 minutes gone, England had scored four tries, although only one was converted by Lawrenson. So, the score was 14–0 to the visitors. Wales hit back briefly with a try by Jenkins converted by Bill Davies.

If the crowd was expecting a lot more tries, they were to be disappointed. Martin Ryan suffered a bad rib injury which disrupted the English backs and they were only able to add a Lawrenson penalty goal and a late Johnson try to complete his hat-trick. Wales could add nothing at all to their total and the *Yorkshire Post* report noted that the 19–5 defeat sent the home crowd home "strangely silent and chastened".

After losing in Marseilles, Wales managed to beat France in Swansea to finish in second place in the International Championship table.

Welshmen in demand

Like most servicemen, Doug Phillips was looking forward to getting back to civilian life. That was not without its problems. The post-war housing shortage meant Oldham was struggling to find suitable accommodation for him and he was forced to live in his old hometown of Swansea. His travel costs to play in the north were proving too great for the club and the Oldham committee decided it was time he moved on. Phillips joined Belle Vue Rangers in early January 1947 for a fee reported to be £1,000, which was said to be a record for a forward moving between rugby league clubs.

The Welsh full-back in the match against France at St Helens, Bill Davies, a pre-war signing from Neath had started out as a centre, but switched to full-back if required after the conflict. His play in the red jersey must have impressed because he was transferred to Dewsbury for a new record fee of £1,650 at the end of January. Cruelly, 12 matches later Davies suffered a compound fracture of the leg which ended his war-interrupted league career.

The George Parsons affair

Any semblances of wartime fraternity were soon dashed in the austere post-war world. Signs of the old distrust and paranoia were soon visible. Newport's George Parsons had won his first Welsh rugby union cap aged just 19 against England when the Five-Nations resumed on 18 January 1947. He should have added a second cap against France in Paris two months later. However, Parsons' decision to leave the police force partway through his probationary course caused an official to believe that he was negotiating with rugby league representatives. That official informed the WRU and that led to Parsons being ordered off the Paris-bound train he had just boarded at Newport by Walter Rees, the WRU secretary. Parsons strongly denied the allegations, but a six-week suspension followed and although subsequently reinstated, those earlier suspicions having proved groundless, Parsons was never to figure again in the WRU selectors' plans. Inevitably, he succumbed to professional offers, receiving a surprisingly large signing-on fee from St Helens for a forward, said to be over £1,000, in January 1948. Parsons took time to settle, but he persevered and went on to make a further five appearances against England under rugby league's banner.

Induction

George Parsons and his Abertillery club-mate, Steve Llewellyn arrived in St Helens on the Friday evening ahead of their debut against Rochdale Hornets the following day. Llewellyn, a young schoolteacher, had been recruited with little fanfare by the Saints at the same time as Parsons. Many years later, Llewellyn recalled in an interview with Alex Service his rather amateurish induction into rugby league. As neither of them had ever seen a league match or gained some familiarity by playing in a trial match, another of Saints' Welsh contingent, Len Constance, was given the job of bringing the pair up to speed on their new game. They got together in Llewellyn's hotel room where Constance demonstrated the 'play-the-ball' with a pillow. Fortunately, both proved quick learners and went on to represent Wales, as did Len Constance.

The next match against England was played early season and utilised as a trial for the upcoming New Zealand tour tests. On the evidence of four club matches at most, the selection committee were expected to choose the team after the international.

Saturday 20 September 1947: England 8 Wales 10
Wigan, 27,000

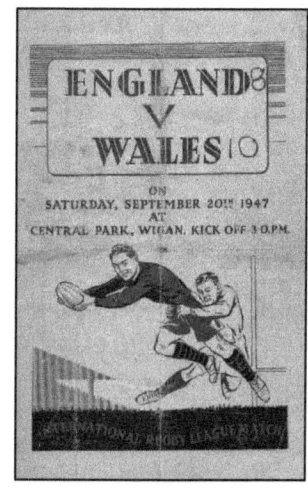

(Courtesy Gary Slater)

One young prop, Dilwyn Harris, was obviously making an impression and he was called up to make his Welsh debut. It was a big step up for Harris who had only made eight appearances in Castleford's first team ahead of the match at Wigan. Swinton's Ralph Morgan was sidelined by an injury and his place at full-back was filled by Joe Jones.

The selectors present watched a disappointing opening match. There was a poor display of back play from both teams which enhanced few reputations. Two tries from Les Thomas, the first of them the result of a memorable passing movement that covered 75 yards, matched two from England. It was Ted Ward's two goals, one more than Ron Rylance, that brought what was the only Welsh win of the season.

When it came to picking a test team, the selectors appeared to have had more questions than answers when Monday's newspapers came out. Although Wales had won, only four Welshmen – Billy Davies, Elwyn Gwyther, Les Thomas and Ted Ward, the latter as captain – were named in the team for the first test. Also included were three English backs – Albert Johnson, Jim Ledgard and Jimmy Stott – who had not figured in the trial.

Great Britain appears

For the first test at Headingley on Saturday 4 October the New Zealanders met the home Test team under its new name – Great Britain. Harking back to the days of the NU, the cover of the programme declared that it was contest between The Rugby Football League and New Zealand.

Inside an article explained that "the appellation of the team representing the RFL has always been the subject of much controversy. All players of British nationality are eligible to play, and it seemed rather incongruous that Welshmen and Scotsmen should be invited to represent England. The Rugby League Council have decided henceforth to refer to this composite team as Great Britain."

With the deciding test of the three-match series two weeks away, England and Wales met again in Swansea. Wales made eight changes to the team which had won at Wigan. England made eight changes to the team that had lost.

Injury ruled out Ernest Ward and the captaincy passed to Joe Egan. Des Clarkson was brought into the England team in place of Len Aston of St Helens.

Saturday 6 December 1947: Wales 7 England 18
Swansea, 10,000

Torrential rain, Swansea Town welcoming a crowd of 16,000 for the visit of Norwich City at the nearby Vetch Field and the end of unrestricted motoring due a national petrol shortage were all blamed for keeping the attendance disappointingly low.

According to the *Bradford Observer* Wales "were beaten in the scrums and unsteady behind". In the rain, handling errors were frequent and it was a disappointing match all round. Wales could only muster a penalty goal from Ted Ward in the first half, supplemented by a Trevor Foster try converted by Ward after the break. England meanwhile had crossed for four tries and kicked three goals to seal a comfortable win. In its report of the match the *Western Mail* commented that "The game generally was not as good as previous rugby league internationals seen at St Helen's, the passing lacking the quickness this type of game demands."

A subsequent home defeat by France ensured Wales finished bottom of the Championship table.

Swansea at bay

There were increasing grounds for concern about the declining attendances at Swansea which were threatening to make the venue uneconomic. There was plenty of competition for the spectator-shilling in the town with the rugby union club getting back to its pre-war standards and Swansea Town gearing up for a promotion push in Division Three (South).

Three internationals were played at St Helen's in 1947–48 and all ended in home defeats. Even worse, the attendances either side of the England match had declined from over 18,000 for the visit of the New Zealand in October to just over 6,000 for the visit of France in March. It was a worrying trend and one that Eddie Waring picked up on in an article for the April issue of *Rugby League Review*. Waring warned that "Preparations for these Welsh games are bad. Things are done in a haphazard way. Players are not assembled, they just roll up as if it were a club game, and the whole atmosphere is not of international standard, but of a club game and a very ordinary one at that." He went on to issue a rallying cry. "One question should be asked. Do we want rugby league football in South Wales? If the answer is 'Yes', then start properly and see that it is a success." St Helen's Field hosted three more International Championship matches – against England and France in 1949 and the Other Nationalities two years later without any obvious improvement.

The Welsh at Wembley

When Bradford Northern and Leeds faced each other at Wembley in the May 1947 Challenge Cup Final, half the players on the pitch were Welsh – Leeds fielding eight and Northern five. Among them were nine Welsh rugby league internationals and two who were soon to be capped. Only two of the 13 players on the pitch were post-war signings. Like at other clubs, the old guard kept soldiering on for Leeds and Bradford Northern, but father time was beginning to catch up with the Welsh pre-war champion team. Leeds's Con Murphy, aged 37, had bowed out after the November 1945 match. Bradford Northern's Frank Whitcombe, aged 33, made his final appearance a year later. His team-mate 'Billy' Davies, age 31, said farewell in September 1947 to be followed by Leeds's Dai Jenkins, 34, and Northern's Alan

Wales versus England at Wigan 22 September 1948. (Courtesy Robert Gate)

Edwards, 32, 12 months later. Between them they left a huge gap for the Welsh selectors to fill in a very short time.

Nearly all of the above had played for one of Bradford Northern, Leeds, Salford or Wigan who had been the keenest and generally most successful pre-war recruiters. In the harsh post-war world, all were finding recruitment much harder.

It was reflected in their contribution to the Welsh XIII; nearly all were pre-war stalwarts who were on the verge of retirement or talking about it along with a few wartime signings. There were few signs of new Welsh blood making a name for itself at any of those clubs.

Wigan, where there was a surfeit of local talent to meet the club's needs, made few Welsh signings, but the other three scouted and tried to recruit as before, but struggled to utilise the fruits of their labour. Scouting in South Wales began to appear as an expensive and mostly futile operation, although that did not prevent clubs making the occasional huge offer for a big-name player. Unless that recruitment situation changed in South Wales, there were bound to be problems down-the-line for the Welsh XIII.

Since the war ended, to aid the country's economic recovery the Government had actively discouraged and then officially banned any matches that were likely to encourage people to leave their places of work on midweek afternoons. Those prohibitions were lifted entirely ahead of 1948–49 and immediately the RFL reverted to midweek international matches in England.

In the next match, in September 1948, England was forced to make a late change, Russ Pepperell replaced Ernest Ward. Wales were not so lucky.

Injury forced Castleford's Len Skidmore to drop out and Joe Mahoney took his place in the centre, Len Constance came in for Dickie Williams and finally Charlie Staines replaced Trevor Foster.

Wednesday 22 September 1948: England 11 Wales 5
Wigan, 12,638

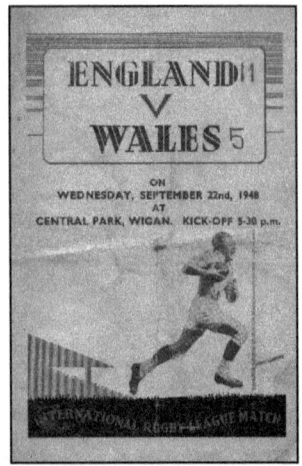

The match was played in persistent rain on a water-logged pitch. Handling was difficult and that pushed the scrum count up to 80 of which England took 46. Combined play was near impossible and both teams struggled to create chances. England scored all their points before the break with tries from Albert Pimblett, Stan McCormick and Gerry Helme and a goal from Harold Palin. Near the end of the match the Welshmen stirred themselves to work a try for Joe Mahoney, converted by Ted Ward to make the score a more respectable 11–5.

The Great Britain selectors met immediately afterwards to pick their team for the first test against the recently arrived Kangaroos at Headingley on Saturday 9 October. Trevor Foster was the sole Welshman chosen.

(Courtesy Gary Slater)

'Dinny' Boocker

The end of the ban on Australians signing for NRL clubs brought an unexpected bonus for Wales. Welsh-born Dennis 'Dinny' Boocker had moved to Australia with his parents when 18 months old. Growing up in Sydney, Boocker had taken up rugby league alongside many other sports and was playing for Newtown when he accepted an offer, reported as £900, to leave for Wakefield. He managed to complete the move just before the ban on signing Australians came back into force in August 1947. Boocker joined up with Trinity two months later and his form soon merited a call up from the Welsh selectors to play against England in Swansea.

Saturday 5 February 1949: Wales 14 England 10
Swansea, 9,553

Having already been defeated by Australia and then France, the Welsh were effectively out of the race for the Championship by the time England arrived at St Helen's for the third international of the season. Press reviews were pessimistic and yet some officials would rate the Welsh performance as their season's best.

Thanks to Frank Osmond's ball-getting in the scrum, Wales had, for a change, plenty of possession to work with. Their backs, ably led by Dickie Williams, showing plenty of pace and guile used it well. It was only Wales's inability to take all the chances they created that meant England finished the first half level at 7–7. Just before the break, Martin Ryan suffered a dislocated shoulder and England struggled to contain the Welshmen in the second half. The Welsh were made to fight, but in the end triumphed 14–10.

Wales had secured what was their only win of the season, but sadly their great performance was witnessed by a poor crowd, just three hundred higher than the one for the visit of the Australians three months earlier.

Despite the doubts about the game's ability to hold spectator allegiance in Swansea, the defeat of England generated enough enthusiasm for some ground-breaking work to be undertaken. The RFL and its Welsh Commission agreed that a promotional tour – featuring Huddersfield and St Helens – would be arranged in three months time.

Wales versus England at Wigan 1 March 1950. (Courtesy Robert Gate)

Two England stars who played against Wales. Left: Joe Egan (Courtesy Robert Gate); right: Martin Ryan (Courtesy *Rugby League Journal*)

Three matches would eventually be played in May at venues across South Wales and the public's response was very positive.

A new beginning in Wales?

The plans hatched in Swansea would lead to an eight-member Welsh League starting in 1949–50. The League's founder members were, Aberavon, Amman Valley, Bridgend, Cardiff, Llanelli, Neath, Welsh Dragons and Ystradgynlais. To help the new league, Bill Fallowfield asked the NRL's clubs not approach its players. However, not all the NRL's clubs were listening. Swinton's officials used the Wales versus France match at Swansea on 12 November 1949 as cover to meet an Ystradgynlais and former Swansea prop, Owen Phillips. Terms were agreed and his move north to Swinton went through without hindrance. At the time the regulations meant that his transfer would cost whatever Phillips negotiated as a signing plus a levy of £250 which was payable to the Welsh League. Having come to terms with his new game, Phillips made his debut in the Welsh XIII a couple of years later.

The return of the Other Nationalities

So many good players had been signed by NRL clubs from Australia and New Zealand since the signing-ban had lapsed at the end of December 1941 that it was possible for the Other Nationalities' team to be reformed. They were included in the International Championship in 1949–50. Their inclusion meant the tournament schedule reverted to a single match between each country each season.

Wales's opening match was held at Abertillery in October. In front of a poor crowd of 2,000, the Other Nationalities won by a single point, having beaten England four weeks earlier. A victory over France at Swansea the following month got the Welsh campaign back on track, but there was then a four month wait before the final match which would decide the title's destination. Both England and Wales needed to win if either was to challenge Other Nationalities' place at the top of the table.

The match was held at Wigan on St David's Day in 1950. With no tour trials being arranged, the international was effectively a final trial for the upcoming tour 'down-under'. Willie Horne was forced to withdraw with a hand injury and was replaced by Wigan's utility man, Jack Cunliffe. In a clear sign of changing times there were six Wigan players, all locals, in the England side. No one from Wigan was chosen for the Welsh XIII which would have been unimaginable before the war.

Wednesday 1 March 1950: England 11 Wales 6
Wigan, 27,500

Both sides tried to play fast, open rugby, but points were elusive. The only ones came from an Arthur Daniels try which put Wales ahead, 3–0, at half-time. A sturdy second half rally saw England take the initiative.

Sixteen minutes in, Jack Hilton got his first try and added a second soon afterwards. Dickie Williams levelled the scores with a try for Wales before a 50-yard run following an interception by Jack Hilton saw him complete his hat-trick seven minutes from time. Ernest Ward added the conversion. This was enough to give England the title and leave Wales in third place. With so much at stake, there was a huge attendance, 27,500, which was a record for an England-Wales match in England that stood for nearly 50 years.

Within 12 hours, the touring party for Australasia was selected. Practically the whole of the English team was selected and four of the Welshmen on duty that day – Arthur Daniels, Frank Osmond, 'Dickie' Williams and Les Williams – were included in the party along with two – Elwyn Gwyther and Doug Phillips – who were not. Unfortunately, Les Williams was not able to make the tour due to work commitments.

The Park, Abertillery

Writing in the *Sunday Pictorial*, the forerunner of the *Sunday Mirror*, on 6 February 1950, Eddie Waring told his readers that the "Future of big rugby league in this area will be under review very shortly, and I would not be surprised to see a different venue in south Wales. This weekend secretary Fallowfield received applications from Abertillery and Bristol." Waring was right. Swansea lost the contract to host internationals and the town, later a city, would lie fallow as far as rugby league was concerned for quite a few years.

Abertillery had already struck a deal with the RFL to host matches at its council owned stadium, The Park, which was the home, but not exclusively, of the town's rugby union club. The town council's willingness to hire out the ground for a good fee inevitably attracted the wrath of the WRU.

The Park, which lay in a picturesque natural bowl at the foot of the Arael Mountain on the edge of the town, was said to have a capacity of 40,000 when it made its debut as an international venue with the visit of Other Nationalities in October 1949. Sadly, it was very much a fair-weather ground with only cover for 650 spectators. This was nowhere near enough on the day, as heavy, icy rain and lightning kept the attendance down to a bare minimum and this made for a significant loss. Unfortunately, the town's location towards the northern end of the Ebbw Fach valley was hardly ideal but the RFL would persevere.

The RFL scheduled the opening match of the next Championship, Wales versus England, at Abertillery on 14 October 1950. Due to its size, The Park would not look full even with a better attendance for England's visit than that seen at the previous year's international.

Both teams were selected at the end of the Lord Derby Memorial Fund match, between a 1950 tourists' XIII and the Rest, at Wigan on Wednesday 5 October. Twelve members of the recently returned tour party were selected – three for Wales and nine for England. For one member of that England contingent, Joe Egan, it had been a busy time since returning home. Wigan had placed him on the transfer list at his request, big-spending Leigh had expressed an interest and he had subsequently signed for them as player-coach for a new record fee of £5,000. Although he arrived at Abertillery as a Leigh player, he was short of recent game-time and had yet to play for his new club.

Saturday 14 October 1950: Wales 4 England 22
Abertillery, 8,000

Many of the Welsh team had played on The Park in their rugby union days, but for George Parsons it was a match to savour as it provided a chance to 'trespass' on his old home ground. A young, uncapped centre from Pontypool was brought into the side for his debut. Don Gullick, who had only made his first team debut for St Helens on 16 September, had just seven league matches under his belt. Wales included a non-NRL player in their ranks; Roy

65

Lambert was chosen from the Neath Rugby League club, one of the members of the eight-club Welsh League.

Hunslet had converted Jack Evans from centre to full-back at the start of the season. Evans changed position so successfully that he not only displaced the club's 'old school' custodian, Tyssul Griffiths, but went on to be selected for Wales and would go on to take over the role for Great Britain the following season. There were a couple of late changes, Jim Featherstone replaced an unwell Ken Gee in the England pack and Joe Mahoney replaced the injured Les Williams as one of the Welsh centres.

Heavy rain had left the pitch soft. Just 10 minutes after the kick-off, Wales's scrum-half, Billy Banks, suffered a facial injury and had to leave the field. With Dickie Williams standing in at scrum-half, Wales mounted a gallant defence. Two penalty goals from Bryn Goldswain were the only points Wales could muster, but England only reached the interval 9–4 ahead. Wales continued to play gallantly, but the unequal struggle proved to be just too much. England went further ahead through a Johnny Lawrenson try seven minutes into the second half. The Welsh defence continued to keep England in check until the last four minutes, when England ran up 10 points to make their win look comfortable. Wales went on to lose both of their following matches and took the wooden spoon.

To take advantage of the light autumn evening, there was a 6pm kick off at Knowsley Road on Tuesday 19 September 1951. There were several changes to the published teams; For the first time in long careers two of England's stalwarts were missing – Ernest Ward was surprisingly over-looked and Joe Egan was unavailable. Late changes affected both teams. For England Gordon Ratcliffe replaced Stan McCormick and 'Ginger' Burnell replaced Workington Town's Albert Pepperell. For Wales, Terry Cook was replaced by Roy Lambert and Les Williams by Joe Mahoney.

Tuesday 19 September 1951: England 35 Wales 11
St Helens, 20,918

Wales were keen to get back to winning ways and initially the omens looked good before injuries to Elwyn Gwyther and Viv Harrison reduced the Welsh team to 11 fit men with 50 minutes left. At that point the Welsh had scored two tries to one and were ahead 8–5, but not even a sporting crowd cheering their every move could prevent the inevitable.

Four minutes before the interval Les White got over a try which Ken Gee converted to give England a 10–8 lead. Wales still had hopes and Dickie Williams grabbed a try four minutes after the restart to reclaim the lead. That it was it for Wales as an attacking force. Twenty-five unanswered points, 20 of them in the last 15 minutes, made the English victory look even more emphatic. A good crowd of over 20,000 produced a profit of £1,492.

After the match, Dickie Williams and Elwyn Gwyther were chosen to play for Great Britain in the first test against the touring Kiwis at Odsal Stadium on 6 October.

Once again Wales lost the next two internationals to finish at the bottom of the Championship table. Worryingly, among the higher echelons of the RFL the feeling was growing that Wales was incapable of fielding a team able to extend the English.

Bradford Northern's directors announced at the start of October 1951 that they were to spend £2,000 to upgrade Odsal Stadium's speedway lights for use at rugby league matches. It was a bold initiative which meant that Bradford Northern gained the honour of becoming the first football club, of any code, to have floodlights outside London. Northern's lights were

Wales versus England at St Helens on 19 September 1951. (Courtey Robert Gate)

ready and switched on for the visit of the New Zealanders on Wednesday 31 October 1951, and drew a very good midweek crowd of 29,072.

Having enjoyed playing under floodlights, the Kiwis requested that another match be arranged if possible and the RL Council considered the options. Essentially a fixture on the Kiwis' itinerary would have to be rearranged to grant their wish. While the RFL continued to believe that the Welsh public were willing to support rugby league, declining attendances at Welsh venues were a cause of concern. In particular, there was unease about the prospects of the New Zealand versus Wales match scheduled for St Helens on Saturday 8 December.

Keen to accommodate the tourists, the RFL announced in mid-November that that match would be held under Odsal's floodlights on the evening of Friday 7 December. The attendance of 8,568, who paid £1,051, while not particularly good, was seen as an improvement on what might have been.

There was a new Cardiff club in the NRL that season, but its home at the newly opened speedway stadium on Penarth Road, with a capacity of 30,000 (2,000 seated), clearly held little attraction for the RFL. Five days after the match at Odsal the Kiwis turned out at Penarth Road to take on Cardiff in front of a paltry afternoon crowd of 1,475.

Decision time in Wales

Losses on representative matches in Wales were compounded by the need for the RFL to subsidise the start-up Cardiff club if it was to complete the season. The high hopes of seven

67

years earlier appeared to be in tatters and there were some strident critics who were keen to push their own Welsh agenda. An article in the February 1952 issue of *Rugby League Review* entitled 'Entrenchment' put the case for ending the game's entanglement in Wales. According to the author, Welsh representative matches were only increasing "the already huge debit account on rugby league football in Wales". For the author the way forward was clear; retrenchment in the northern counties should be a priority.

It had not been realised at the time, but the Welsh team had already played its last international match in the Principality for over 20 years. It had happened at Abertillery on Saturday 1 December 1951 when Wales had taken on the Other Nationalities in front of a crowd estimated by the press at 10,000 yet reported officially as 3,386.

Something had to be done to stem the losses and the RFL's international selection committee meeting at the end of April 1952 took what it probably thought was the only sensible decision. For the coming season it would cease using Welsh venues and arrange all Wales's home matches in the north of England.

There were some in the north of England who welcomed this decision. A regular contributor to *Rugby League Review*, Vincent Firth, spoke for them when he commented "It is gratifying to learn that it has at long last been realised that the playing of 'home' Welsh international matches in Wales is a shameful waste of time and money, and that these games will in future be played in the North." A small, but enthusiastic, band of Welsh supporters had effectively been left high and dry.

The following season's International Championship opened once again with England taking on Wales. This time the match returned to Wigan's Central Park, which was celebrating its Golden Jubilee, on 17 September 1952, play getting underway at 6pm.

There were the usual pre-match changes. Seventeen-year-old Terry O'Grady replaced Huddersfield's Dick Cracknell on England's right wing.

There were three changes for Wales – Sydney Williams came in to replace Jack Evans, Don Gullick replaced Salford's Jack Davies and Mike Condon replaced Owen Phillips.

Wednesday 17 September 1952: England 19 Wales 8
Wigan, 13,503

Neither side showed much cohesion. For once, the scoring did not reflect the scrum count. In the first half Wales took the scrums 16–8, but with Willie Horne running the play England managed to create tries for Charlie Pawsey, Alf Burnell and Ernest Ward to one from Roy Lambert to deservedly lead 13–5 at the break. In the second half, England took the scrums 21–12 but could only manage two tries from Dougie Greenall and Alf Burnell to one from Ray Price for Wales. England finished as winners 19–8.

The selectors had seen enough and Great Britain's line-up for the first test against the touring Australians, on 4 October, was announced the following day. Just two Welshmen, Jack Evans – who had not played at Central Park – and Arthur Daniels, were named in it.

After losing at Wigan, Wales confounded their critics. They went on to beat France at Headingley the following month which meant the title would be decided by the outcome of their match against the unbeaten Other Nationalities at Warrington in mid-April. The Welsh won that one too, which meant that the three teams were tied at the top of the table with two wins apiece. Points' difference had to be used to separate them; the Other Nationalities finishing as champions with +24, Wales second on –3 and England third on –6.

Welsh hopes of an even better campaign received a setback almost as soon as the new season got underway. It was confirmed that the Principality's biggest-name, Lewis Jones, was struggling to recover after injury and was not playing well enough to warrant selection. Eighteen months on from a severe knee injury, 'Dickie' Williams was still struggling to regain his best form and full fitness. Realising he was short of both, Williams stood down from the opening match, England versus Wales, at Knowsley Road on Wednesday 16 September 1953. His withdrawal had limited impact as stand-off was a position where Wales had some real depth; Ray Price coming back into the team in Williams's place.

Except on a few occasions when injury had ruled him out of contention, Ernest Ward had been an automatic choice as an England centre ever since the war. Now, at the veteran stage, he found himself embroiled in a dispute with Bradford Northern over a transfer to Castleford and a move into coaching.

Unable to play for either club he was ruled out of selection for this match and a last chance to face Wales was gone. For England, the experienced Ken Traill replaced a young Johnny Whiteley at loose forward.

Joe Humphreys in his preview of the match in the *Daily Mirror* gave details of the players' payments for the match. They were due to receive £10 for a win, £8 for a draw and £7 in defeat which compared unfavourably with those offered by the FA for their internationals.

Wednesday 16 September 1953: England 24 Wales 5
St Helens, 19,357

This was another early evening kick off and it attracted another good crowd to Knowsley Road. Saints supplied two players to England – Stan McCormick and Dougie Greenall – and two to Wales – Don Gullick and George Parsons. Greenall and Gullick were once again in direct opposition and a full-blooded contest ensued with the former enjoying a better evening by scoring a try. Other members of Saints' Welsh contingent – Ray Cale, Steve Llewellyn and Glyn Moses – could only watch on from the stand as an England team with an accent on youth played well. England took the first half scrums 20–12, but could only register a Dick Cracknell try to lead 3–0 at the break.

Wales just shaded the scrum count in the second half, but England overran the Welsh defence running in five more tries in a total of 21 points to take home the winning pay. Wales only response was an Arthur Daniels try, converted by Jack Evans. It was a convincing victory over what was reckoned to be a near full-strength Welsh side.

Wales were unable to find any better form against the Other Nationalities at Odsal Stadium four weeks later. The Championship campaign concluded in the Marseilles Velodrome where the Welsh suffered the narrowest of defeats. A winless Wales received the wooden spoon once more. An undefeated England took the title. The Welsh glory of the late-1930s was by then a distant memory in both the north of England and South Wales.

BBC television

Although the BBC television service was resumed in 1946, its coverage was not extended to the north of England until the switching on of the Holme Moss transmitter in October 1951. Almost immediately, the BBC began to broadcast coverage of rugby league matches. The second half of the Wales versus Other Nationalities match at Odsal Stadium, which was played under floodlights in October 1953, was covered by the BBC. Although television sets were not that common in both northern England and South Wales in 1953, that broadcast provided some rugby league fans with what turned out to be the last chance to catch a glimpse of the Welsh team in action for many years.

A changing emphasis

To accommodate rugby league's inaugural World Cup tournament, which was held in France between 30 October and 13 November 1954, the International Championship was suspended for a year. While in abeyance, the Rugby League Council decided in February 1955 that Wales, due to declining levels of recruitment, was no longer strong enough to maintain an independent existence in the International Championship. Wales was effectively wiped off the rugby league map.

The meetings of England and Wales which had enabled rugby league supporters to see its best players playing at the highest representative level over many purely domestic seasons were consigned to history. Those fixtures had also offered an incentive for rugby union players to turn professional by offering a much-desired chance to play for national pride. They had also given rugby league a showcase for those rugby supporters outside its heartland to check how its new law changes had worked out and to what extent professionalism had improved fitness and the quality of play. They would be missed.

Wales was merged into the Other Nationalities when the International Championship was restarted in 1955–56. The Other Nationalities finished that season as champions with a team that included eight Welsh players – Billy Banks (Huddersfield), Billy Boston (Wigan), Bryn Goldswain (Oldham), Granville James (Hunslet), Lewis Jones (Leeds), Glyn Moses (St Helens), Ray Price (Warrington) and John Thorley (Halifax). Believing it also to be a declining force due to the inevitable effect of the signing-ban on Australians and New Zealanders which had been extended for a further five years in 1954, the RFL disbanded the Other Nationalities side at the end of the 1955–56 season. The International Championship was also suspended to be replaced by an annual series of test matches between France and Great Britain.

8. The scale of the challenge in South Wales

The scale of the challenge facing the Welsh XIII in South Wales should not be minimised. There was a different balance of power between the football codes after the war. Rugby union writer JBG Thomas noted it in the *Playfair Annual* for 1948–49. Reviewing the domestic situation Thomas wrote "Today, the rugby union's greatest rival in Wales is not the rugby league but association football, particularly in the West, although the Australian tourists and Cardiff's continued brilliance did much to counter the opposition of the rival code." Crowds were flocking to Ninian Park and the Vetch Field. At the former, Cardiff City was in the process of rising from Division Three (South) to the Football League's First Division in just five years while in Swansea there was a return to Division Two. With the association and rugby union games going head-to-head, rugby league became collateral damage as it was squeezed into insignificance.

The start of the 1950s saw a revival of the Welsh XV under the leadership of John Gwilliam. His teams were hard to beat, if hardly exciting, but for a short spell they were successful and reconnected with post-war sports fans. Transformed from wooden-spoon recipients the previous year, Gwilliam's men delivered the first Grand Slam for Wales since 1911 in 1950. When the fourth Springboks arrived at the Arms Park on 22 December 1951, they were greeted by a crowd of 55,000. The next home match, which brought Scotland to the Arms Park on Saturday 2 February 1952, drew a ground record crowd of 56,000 with receipts of £14,506. The Welsh closed their Five-Nations campaign with the visit of France to an extended St Helen's Field in March. A staid performance was enough to deliver victory and a second Grand Slam.

While Gwilliam's teams might have only enjoyed a brief period of success, interest in the Welsh XV grew massively and had an impact across Britain. The quest for the first Grand Slam started at Twickenham in mid-January 1950 where an estimated 25,000 Welsh were part of a record 75,500 inside the ground and thousands locked outside. Thirteen months later, it was estimated that 20,000 made the trip to Murrayfield to be part of a record 80,000 crowd there. By the time Wales returned to Twickenham in January 1952, the RFU had made the venue all-ticket. Even so when the gates had to be closed there were 73,000 inside and once again thousands were locked out.

In his preview of the upcoming rugby league international published in the *Daily Mirror* on Wednesday 17 September 1952, Joe Humphreys could only wonder at the difference in attendances: "To watch a Welsh rugby union XV play, the pit workers and steel rollers from the valleys of South Wales travel in their thousands. Dublin, Murrayfield or Twickenham, it makes no difference. But they won't turn up to see England play Wales at rugby league in Wigan. And because of this apathy towards the professional game the rugby league's international games fall flat. Left to support Wales are only the Welshmen exiled in the north." Humphreys declined to offer any suggestions as to how the problem might be fixed.

Spurning the offers

The biggest 'names' in that Welsh Grand Slam team – Bleddyn Williams, Lewis Jones, and Cliff Morgan – would prove difficult to recruit. The agents tried their best, making offer after offer but found little encouragement. Larger and larger sums were mentioned, but with the economy picking up, the leading players had alternatives to 'going north' to consider. Not long after returning from the 1950 British Lions tour of Australasia, Bleddyn Williams, who had been the subject of a large amount of interest from Wigan, disclosed that he had received an offer of £6,500 from an unnamed rugby league club, a huge amount for a player in his late 20s. DE 'Danny' Davies recounts in his book, the centenary history of Cardiff, talking over the offer with Williams as the team travelled to play Newport on 11 November. Besides letting him know how much the team would miss his stylish centre play, Davies focused Williams' attention on the advantages to be gained from his Rydal scholarship and the "important occupational and professional prizes to be gained as an amateur, broadcasting and writing for example". Having considered his options, Williams decided to reject the offer. Williams continued to resist offers rising allegedly to £10,000 for a three-year contract plus a job. Having captained his country, he retired in 1955, still beyond the clutches of the scouts, having followed Davies's advice, moving into journalism and writing regularly for the *Sunday People.*

Many others would try and follow his lead over the coming years, taking jobs in the media, banking and finance as the union game sought to protect its greatest talents. For many others the resurgent Welsh economy would provide enough opportunities to make a move across the Severn unnecessary.

Rising fees weaken the team

While the leading players might still listen to offers, there seemed to be little interest. They seemed reluctant to turn professional despite the large sums being quoted which were hugely inflated compared to those offered pre-war. As a result, the recent Welsh rugby league teams, even though they had never had a high proportion of Welsh rugby union caps in their ranks, lacked glamour and stature compared to their pre-war heyday.

Peter Dimmock's Sportsview Annual for 1955 had this to say on the changing situation: "For many years, until very recently, there was a regular influx of Welshmen travelling north for trials with the 'pro' clubs. Of late this stream has become less steady and only the 'big' names are being chased. It is unlikely that the £6,000 paid to Lewis Jones of Gorseinon will be passed. For even Rugby League clubs are finding expenses just a little too much to spend as freely as they once did in the Welsh valleys."

While France showed an occasional interest in meeting Welsh teams in the late 1950s and early 1960s, no other fixtures were possible as the England XIII also practically disappeared from the international stage for the next 15 years. It meant that neither Lewis Jones, nor another supremely talented young Welshman, Billy Boston, would ever have the chance to wear the red shirt of Wales against England in a rugby league international.

Lewis Jones and Billy Boston

Lewis Jones was the one big-name who would eventually be tempted by the northern-pound. His initial reluctance would eventually cost him dear in terms of future Welsh caps. The 21-year-old Jones was finally convinced to go north by Leeds for £6,000 on a nine-year contract in November 1952. This substantial sum, which equated to around 12 years salary for a professionally qualified man, was far higher than any previously paid to a union convert and was even higher than the NRL's transfer record. The fee was backed up by match terms of £12 for a win, £8 for a defeat plus additional bonuses for cup-ties. When he finally put pen to paper it was big news. After only seven matches, Jones was ruled out of action by a broken arm and it was not until the start of the 1953–54 season that he resumed his career in the 'A' team. It meant he was unable to stake his claim for a place against England until after the last match was played in September 1953. In spring 1964, Jones departed to start a new life in Sydney well before Wales resumed playing.

While some Welshmen accepted rugby league offers in a blaze of publicity others, the comparatively unknown and mostly uncapped, would be deemed worthy of little more than a few lines in the press. That was the fate of the second of rugby league's biggest names in the 1950s and 1960s, Billy Boston. His performances for the Army XV were little known outside the game, but he would develop to become rated by many as one of the finest, if not the finest, Welsh rugby league player of all time. The timing of his entry into rugby league, however, was awful from the point of view of winning a Welsh rugby league cap. The 19-year-old made his debut for Wigan on 21 November 1953 two months after Wales had played England for the last time. Ten matches later he was on his way to Australia as a 1954 British tourist. With age and injuries catching up on him he called time on his Wigan career, announcing his retirement and played what he said would be his last match at the end of April 1968, five months before the decision was made to bring the Welsh team back into life. Throughout that long and very successful career, Boston had never been able to don the red jersey in an official international against England.

A declining Welsh presence

There had once been a strong Welsh presence in the touring parties heading 'down under', but in the mid-1950s and beyond that was much reduced. Billy Boston and Lewis Jones were both included alongside Tommy Harris (Hull) and Ray Price (Warrington) in the 1954 party which was led by Hunslet's 'Dickie' Williams. Four years later there were just two – Tommy Harris (Hull) and Glyn Moses (St Helens) – and no Welsh half-back for the first time ever. The next party in 1962 included just one, Billy Boston (Wigan). This was due as much to the fact that rugby league was changing on the field as to the paucity of recruitment activity off it. One notable recruit was international full-back Garfield Owen, who joined Halifax in 1956. He signed for the club live on BBC's Sportsview programme.

A changing game

Full-back play, which had remained very similar to that found in rugby union, changed significantly after Jim Sullivan hung up his boots. In Sullivan's prime, the last line of defence had to have a safe pair of hands under the high ball and an ability to return kicks far down field to put their opponents on the defensive and, if possible, force a handling error or find touch. Kicking duels between full-backs were a regular feature of play in the NRL. A safe pair of hands was still important, but the attitude had grown that kicking away possession was the wrong thing to do. Full-back play had to change and the days of the old style were numbered.

A few Welsh full-backs were still signed and Jack Evans, a former Newport centre, gained test honours at the start of the 1950s before they were superseded by the out-and-out running full-back pioneered by Martin Ryan at Wigan under Jim Sullivan's coaching. Recruitment of Welsh full-backs was much reduced until rugby union adopted a similar style most famously in the form of JPR Williams.

73

1959 Wales team which played France in a friendly. (Courtesy *Rugby League Journal*)

Welsh forwards also anticipated largish pay days, but their chances of successfully converting to League were plummeting. Since the end of the Second World War, league coaches, like Jim Sullivan at Wigan, had placed a greater and greater emphasis on handling skills and pace up front. Scrummaging alone was no longer enough. Forwards, like Welsh hooker Tommy Harris, had to be good in loose play and back-row forwards needed to be powerful, pacey ball carriers. The other essential change was to stop following the ball in the event of needing to ruck or tackle and instead stay in the line and wait for the ball to come their way. There was little understanding of those differences in Welsh rugby union at the time and the recruitment of forwards, even those with a good reputation, became prone to failure.

Welsh coaches

While the Welsh presence might have been declining on the field, it had probably never been greater in club affairs. Most clubs had by now appointed manager-coaches, and many of them were former Welsh internationals. For 1960–61, Welsh coaches were preparing the following teams to play the new evolving style of rugby league: Bradford Northern (Dai Rees), Doncaster (Bryn Goldswain), Halifax (Griff Jenkins), Hull (Roy Francis), Leeds (Dai Prosser), Oldham (Gus Risman), Rochdale Hornets (Jim Sullivan), Salford (George Parsons) and Swinton (Cliff Evans). It was a list that bore testimony to the enormous contribution that some Welshmen had made to the rugby league game over the years.

9. The times they are a-changing

In the mid-1960s, the opinion in the north of England was that the Welsh did not want to watch rugby league and their best players did not even want to seriously discuss playing it. The first issue of the *Leeds RLFC Supporters Yearbook,* published in 1965, included a contribution from the club's general-manager, Joe Warham. Drawing on his wealth of experience he let his readers know that the approach to teambuilding had had to change: "Never was the junior field more assiduously combed than it is today. With the ban on overseas signings and because the welfare state has removed much of the compulsion to leave South Wales, clubs largely confine themselves to recruitment from Lancashire, Yorkshire and Cumberland." If a club like Leeds with its spending power and traditional allure for Welsh players thought it could no longer succeed, then the chances of new stars arriving from the Principality looked remote. While Warham and the Leeds board might be focusing their recruitment nearer to home, some other northern clubs still lived in hope of bringing some talented Welshmen north.

Terry Price and David Watkins

Not long after Warham's comments were published, there seemed a new optimism about the Welsh market. Writing in Huddersfield's *Yearbook* for 1967, the chairman of the club's football committee, George Armitage, said that the old methods of strengthening the side would be used again. "Already deputations have been into South Wales to see recommendations but at the time of writing no direct signings have been made." It is doubtful that Huddersfield had either the ambition or the budget big enough to pull off a big-name signing whereas a couple of once powerful NRL clubs – Bradford Northern and Salford – fared far better.

Before Armitage's intentions were committed to print, the headline in the local paper in late April 1967 had proclaimed "Welsh Wonder Boy signs for Northern". The article revealed that after weeks of secret negotiations, Bradford Northern had secured the services of Llanelli's full-back Terry Price for a club record fee of £8,000. Price had made his debut for Wales against England two years earlier while still a teenager. His potential was clear and he looked certain to be a Welsh star for many years to come but in the Five-Nations' tournament which had just completed, he seemed to be struggling in a struggling team. Three months later Salford announced the signing of David Watkins for £16,000. A fast, elusive running stand-off with a good kicking game, Watkins was a proven leader who had captained Newport, Wales and the British Lions in the past five years. Although out of favour for a while with Welsh selectors, he had fought his way back into the national side at the end of the previous season and looked back to his imperious best.

These were the sort of high-profile signings that had not been made by a rugby league club since Leeds secured Lewis Jones 15 years earlier. As with the signing of Lewis Jones, both Bradford Northern and Salford were looking to their new Welsh stars to increase their profile and demonstrate that there was real ambition in their respective boardrooms. Both clubs had to hope that their stars made a successful conversion into a much different game. Both players would have to refine their skills, retune their instincts and realign their tactical understanding. Both managed it well. Price made his debut for Northern on 27 August and went on to play test match rugby league. The 25-year-old Watkins made his Salford debut on 20 October and went on to win six Great Britain caps.

Their presence raised the profile of rugby league nationally and led to the possibility of the Welsh team being revived. Previous failures had left their mark on the RFL and the committee decided to 'test the water' in South Wales before going further. Bradford Northern and Salford agreed to take part in an exhibition match on Saturday 1 June 1968. The venue appropriately would be The Park at Abertillery. It was an enjoyable return to his homeland for Terry Price who contributed 26 points – four tries and seven goals – towards Northern's 46–20 victory. The attendance, 10,000, boosted confidence and the RFL proceeded to re-awaken the Welsh XIII from its long hibernation three months later.

A survey was conducted which showed that there were 37 Welsh players registered with the NRL, and the good news was that although there was a preponderance of wingers, the players identified covered all the positions. There was even an international class hooker available – Tony Fisher had left the RAF and followed in his brother Idwal's footsteps to Bradford Northern.

Sixty years earlier, the England versus Wales matches had got underway not long after the NU had made major changes to create its own version of the handling code. The restart of that series of matches took place under an updated and quite distinct version of rugby league. At least this time interested rugby fans in Wales had through television coverage a clearer idea of how rugby league had changed.

Limited tackles

It had become obvious that monotonous and predictable play was losing supporters and plunging the game into crisis. Attention focused on the play-the-ball which might have been designed to provide a contest for the ball, but had changed over the years to allow the ball carrier's team to inevitably retain possession. It was a development that provided no adequate reward for the tackler's team. Some radical thinking was needed to stem the decline.

At a management committee meeting in late September 1966, Bill Fallowfield presented a statistical report detailing the functioning of the tackle law which highlighted the ability of sides to retain possession for long periods. It was felt something had to be done and Fallowfield proposed that the number of successive tackles a team in possession could enjoy should be limited. Ignoring the fact that the season had been underway for over a month, it was decided that from October onwards clubs could choose to use the reformed law. This stipulated that after a team was tackled three consecutive times, a scrum would be formed to give their opponents a chance of gaining possession.

Overall, there was a positive response and that was sufficient for clubs to agree to use the new rule in all NRL matches from November. Many coaches and players were less positive as they struggled to adjust and many spectators were still to be convinced, especially as the number of scrums increased.

Nevertheless, an emergency meeting of NRL clubs, while supporting the limited tackle idea, agreed to increase the tackle limit to four in December. That number proved acceptable and the change would be written into the laws of the game at the 1967 RFL AGM by a near unanimous vote. It was the radical move the game needed and would change its emphasis significantly from possession to field position.

Substitutes

While the Welsh team was in abeyance the RFL, like the WRU, amended its rules on substitutes to try and end the old problem of injuries leaving teams to play on short-handed. When international matches restarted, the rules provided for up to two substitutes being allowed as replacements for any reason before the second-half started. By the following year rumours of abuse had become so rife that the rule was amended to allow the tactical substitution of up to two players at any point in the match. Over the coming years the rules would evolve further towards the multiple player interchanges that would become the norm in both rugby codes.

Back on the field

The Welsh XIII returned to action in Salford on the evening of 7 November 1968. For many of the NRL's Welsh players, the dream of wearing the red shirt had come true at last. John Mantle was made captain of a new look Welsh team. Kel Coslett, who had been the Welsh XV's full-back six years earlier, was selected as loose-forward, a position to which he had successfully converted after recovering from a broken leg. Coslett and Mantle were joined by four other Welsh rugby union caps – Terry Price, David Watkins and John Warlow with Bobby Wanbon, who had played at Twickenham at the start of the year, on the bench. Four– John Mantle, Graham Rees, Clive Sullivan and John Warlow – were also Great Britain test caps.

The selectors had some unwanted news in the run up to the match. Both Castleford's Alan Hardisty and Hull KR's Alan Burwell withdrew and had to be replaced by Billy Benyon and Chris Hesketh. Then, on the morning of the match, Alex Murphy also withdrew. Tommy Bishop was the selectors' choice to replace him, but he was un-contactable through work. With time running it was decided to play the reserve back, Leeds's Mike Shoebottom, normally a stand-off in the less familiar role of scrum-half.

As the band struck up *Men of Harlech,* the re-born Welsh XIII took to the field under The Willows' floodlights. BBC cameras were on hand and the match featured later that night on the *Sportsnight* programme.

Thursday 7 November 1968: England 17 Wales 24
Salford, 6,002

The Welsh were primed for action and were quicker and better handlers of the ball from the start. Their forwards broke through to send Colin Dixon in for a try within the first minute. Eleven minutes later, the Welsh forwards burst through again to send another of their number, Graham Rees, over for a try. Terry Price converted both of them and the Welsh were 10–0 up with barely a quarter of an hour gone. England struck back with a try by John Atkinson, converted by Brian Jefferson to halve the deficit. Wales were awarded a penalty try when Watkins was obstructed, Terry Price converting. Kevin Taylor responded with England's second try on 22 minutes. Welsh pressure

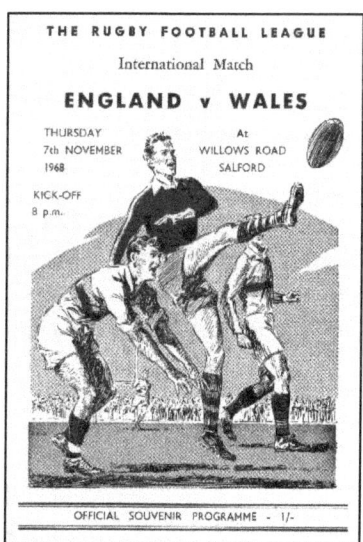

kept England on the back foot and with a couple of penalty goals, the Celts were 19–8 ahead at half time.

Wales's fourth try, which came immediately after the break, was a spectacular effort from Clive Sullivan. Once again, Price converted. England had the better of the rest of the half, scoring a further three tries, two of them from Alan Smith and one from Cliff Watson, but it was not enough. Although England had outscored the Welsh by five tries to four, it was Terry Price's goalkicking, six from seven attempts, that proved decisive. His opposite number, Brian Jefferson, managed to convert only one of his eight attempts.

An immediate victory over England, the first for nearly 20 years, appeared to be exactly the start needed to inspire the Welsh. Colin Dixon's storming display for Wales brought him a Great Britain cap three weeks later and led to his transfer to Salford in mid-December in a deal reckoned to be worth £15,000, a new record. Wales narrowly lost in Paris in March to bring down the curtain on a very successful season.

One of the new caps in 1968 was the multi-qualified Alex Kersey-Brown. He was born in Bristol, but had a Welsh mother and a Scottish father. He had joined Huddersfield from London Welsh. The following year the Cornish-born Peter Rowe, who had grown up in Wales and captained the Welsh under–19 team in union, made his debut.

International confusion

After the completion of the 1968 World Cup, the RLIB addressed the international timetable and decided the next tournament would be held in England and France in October 1969. There were even thoughts about including Wales in that competition. Those plans were soon abandoned and into their place came a restart of the International Championship, rebranded as the European Championship with the Welsh XIII involved. Bill Fallowfield, the RFL's general secretary, appeared to downplay the latter possibility saying that there were not enough Welsh players to cover a crop of injuries and crucially there was only one hooker among them. Ignoring Fallowfield's concerns, Wales, having put up a good performance against France in March 1969, was included when the European Championship was relaunched for the following season. Wales versus England at Headingley on 18 October 1969 was the Championship's opening match.

As an 18-year-old, Keith Jarrett had made a sensational debut for the Welsh rugby union side against England in April 1967 scoring a record-equalling 19 points. It was a performance that immediately made him the target of rugby league offers. Finally, two years later, Jarrett accepted a deal worth £14,000 over five years and made an impressive try-scoring debut for Barrow against Wigan on Friday 3 October 1969. On the basis of that one performance, the selectors hoped to play him against England but he was forced to declare himself unavailable with a hamstring injury. Injury also ruled out Gordon Lewis, David Watkins and Keri Jones. Alex Murphy was forced to rule himself out due to injury and there was a further late change for England, John Atkinson replaced the unlucky Alan Burwell.

Saturday 18 October 1969: England 40 Wales 23
Leeds, 8,355

Both teams set out to attack and the lead changed hands three times in the first half-hour. Roger Millward opened the scoring with a penalty goal to put England ahead. A Peter Rowe try took the lead back for Wales.

Syd Hynes, Roger Millward and Bill Burgess after England have scored against Wales on 18 October 1969. (Courtesy *Rugby League Journal*)

Ray Batten's try took it back for England before a Terry Price penalty goal levelled the scores at 5–5. A David Jones try, converted by Price then put the Welsh ahead only for them to be pegged back by a Syd Hynes try, converted by Millward. The final try of the half came from Colin Dixon. There was a final penalty goal from Millward to leave Wales in front by a point, 13–12, at the break. Once play restarted, it was clear that England were keen to take control of the match. Tries by Alex Murphy and Syd Hynes, the former converted by Millward gave England the lead. A Clive Sullivan try closed the gap, but it soon widened further as Ray Batten and Syd Hynes touched down, the former converted by Millward. Alex Murphy added a drop-goal to put England 11 points ahead. Wales rallied and scored a late try through Phil Morgan, converted by Price who then added a penalty goal. Wales could get no closer and before the end, Bob Haigh added a try, converted by Millward. So England won 40–23.

Wales went on to lose in France before England and France drew at Wigan. With England and France tied at the top, a win apiece, the Championship's round of matches had not produced a conclusive winner. So, the French proposed that a second series be organised. As France had already scheduled visits from England and Wales it only left the RFL to arrange a second meeting between England and Wales. There ought to have been a home match for Wales in this second series, however, at short notice there was no realistic prospect of that. Football League and WRU grounds were out of bounds and older options like Cardiff's White City was lying derelict, while the Penarth Road Stadium was in the hands of developers.

As plans were formulated for the second series, Trevor Foster, who had been keen to get involved, was interviewed by Brian Bearshaw for the *Manchester Evening News*. Foster obviously felt the England match was a missed opportunity. So much more could and should have been achieved. "There was no atmosphere. It was very sad. I was in the dressing-room to rub one or two players down. I felt cold. There seemed a lack of enthusiasm among some, and two of the players weren't fit. The two substitutes ... were itching to get on the field. They badly wanted to play, yet they had to sit on the bench for the whole match. It was said that the rugby league couldn't find a team manager for our international side. But this is ridiculous. There are many of us about who'd be only too happy to take it on. The importance seems to be going out of these matches, unfortunately. Let's build them up again, get the players together, get Welshmen together, organise meetings and restore interest."

Wales opened the second series with a morale boosting win at Perpignan. Their second and final outing, the Championship's penultimate match, saw them take on England, once more at Headingley, on 24 February. The Welsh had to win by a large margin and hope England could only draw with France at Toulouse in a month's time for them to become champions. The referee for the match was RL Thomas who was the grandson of one of the earliest Welshmen to take the road north after the 'split'. His granddad was Richard Llewellyn Thomas, who after playing full-back for Pill Harriers and Newport arrived in Oldham in August 1897. He gave a decade of great service to his new club.

England included five backs from the high-flying Leeds club whose skills and fitness had been honed by Roy Francis. Graham Rees stepped into the Welsh team in place of John Mantle. Both teams were eager to impress with selection for the tour 'down under' imminent.

Tuesday 24 February 1970: Wales 7 England 26
Leeds, 9,393

Having so many players from Leeds among the backs brought cohesion to England's play. Between the five of them they accounted for five of England's six tries. Hull KR's Phil Lowe got England's sixth try and Ray Dutton kicked four goals. Wales's only points came from a Keith Jarrett try and two Stuart Ferguson goals. England had recorded a comfortable win, but their subsequent defeat at Toulouse meant that even after playing the second series there was still no clear winner so the title went to the nation with the best points scoring average. That was England with 1.56, ahead of France with 1.18.

An uninteresting series was cited as the reason for suspending the Championship after just one season, but by then it had been confirmed that a World Cup tournament would be held in England in October and November 1970. A Kiwi tour the following season, a World Cup tournament in France in October and November 1972, to be followed by a Kangaroo tour in 1973–74 left no space for the European Championship and it was suspended.

Six-tackles and new scoring values

While the Welsh XIII was once again inactive, some significant changes were made to rugby league. The belief that allowing only four tackles before ball-release was leading to 'panic' rugby grew and so did calls for change. More time to mount a planned attack was needed, but change came about slowly. The NSW Rugby League was the first to bow to the pressure, officially introducing a six-tackle limit in 1972. For the 1972–73 season, the number of consecutive tackles in British rugby league also increased from four to six. A reduction in the value of the drop-goal to one point was agreed by the RLIB in January 1974. That change was approved by the RFL at its AGM in June 1974. That AGM, however, rejected an increase in the points for a try to four, which had also been agreed at the January 1974 RLIB meeting. That change would not finally be made until 1983.

10. The RLIB resurrects the Welsh XIII

The RLIB, in a bid to widen the game's international presence, began moving towards a new competition in 1975. The plan was for a five-nation championship which would include separate English and Welsh entries. It was not a plan that appealed to the RL Council when it was considered in October 1974, but finding itself in a minority of one it reconsidered and accepted it the following month.

The European Championship was quickly restarted despite initial concerns about raising a strong Welsh team. Unfortunately, some key players, such as Terry Price, Phil Morgan and Keith Jarrett had moved on, leaving some significant positions to fill. To allay any fears regarding Welsh strength, the RFL futuristically agreed to include players of Welsh descent in the national team. A Welsh parent or grandparent was required, and a search of the NRL's rosters turned up a number of possible players.

The response to Welsh-heritage inquiries was very positive and soon there was a list of excellent new Anglo-Welsh players such as Peter Banner, Harold Box, Eddie Cunningham, Bill Francis, Trevor Skerrett and David Treasure to factor into future team-building plans. England also appear to have benefited, the Peebles-born George Fairbairn who had represented the South of Scotland rugby union representative team, becoming available, allegedly qualifying by virtue of an English grandmother. While this was relatively controversial at the time, it became standard practice in many sports over the next few years.

Recognising the need for better organisation, the RFL appointed Ron Simpson, the former Castleford chairman, who had recently stepped down as chairman of the RL Council, as the first manager of a very experienced Welsh squad in January 1975. Further independence came in the form of a separate selection committee, even if they were all English to begin with. Reg Parker, Ron Simpson, Dick Gemmell and Mike Lamb of Dewsbury were the selectors. Les Pearce, the coach of Halifax, the club he had joined from Swansea after appearing in Welsh rugby union trials in August 1949, was appointed as coach of the Welsh XIII. Time was allotted for training sessions. Time and injuries might have been taking their toll, but David Watkins was the obvious choice as captain. He accepted which bestowed on him the honour of having led his country in both rugby union and rugby league. Bill Oxley, a Barrow director and member of the RL Council, took on the job of England manager in partnership with Warrington's Alex Murphy as coach.

A new 'Golden Era'

The rebirth of the Welsh XIII came as Welsh rugby union was enjoying another 'Golden Era'. It had begun with Triple Crown and Grand Slam success in 1968 and followed by another Triple Crown the next year. Over the 'Era', which lasted until 1980, the Welsh team collected six Triple Crowns, three Grand Slams and perhaps more importantly beat England on 10 out of a possible 12 occasions.

Besides innate talent, the success of the latest 'Golden Era' was based on a businesslike spirit similar to the one that animated the original. Taking advantage of an increasingly flexible amateurism, the WRU looked for success through thorough preparation, relying on unprecedented levels of coaching provided by a national coach, national squads and squad sessions. Over those dozen heady seasons, the WRU's approach delivered a supremely confident attacking combination that was thought to exude Welsh style and delivered exemplary success.

In those years the Welsh side virtually picked itself, which placed huge demands on the core members of the national squad. Its most iconic figures – Gareth Edwards, Barry John, Phil Bennett, Gerald Davies, JPR Williams, Ray Gravelle and Mervyn Davies – became household names both in Wales and across Britain. They all received good offers to 'go north' and one or two hesitated before saying 'no' and staying loyal to the team. For many of them, offers of well paid, flexible employment outside the game kept them safely at home.

During that spell of great success a few of the Welsh squad still found the challenge of rugby league appealing. Of them, three wingers – Maurice Richards (joined Salford October 1969), Roy Mathias (joined St Helens August 1972) and John Bevan (joined Warrington September 1973) went on to achieve great success in rugby league. Injury blighted the chances of Clive Griffiths, who joined St Helens in August 1979, from achieving similar success in the new game.

Return to Swansea and Salford

International rugby league returned to Wales after an absence of 24 years as part of the re-launched European Championship. Swansea's St Helen's Field was hired for the visit of France on Sunday 16 February 1975. Public interest was huge and there were still people queuing outside the ground 15 minutes after kick off. The gates were opened and around 3,000 let in for free. That attendance, given officially as 15,000, provided a huge boost for international rugby league. Next up for Wales were the English at The Willows in nine days time. That evening clash would decide the European title's destination.

The Welsh selectors made just one change to their starting line-up. Stuart Gallacher came in for Mike Nicholas. David Watkins led out an experienced Welsh team at his home club ground. The starting line-up contained three 'Anglos' and there were two relatively recent recruits from the ranks of the successful Welsh rugby union squad – Cardiff's John Bevan and Llanelli's Roy Mathias – who were proving to be 'natural' rugby league players. Glyn Turner, who had only signed for Hull KR a month earlier, was on the Welsh bench.

England's coach, Alex Murphy, let the press know that this match was being treated as a trial for the World Championship. It explained why the selection was somewhat controversial; two players, both struggling to overcome injuries, had been chosen. And it soon turned out that the doubts were valid as both Steve Nash and John Walsh withdrew from the team and had to be replaced by Roger Millward and Derek Noonan. There were two more late changes – Ged Dunn came in for Salford's Keith Fielding and Mick Morgan for George Nicholls. The captaincy also passed from John Walsh to Roger Millward. For Wales the only late change was Dick Evans taking over at hooker from Tony Fisher. Hoping to build on his team's emphatic victory in Swansea, Les Pearce said he was hoping to give the English "a very good run for their money."

Tuesday 25 February 1975: England 12 Wales 8
Salford, 8,494

David Watkins opened the scoring with a drop-goal, but that narrowest of leads did not last for long. England responded with tries from Derek Noonan and John Atkinson.

John Atkinson scoring for England against Wales on 25 February 1975.
(Courtesy *Rugby League Journal*)

Both were converted by John Gray. The first half's scoring was completed by Kel Coslett who succeeded with one of his three penalty kicks at goal to leave his side trailing 10–3 at the break.

A spell of fierce tackling opened the second half and led to a severe blow to Welsh hopes. Following an incident with Mike Coulman, Jim Mills was dismissed for striking. Despite being a man down, David Watkins led by example; he scored a try which he then converted to put Wales within two points of England.

The gap could not be narrowed any further before John Gray added a penalty goal to England's total. This made the final score 12–8. Wales may have lost, but a runner-up finish in the Championship was a satisfactory prelude to the impending World Championship.

The 1975 World Championship

Instead of a World Cup tournament, a new format World Championship was introduced. The Championship stretched across Europe and Australasia and ran from March through to November. Wales, one of the five entrants, kicked off the competition in Toulouse at the start of March, then headed to Australia for the months of May and June before drawing down the curtain on the whole event in Salford at the start of November. Fixtures would be home and away which meant England and Wales would meet twice in the tournament. No final was planned, the final placings were to be decided by a league table.

England got off to a great start by beating France at Headingley in mid-March. A week earlier Wales had lost to France in Toulouse. Both sets of selectors then sat down to pick parties of around 20 players to make the month-long trip 'down under'. Two of the most potent scoring threats in world rugby, Maurice Richards, who had appeared in the opening match, and John Bevan declined to be part of the Welsh party which headed to the Antipodes. For England the changing balance of power in the global game was a major concern. Their hopes would rest on a squad weakened by the exodus of a handful of Great Britain forwards – Bill Ashurst and Mike Stephenson (Penrith), Phil Lowe and Mal Reilly (Manly-Warringah) and Brian Lockwood (Balmain) – to the Sydney Premiership. There was a further blow when they lost the services of John Gray to North Sydney before the squads set off south.

The first of the England-Wales meetings, the 50th time the two countries had met, was technically the Welsh home match. It was held, however, in the unfamiliar semi-tropical surroundings of south Queensland. To get ready for the fray, the Welsh arranged two warm-up matches. The first was a benefit match on the evening of Wednesday 21 May. It was played under floodlights at Dewsbury's old Crown Flatt ground where a Welsh rugby team had first beaten England 85 years earlier. A second victory followed at Ipswich in Queensland on Thursday 5 June. England meanwhile used matches in Perth and Toowoomba, both won, to sharpen up for the critical fixtures that lay ahead.

Ready or not, the English met the Welsh under lights in Brisbane on 10 June. The venue was Lang Park which after a major re-development would become the home of the Brisbane Broncos, the Suncorp Stadium.

Tuesday 10 June 1975: England 7 Wales 12
Brisbane, 6,000

Local television was enlivened over the run up to the match by the outpourings of Alex Murphy, the England coach. Murphy was at his outspoken best, informing the viewers that among other things not one of the Welsh squad was good enough to find a place in his England team. He also claimed that as a rugby league coach, Les Pearce might make a good greyhound trainer. Murphy's goading was seized upon by Pearce. He used it to motivate his team and turn the clash into a grudge match. Pearce's game-plan was simple, keep play forward-based and hope that Wales's rugged pack would get the better of their English opponents. Back play would hardly figure.

It was soon clear that the Welsh pack was better equipped for a physical battle and Pearce's game-plan proved to be a winner, but it led to some ugly, vicious incidents. England were unable to play to their own strengths and struggled to put points on the board. David Treasure scored the only try of the first half, which along with a David Watkins penalty goal gave Wales a 5–2 lead at the interval.

After the restart, an opportunist try by Clive Sullivan and more penalty goals from David Watkins gave Wales a healthy lead. With 10 minutes remaining, Tommy Martyn got over for a try and George Fairbairn kicked a second goal, but time was against them. Following a brawl in the late stages of the match, England's centre, Les Dyl, was dismissed for kicking David Watkins. After the match the referee defended his decision: "I could have sent off half-a-dozen players off. ... Eventually one had to go but the match was all over by then."

The on-field ill-feeling persisted and the two sides refused to socialise after the match. Wales had inflicted an unexpected defeat on England which eventually fatally undermined their hopes of winning the Championship. The pouring rain had deterred the locals from attending in any number and the receipts were much lower than expected.

That was as good as it got 'down-under' for Wales. The next match against Australia in Sydney was lost, as was the one against New Zealand in Auckland. The latter took place during a six-match tour of the 'Land of the Long White Cloud'. Things went much better for the English party. During June they managed to draw with New Zealand in Auckland and then a week later achieve a similar result against Australia in Sydney. After a series of matches in Australia and Papua New Guinea they too headed home.

The two British squads then had a couple of months break from international action before the Championship's second stage got underway in Europe. To drum up interest, both the England and Wales squads recorded singles. England's record was titled *Up and Under* while *Hear the Mighty Dragon's Roar* was Wales's offering.

The Championship got underway again on 20 September when England and Wales resumed hostilities at Warrington's old Wilderspool home. Three months had passed since Brisbane and team changes were inevitable. A knee injury side-lined Jim Mills and Mel James was brought in.

John Mantle, Brian Gregory and Frank Wilson replaced Bobby Wanbon, Colin Dixon and Dave Willicombe respectively. There was also a further late change in the Welsh line up, Clive Sullivan replacing Roy Mathias.

Alex Murphy's Warrington squad supplied nine players to the World Championship, five for England and, by September, four for Wales. However, only one of them, John Bevan, figured in the match at Wilderspool.

The England selectors were keen to exact some revenge on the Welsh. They kept only four of Brisbane's starting line-up – George Fairbairn, Keith Fielding, John Atkinson and Roger Millward. The whole pack was discarded and a new group of forwards brought in. There was a lot for Alex Murphy to do ahead of kick off.

Saturday 20 September 1975: Wales 16 England 22
Warrington, 5,034

England could not have had a better start. They caught Wales cold and had their first points on the board, a penalty goal by George Fairbairn, in the first minute. Two flowing passing movements followed, producing tries for Keith Fielding and John Holmes. The latter was converted by Fairbairn to put England 10–0 up in nearly as many minutes. A further penalty goal from George Fairbairn extended England's lead. With the deficit mounting, Wales got organised and replied through a David Watkins penalty goal and a Peter Banner try, converted by Watkins. The only other scores of an entertaining first half were penalty goals from Fairbairn and Watkins which left the score at half-time 14–9 to England.

Once play restarted, Wales grabbed the initiative and got their reward after 12 minutes when Kel Coslett powered his way over. Watkins converted to level the scores at 14–14. Fairbairn and Watkins went on to add penalty goals to their country's totals as each side strove to gain the advantage.

RUGBY LEAGUE   1975
World Championship
WALES V ENGLAND
Wilderspool, Warrington.
Sat. Sept. 20th
Official Programme 15p

(Courtesy *Rugby League Journal*)

It was England, well-marshalled by Ken Gill and Roger Millward, who made the breakthrough. Another Fairbairn penalty, a try from Eric Hughes and a drop-goal from Keith Bridges put England through to victory. Sadly, there was a poor turnout to watch England win an exciting, closely contested match 22–16.

England were building momentum and managed to beat New Zealand at Bradford and then at the start of November Australia at Wigan. That wound up what had been in many ways a very successful campaign for the English, but the draw against New Zealand and the defeat by Wales left them one point behind the champions, Australia, in the World Championship table. Having lost to Australia in Swansea in mid-October, the Welsh XIII bounced back to beat New Zealand at Swansea and then finally overcame France at Salford to claim third spot in the table.

To accommodate the World Championship, there was no European Championship in 1975–76. There was some bad news in April 1976 when the RL Council decided that there were not enough Welsh players and agreed to merge England and Wales into the Great Britain team for the next World Cup tournament which was to be held in Australia and New Zealand in June 1977. This was accepted by the RLIB in the following October.

The good news was that the European Championship was to be restarted once more and it opened with the meeting of England and Wales at Headingley on 29 January 1977. Sections of the press carried details of an invitation to Prince Charles to attend the match. Those hopes were soon dashed when it was discovered that the Prince had other engagements.

Bill Francis and David Watkins were put in charge of the Welsh team's preparation as joint player-coaches. Watkins also doubled up as the Welsh captain. Bradford Northern's Peter Fox was handed the England coaching job. When the squads were announced a week before Christmas Peter Fox had doubts about a lack of balance in the England ranks. Some of the squad's senior players harboured doubts about Fox's highly structured rugby. Late changes were minimal; Doug Laughton replaced Hull FC's Steve Norton in the English line-up. Hull KR's Phil Lowe also eventually withdrew to be replaced by Jeff Grayshon.

Saturday 29 January 1977: England 2 Wales 6
Leeds, 6,472

A very close match had been predicted and a good crowd was anticipated. It was certainly a keenly fought match, but a conflicted England XIII struggled to live up to its pre-match billing as favourites. There were only a couple of real scoring opportunities in the first half; David Watkins sent a penalty right in front of the posts wide and Stuart Wright almost got over in the corner for England. No one else came close and the half finished 0–0.

With the second half live on BBC Television's *Grandstand,* the small crowd had to hope that play would improve for the viewers at home. It was, however, an English mistake that would determine the outcome. A dropped ball was seized upon by Eddie Cunningham who dashed in for the only try of the match which Paul Woods converted from the touchline. George Fairbairn kicked a penalty and Peter Rowe a drop-goal to bring a disappointing match to a close. Afterwards an elated Ronnie Simpson summed up the afternoon for Arthur Brooks of the *Daily Mirror:* "We could have played better, but England were simply awful."

The title appeared to be there for the taking, but the French proved too strong in Toulouse three weeks later. A subsequent English defeat in Carcassonne meant the Welsh finished as runners-up, with the Anglo-Saxons below them.

Roger Millward scoring for England against Wales at St Helens in May 1978.
(Courtesy *Rugby League Journal*)

Left: Jeff Grayshon, in Featherstone kit, who made five appearances for England against Wales between September 1975 and November 1981. (Courtesy *Rugby League Journal*)

Two decades earlier, the WRU had decided that only Cardiff Arms Park was capable of hosting international matches and had duly abandoned St Helen's Field. Since then, it had been underused, a situation that did not sit well with the Swansea Corporation. They made it available once more and the RFL arranged for two matches to be played there as part of the 1975 World Championship. Three years on, the Wales versus England match was scheduled to be played there on 19 February 1978. Having beaten France at Widnes in mid-January, the Welsh team, coached by Bill Francis and John Mantle, headed to Swansea full of confidence. Unfortunately, a heavy overnight snowfall brought South Wales to a standstill and forced the match to be called off.

A move to play the match at Headingley the following evening was abandoned after police advised against trying to make the journey until the roads were cleared. Continuing bad weather and the ensuing fixture congestion meant the match had to be postponed.

The re-scheduling took so long that St Helen's had been handed over to its summer tenants, Glamorgan County Cricket Club. The Championship decider eventually took place, on a Sunday for the first time, at Knowsley Road in the middle of the Spring Bank Holiday weekend.

With the honours and medals accounted for, the teams were announced on Monday 22 May. England had to replace two forwards, Phil Lowe and Mick Adams. With George Fairbairn ruled out by injury, 32-year-old Geoff Pimblett was called up for his international debut. Late season injuries also hit Wales hard with Colin Dixon, Mike Nicholas and Glyn Shaw all ruled out. To partially offset those losses John Mantle was coaxed out of international retirement. Kel Coslett was unable to prepare the Welsh team so the job fell to the players – Bill Francis taking responsibility for the backs and John Mantle the forwards.

Sunday 28 May 1978: England 60 Wales 13
St Helens, 9,759

With the temperature pushing 25°C, this was summer rugby long before summer rugby came along. Wales looked disappointingly out of condition and were just too slow to be competitive. A one-sided first half ended 28–2 to England. Wales's only response was a penalty goal. There were signs of the old pride after the break, Wales showing enough fight to run in three tries. England, however, had run through them at will to score 14 tries in total.

In so doing, they also wrote a couple of new entries into the record book; this was both a record defeat and also a record margin of defeat for a Welsh team which still managed to finish as runners-up once more. Such a heavy defeat led Ron Simpson to reflect afterwards that "The future of Wales must be very dicey. We just do not have the forwards capable of putting up an international show." Alarm bells immediately started to sound at the thought of Wales being demolished if the planned meeting with the Kangaroos went ahead the following autumn. The RFL held its nerve and Wales did extremely well to hold Australia to 8–3 at Swansea in October 1978.

Kel Coslett, who was Rochdale Hornets' player-coach, was appointed as the Welsh coach for 1978–79. A Welsh team, depleted by the loss of five forwards through suspension and injury, played bravely but could not get the better of a strong French side at Narbonne in January. Then, it was time to dispel any lingering memories of the hammering at Knowsley Road and prepare to take on the English again on the evening of 16 March 1979 in Widnes. Naughton Park, as the ground was then known, was a new venue for the meeting of England and Wales.

Time was catching up with David Watkins' body and he withdrew to be replaced in the squad by Ray Wilkins. The captain's armband was passed to Bill Francis. Due to illness, Hull FC's Keith Tindall was forced to withdraw shortly after selection and was replaced in the England pack by Harry Beverley. There was a late reorganisation of the English team; Hull KR's Phil Hogan had not recovered from an injury and he was forced to drop out. Mick Adams dropped back to replace Hogan at loose-forward and Tommy Martyn was brought in to fill the vacancy in the second-row.

Snow caused problems on the day of the match. With trans-Pennine routes blocked, the appointed referee, Fred Lindop, was unable to travel over from Wakefield and Ron Campbell, who lived locally, stepped in. England's kit was stuck in transit in the car of David Howes, the RFL's Public Relations Officer, and England had to take the field in Widnes's black and white strip. With selection for the upcoming tour of Australia and New Zealand looming there was a lot at stake for both teams.

Friday 16 March 1979: England 15 Wales 7
Widnes, 5,099

In very poor conditions, with continuous sleet driving across a treacherous surface, both teams put up a spirited performance. A fiery opening saw Welsh hooker Tommy Cunningham dispatched to hospital with a broken nose and forced some reorganisation in the Welsh ranks. Wales could, and probably should, have built an early lead, but Paul Woods missed three attempts at goal early on. England struck first with a Keith Mumby penalty goal before his opposite number, Harold Box, replied with a try and conversion to put Wales ahead by three points after a quarter-of-an-hour. Ten minutes later, Keith Smith got a try for England and an evenly balanced first half ended all-square, 5–5.

After the break, England generally handled the atrocious conditions better than the Welsh. Ten minutes after the restart, England took the lead through a John Woods try, but the gap was reduced to a single point by a Harold Box penalty. In the last 15 minutes England got a try from Mumby to which John Woods added the conversion and a later penalty goal to make a 15–7 victory look easier than it had been. A second defeat meant Wales finished bottom of the table. England went on to beat France the following weekend and claimed the title.

Five 'Anglos' – Harold Box, Gus Risman's son John, Bill Francis, Tommy Cunningham and Trevor Skerrett – had been included in the Welsh team which was one less than in the earlier match at Narbonne. In his 1980 autobiography, David Watkins wrote that he was unsure about having too many 'Anglos' in the team as it would detract from the authentic nature of a Welsh XIII and that 'discovering' a Welsh ancestry had become a bandwagon for ambitious players. While this was partly due to an understandable desire for international honours, Watkins also felt that it was partly because the match fee had by then risen to £75. The number of 'Anglos' selected would fluctuate, but would remain an essential feature of the Welsh XIII going forward.

Blackpool Borough's chairman, Reg Parker, who had managed the Great Britain tour parties to Australasia in 1974 and 1977, took over as the Welsh team-manager. Kel Coslett, recently appointed as coach at relegation threatened Wigan, found the time to continue as Wales's coach. St Helen's coach, Eric Ashton MBE, who had just returned from the tour of Australia and New Zealand, was appointed as England's coach.

Friday 29 February 1980: England 26 Wales 9
Hull, 7,557

With the City of Kingston-upon-Hull enjoying a rugby league boom, the RFL announced in the middle of February that the meeting of England and Wales would return to Hull KR's then home, Craven Park, after an absence of 44 years. When the teams were announced on 17 February, they included four Hull FC players – one for England and three for Wales – which was a record number for the 'Airlie Birds'. The record proved short-lived as one of them, Keith Tindall, had to withdraw, this time due to injury. His place in the England team was filled by Keith Rayne. Hull KR provided three players to England. It was an inexperienced England team containing seven new caps and an average age for the team of 25.

There was a lot for both teams to play for as the RFL was considering the possibility of sending England and Wales on a promotional tour of the USA for a three-match series in June. Some critics aired their doubts and certainly the USRL seemed unwilling to put up the requested guarantee of £50,000. Like many other North American schemes for rugby league, it all proved to be mere speculation.

Play was fairly even for nearly half-an-hour as England struggled to rid their play of errors and Wales looked almost in vain for combination. An early exchange of kicks put England ahead, 3–2, thanks to a George Fairbairn penalty and a Harry Pinner drop-goal against a Paul Woods' penalty. A Roy Holdstock try, converted by Fairbairn, on 20 minutes opened a wider gap, made wider still when John Joyner crossed 10 minutes later. Fairbairn converted. Wales only response was a second Woods penalty goal to leave England comfortably ahead 13–4 at the break.

In the second half, Wales's play improved. A Pinner drop-goal made the slightest improvement to England's lead before some smart interplay sent Brian Juliff over for a try, converted by Woods. Wales

90

could not close the gap further and it remained at five points until the 70th minute. Then George Fairbairn dived over for a try, Paul Woods stamped on his hand and was shown a yellow card. Fairbairn added the conversion and a further two point penalty for the foul. Two minutes from time, Keith Rayne added a further try and that might have closed the scoring. It did not because Paul Woods stiff-armed Steve Evans which not only saw him dismissed, but allowed Fairbairn to add another two points to England's total in injury time.

Having already lost to France at Widnes, Wales again finished bottom of the Championship table.

The passing of the old guard

A group of veteran Welsh players had retired, which forced Wales to start rebuilding at the end of the 1970s. Filling the vacancies left by the likes of John Mantle, who bade farewell after the heavy defeat in 1978, and two other titans of a great Welsh pack, Jim Mills and Mike Nicholas, who both made their last appearances the following year, would never be easy to do.

That forward weakness would be covered by a few big, bustling wingers, some nearing the veteran stage such as John Bevan, Roy Mathias and Brian Juliff finding a place in the Welsh pack. Replacements were also needed in the back division for David Watkins and Clive Sullivan, who also made their last appearances against England in 1979. Age caught up with Bill Francis in 1980 to make the rebuilding process even more demanding. Losing so much experience and talent in such a short space of time was bound to deal a huge blow to the team, but at least the selectors had the consolation that there was some new talent coming into the NRL to work with.

Although he had ultimately failed to stave off relegation at Wigan, Kel Coslett's work had not gone un-noticed and he had been recruited by St Helens as their coach. Once again, he found time to continue as the coach of Wales. The international match returned once more to east Hull. With both teams having lost their opening matches, the title already belonged to the French. The clash of the two Home Nations at Craven Park on 18 March 1981 was therefore to decide which of them took home the wooden spoon.

When the teams were announced earlier in the month, there were five players each from Hull FC and Hull KR. By the time the teams took the field, that number had been reduced to four each; Steve Nash was recalled in place of Hull KR's Paul Harkin for England and Brian Juliff replaced Hull FC's Paul Prendiville. There were two other changes; Leigh's Des Drummond withdrew and the England selectors replaced him with Terry Richardson. Steve Rule was a late call up to replace Clive Griffiths in the Welsh line-up. Hull KR's Colin Dixon was a surprise recall for the Welsh. Two members of the Welsh squad, Adrian Cambriani and Martin Herdman, were selected from the new Fulham club which was pioneering professional rugby league in London. For the latter it was a major step up; Martin Herdman, who qualified thanks to a Welsh grandmother, had only managed half-a-dozen first-team appearances. He was the first Londoner to play for Fulham.

Wednesday 18 March 1981: England 17 Wales 4
Hull, 4,786

The match reports said that England coasted to victory and they were certainly the better team throughout. In testing conditions, the creative work of Ken Kelly and Steve Norton in midfield made all the difference. Tries from John Joyner and Ken Kelly in the first half put England comfortably in front. A further try from John Woods in injury time and four George Fairbairn goals sealed the victory. Wales never really looked like a scoring a try and Steve Rule's brace of penalty goals provided all their points.

Wales having again lost both its matches for the third season in a row, the Championship, which France had regained to end England's hopes of a fifth consecutive title, was suspended. The timing of that decision would prove to be poor to say the least.

11. Friendlies in the 1980s

Bob Grogan had used his company, the Newcastle-upon-Tyne-based Kenton Utilities, a civil engineering concern, to buy the bankrupt Cardiff City Football Club in 1977. With no fixtures for City's reserve and youth teams in 1981, the Ninian Park pitch was standing idle far too often. With the Football League open to ground-sharing, Grogan, City's chairman, discussed Fulham's rugby league activities with its chairman Ernie Clay and decided to follow suit.

Cardiff City's board announced plans to apply for a place in the Rugby Football League by the end of April. A deputation visited Cardiff to check on the arrangements for the rugby league side, named the Cardiff City Blue Dragons, who would share the Ninian Park Stadium with the Cardiff City association football 'Bluebirds'. A good report from the deputation meant the Blue Dragons were admitted into the NRL on 6 May, rebuilding a connection with the city lost nearly 30 years before.

Appointed as managing director, David Watkins's job was to recruit a Dragons squad, some based in South Wales and some in the north of England – the latter organised by John Mantle – that could mount a real challenge when the league fixtures got underway in three months' time. A few high-profile rugby union players were targeted and three of them accepted offers. Llanelli's Paul Ringer and Bridgend's Steve Fenwick had fallen out of favour with the Welsh selectors the previous season, the latter after leading his country in three internationals. Pontypridd's Tommy David had been out of favour for five years. All three were on the wrong side of 30. However, they provided the catalyst both for the launch of the Dragons and the re-launch of the Welsh XIII.

All three of the Dragons' big-name signings went on to become dual code internationals. With no European Championship matches scheduled, the RFL organised an international match to assist the Dragons' promotional efforts. David Watkins assumed the role of Welsh team-manager and he retained Kel Coslett as coach.

England's first visit to Wales since 1950 saw them in action for only the second time in Cardiff. The meeting at Ninian Park on 8 November 1981 was the first time that an international had been played on a Welsh Rugby League club's home ground for 70 years. Martin Herdman replaced Trevor Skerrett in the Welsh pack.

Sunday 8 November 1981 Wales 15 England 20
Cardiff, 13,173

A good crowd saw Wales mount a strong challenge to the English. A try by Des Drummond, converted by George Fairbairn, gave England a slender advantage which was nullified later thanks to two penalty goals from Steve Fenwick and a drop-goal from Danny Wilson. The two sides turned around level 5–5 with all to play for. England stamped their authority on the match through the pack when play resumed. Tries followed from Jeff Grayshon, Peter Gorley and Henderson Gill. Fairbairn's touch having failed him in the first half, the kicking duties were taken over by John Woods who added two conversions and a penalty goal to make the score 20–7. Wales's woke up in the final 10 minutes and applied real pressure to the English line. Ness Flowers and Paul Prendiville scored tries and Fenwick added a conversion, but the final whistle came before the Welsh could get any closer to England's total. The final score was 20–15 to England. In his autobiography, Steve Fenwick recalls that

Wales versus England in 1981 at Cardiff's Ninian Park ground.

England versus Wales in 1981 at Cardiff. (Both photos Courtesy *Rugby League Journal*)

"We only lost to England by a small margin and we earned respect from the English players who thought they were going to hammer us."

Fenwick had made a successful transition to his new code in a very short space of time was voted Welsh 'man of the match'. Tommy David also had a very good game, which led many to ponder what a great rugby league forward he might have become if he accepted any of the offers he had received to turn professional in the mid-1970s.

After initially being given as 8,102, the attendance was revised upwards by officials to 13,173.

The Dragons' fire burns out

Rugby league's allure grew with the establishment of the Blue Dragons. Over the next decade, 18 capped players and others on the fringe of the national team negotiated contracts that took them north.

After a poorly attended match against the all-conquering Kangaroos at Ninian Park in October 1982, the Welsh XIII was allowed to slip into inactivity. By the summer of 1984, Wales's standing in rugby league appeared to have dropped to an all-time low. For the first time, not one Welshman had been selected for the tour 'down under'. There was more bad news in July when the ailing Cardiff City Blue Dragons were forced to leave Ninian Park, which was being considered as a permanent headquarters for the Welsh FA and find a new home. The club, which was facing liquidation after incurring considerable losses, was bought from Kenton Utilities by a group of businessmen in August 1984. The rescued Blue Dragons, without David, Fenwick and Ringer who had all retired, found a new home at the Bridgend football club.

Eugene Cross Park, Ebbw Vale

With Welsh club rugby league seemingly on its last legs, another promotional international match was arranged for 14 October 1984. It was not to be held at the Blue Dragons' new home in Bridgend, but in Ebbw Vale. Over 70 years had passed since the last international was played in the town.

The same ground under a different name would be used. The Bridgend Field had been renamed the Eugene Cross Park in 1974 in honour of the man who had been chairman of the town's welfare association for 50 years. Seven years later the ownership of the complex which was home to the town's cricket, football and rugby union clubs passed to a public trust who reached agreement with the RFL to stage the match.

The ever-willing David Watkins took on the task of preparing the Welsh team for which Bridgend Blue Dragons, a woefully weak Second Division combination, provided six players. Following an extremely disappointing Antipodean tour which had seen the Lions whitewashed in both Australia and New Zealand, there were demands for new blood.

The selectors appeared to take heed; there were seven debutants in a youthful England team and as no coach was appointed, it fell to Reg Parker, the former Welsh manager, to get them into a working combination. Mick Burke was called in to replace Bradford Northern's Keith Mumby. Mumby had been appointed as England captain and that job was passed to Steve Donlan.

Sunday 14 October 1984: Wales 9 England 28
Ebbw Vale, 2,111

Live television coverage across Wales of the whole match inevitably kept the crowd down on a damp afternoon. Fears that the weak Welsh team would be overrun looked likely to prove correct. The first half saw largely one-way traffic heading towards the Welsh end. The Welsh could not compete in the scrums, where Kevin Beardmore virtually monopolised possession and this placed extra demands on the Welsh defence. England's left winger, Garry Clark, got the first try after three minutes and completed his hat-trick halfway through the half. A fourth try from Ellery Hanley and six points from the boot of Mick Burke put England 22–0 up at the break.

With a motivational speech still ringing in their ears, the Welsh upped their commitment. Danny Wilson stepped up a gear and through his prompting the Welshmen put up a more spirited fight. Six minutes after the restart Wilson dummied his way over for a try which Hallett converted. A Wilson drop-goal and Hallett penalty restored further pride to the Welsh side. The Welsh threat receded after Wilson was forced to leave the field after aggravating a hamstring injury. Mick Burke completed the scoring for a coasting England with a try which he converted himself. At the final whistle, the score, 28–9 to England, at least looked semi-respectable. For his efforts Wilson received the Welsh 'man-of-the-match' award.

In the aftermath of that match, Paul Fitzpatrick, bemoaning the lack of build-up, wrote in *Open Rugby* that "It is not enough to rent a decent ground, hire a well-drilled band, produce a programme, call it an international and then hope that spectators will turn up in their thousands." Despite the day's disappointments, he was happy to admit that "the match turned out if not quite a resounding success, then an enjoyable, worthwhile exercise. Perhaps those of us who had viewed it with a degree of pessimism should have shown a little more of the faith that sustains David Watkins." The scoreline was, however, a setback for the Welsh and dashed hopes of further matches or even a revival of the European Championship.

Although Bridgend Blue Dragons were included in the NRL's fixtures for 1985-86 there were major concerns about their situation. Finally, only a few days before the start of the new season the Blue Dragons were removed from the fixture list because of their failure to secure a ground at Maesteg. With their demise and the national team in abeyance, rugby league had disappeared from the South Wales sporting scene once more. As before, it was gone but not forgotten.

12. Enter the 'Codebreaker'

The winter of 1987–88 saw a revival in the fortunes of the Welsh rugby union team. Three successive victories brought the Triple Crown to Wales for the first time in nine years. It appeared the team's fortunes were looking up. They were until the biggest name in that side – Llanelli's Jonathan Davies – decided to switch codes. The news of his decision to go north was announced on Friday 7 January 1989 and captured the attention of the national media. After rejecting many previous offers, Davies had signed a four-year contract with Widnes for an undisclosed, but reportedly record fee of £150,000. Just three weeks before the opening round of the Five-Nations tournament, Davies, Wales's stand-off and captain, despairing of the unresolved problems circling around the national team, had decided the offer would secure his family's future and was just too good to refuse.

Where Davies had led, many more members of the Welsh rugby union squad – David Bishop, Adrian Hadley, John Devereux, Jonathan Griffiths, Paul Moriarty, Rowland Phillips and David Young among them – would follow, proving that 'going north' still held strong attractions as they snapped up the best offers coming their way. For the Morriston born Moriarty, it was a chance to return to his Kirkby-born father's roots, but it did not lead to any change in his allegiance. The English XV were not slow to take full advantage. Wales suffered a dismal defeat at Twickenham in February 1990 – England running in four tries, a feat they had not managed for nearly 70 years. England's superiority was clearer the following January when they won at the Arms Park for the first time in 28 years.

With the Welsh XV failing to live up to expectations, there was an opportunity for the Welsh league exiles to remind the people back home of their strengths. Jonathan Davies's successful career in the NRL and the growing number of talented Welshmen following in his footsteps saw the volume of calls for the Welsh XIII to be revived grow ever louder. Finally, they were heeded and after seven years in hibernation, the Welsh XIII was brought back to life in 1991. Having made a successful debut hosting the demolition of Papua New Guinea under lights in October that year, Swansea City's home ground, the Vetch Field, was hired for a further two matches in 1992.

Jim Mills, who had moved into the boardroom at Widnes since he hung up his boots, accepted the position of team manager and Warrington's highly regarded assistant coach, Clive Griffiths, once of Llanelli, took over the preparation of the Welsh team. Griffiths faced some major problems in getting his team ready. He later recalled in an interview for *Tries in the Valleys* that the team was selected from a pool of just 24 players. There was further insight in an interview for the match programme where John Devereux explained that the team had only managed four training sessions since playing France. It was hardly ideal preparation to take on an England combination that was essentially the Great Britain test team.

Friday 27 November 1992: Wales 11 England 36
Swansea, 10,243

Eight months after the French had been overrun, England, the favourites, arrived at the Vetch Field to be given a partisan reception by a sizeable crowd. Sadly, they would not face Jonathan Davies who was recovering following a groin operation.
Left: Jonathan Davies in Welsh kit (rlphotos.com)

Left: Mike Nicholas and Jonathan Davies.

Below: An informal Welsh team group in the early 1990s, including Mike Nicholas, Clive Griffiths and Jonathan Davies. (Both courtesy Gary Slater)

Phil Ford was the only Welsh survivor from the last meeting with England at Ebbw Vale. Ellery Hanley and Garry Schofield were the English survivors from that encounter. It was a strong Welsh line-up containing 10 Great Britain test caps, but it suffered a setback when Barry Williams, the Carlisle hooker, withdrew and was replaced by a less than match-fit David Bishop.

Despite rain throughout the day and live coverage on satellite television, a good crowd of over 10 thousand showed up.

A close match was anticipated, but things did not go well for Wales from the start. England had the better of the opening exchanges. Ellery Hanley and Mike Ford scored tries and Lee Crooks kicked two goals to give England an early 12–0 lead. To make matters worse, a broken jaw forced Gerald Cordle off the field. The setbacks, however, only seemed to inspire a fight back from the Welshmen.

Good Welsh pressure produced tries for Jonathan Griffiths and Mark Jones, to which John Devereux added a conversion and Kevin Ellis a drop-goal to close the gap on England to one point. Then, just a minute before half-time, a Welsh fumble allowed Crooks to dive over for a try which he converted to rebuild England's lead to seven points as the teams trooped off.

The second half saw England control the play and dominate possession, but that was not translated into points for the first quarter of an hour. All the defensive effort began to tell on the Welsh and England took advantage. Offiah, twice, Newlove and Schofield touched down and Crooks added a final conversion to give England a 36–11 victory.

Changing up a gear

As the England-Wales matches got underway again, changes were coming to fruition that upped the tempo of the rugby league game. Since the match at Ebbw Vale the number of scrums per match was much reduced thanks to the turnover of possession after the sixth tackle.

With the scrum much less significant, it was now just a way of restarting play as quickly as possible after certain infringements; it was tacitly de-powered. With fewer scrums, breaks in play were far less frequent and the ball was now in play much longer meaning that fitness would become paramount. In a bid to allow the attacking side more space to launch moves, the RFL had taken the lead in pushing back the offside line from five to 10 metres at the play-the-ball. Taken all together these changes would reshape the game.

Welsh rugby league

Although Wales voted four-to-one against devolution in 1979, the tide of nationalist sentiment would not abate, bringing a new assertiveness to the Welsh language and an edge to popular culture that washed over into the rugby game. There was a boost to Welsh identity when John Major's Conservative Government passed the Welsh Language Act in 1993, giving equal status to English and Welsh.

There was a need for sporting bodies to publicly embrace the changing national identity and language and the RFL did both with establishment of Cynghrair Cymru Rygbi / Welsh Rugby League as the game's independent authority in the Principality.

The last Welsh international to go north in the 'amateur' period

It looked likely that a place in the history books as the last Welsh rugby union international to switch to rugby league in the 'amateur era' would be occupied by Scott Gibbs when he signed for St Helens in April 1994. It was a decision that saw all the old bitterness and anger pour out – the chairman of Swansea labelling him a 'rugby parasite' for capitalising on his talents. That place in the history books would in fact be occupied by Scott Quinnell. He left Llanelli to sign for the dominant Wigan team not long after they had won the World Club Challenge at the start of June 1994. He was the 164th Welsh international to go north.

Since then, Gareth Thomas, a Welsh union international in the professional era, played rugby league for Crusaders in Super League and also played for Wales. Gavin Henson also played briefly for West Wales Raiders.

New life was breathed into the European Championship once more. Mike Nicholas succeeded his old team-mate Jim Mills as team manager and Clive Griffiths resumed as Welsh coach. Griffiths benefitted greatly from the RFL's decision to accept the Welsh management's request to allow grandparents to count towards qualification for Welsh selection. No less than eight Anglos – seven in the starting line-up and one on the bench – would qualify by that route for the match on 1 February 1995. One of them was Richie Eyres who, since making a 'Man-of-the-Match' winning appearance for England in 1992, had discovered a Welsh grandfather and decided to switch allegiance. Another of the starting seven was the very Welsh sounding Iestyn Harris. Although born and raised in Oldham, the 18-year-old Harris strongly identified with his Welsh heritage and seized the opportunity to follow his grandfather, Norman, into the Welsh XIII. Similarly, the Wigan front-row had also found themselves qualified for Wales.

Jonathan Davies led the Welsh XIII against England for the first time in this match. In doing so he became the third man – and the second in peace-time – to have led both the Welsh XIII and the Welsh XV against the Anglo-Saxons. Four of England's first choice players were unavailable – Denis Betts, Lee Jackson, Chris Joynt and Martin Offiah were all included in the Great Britain squad which had already departed for the Coca Cola World Sevens tournament in Sydney. Injuries ruled out Shaun Edwards, who was replaced by Deryck Fox, and his team-mate Gary Connolly, who was replaced by Daryl Powell. Ellery Hanley, the England coach, was still able to put out a strong team.

Wednesday 1 February 1995: Wales 18 England 16
Cardiff, 6,252

There was a reasonable crowd on a wet night for a match played under Ninian Park's floodlights. The Welsh XIII started well, scoring first with a Kevin Ellis try, converted by Jonathan Davies. In reply, England got Richard Gay over the try-line and Deryck Fox kicked a penalty. Only a Jonathan Davies penalty goal separated the two teams at the break.

When play resumed, England surged into the lead with tries from Deryck Fox and Jason Robinson. Welsh defence prevented further scores and eventually Wales, trailing 16–8, regained the initiative. A second try by Kevin Ellis and two penalty goals from Jonathan Davies brought the scores level. With 10 minutes remaining, Rowland Phillips and Anthony Sullivan combined to carry the ball downfield before setting up Jonathan Davies for a successful drop at goal. With only a point in it, the tension mounted. England's hopes of victory were finally quashed when with two minutes remaining Davies sent over a second drop-goal to bring Wales its first victory over England for 18 years.

Summing up the impact of the match, *Open Rugby* commented: "Wales's victory gave rugby league in the Principality its biggest boost for many years. The reaction of the Welsh team and the spectators at last proved that the country of Wales can be become emotional about rugby league. The *hywl* was there." There was even more to be emotional about when Wales subsequently beat France in Carcassonne at the start of March to become European champions for the first time in 57 years.

The 1995 World Cup

As part of Rugby League's centenary celebrations, a World Cup tournament was planned for the autumn of 1995. Wales's management had been led to believe that if victories were recorded over Papua New Guinea and France in 1992, that they would secure a World Cup place. When it was realised in June 1993 that those two victories would not count and Wales did not figure in the plans, Jim Mills resigned in protest. Trevor Foster, then the President of the Wales Rugby League Players Association, sprang into action. In a letter to Maurice Lindsay, the chief executive of the RFL, he called for the inclusion of Wales, emphasising that "Wales may not have the playing resources at their disposal in comparison to Australia, New Zealand or Great Britain, but have proved over the last two years that they are able to compete on level terms with any nation, and certainly are capable of competing in any seeded or 'pool' competition which would involve France, Fiji, Tonga and Western Samoa, for example."

That letter achieved the change of heart its author intended when on 24 January 1994 the RFL announced that the tournament would be organised across England and Wales and that the Welsh team would be included as one of the 10 entrants. Clive Griffiths continued his stint as the Welsh coach.

Although Jonathan Davies was away for the summer playing for North Queensland Cowboys, a strong squad was assembled for a short visit to Philadelphia in June. Two wins, both by large margins, were recorded against the USA national team.

Jonathan Davies was back in time to resume the captaincy ahead of the World Cup. By the time the competition came around there was a lot of speculation about his future. The decision of rugby union to allow professionalism paved the way for players who had 'gone north' to return to their original code.

Home victories over France and then Western Samoa in front of full houses in Cardiff and Swansea propelled the Welsh team to the top of their group and a place in the semi-finals. England had opened the tournament with a morale boosting victory over a depleted Australia at Wembley and followed up with further victories over Fiji and South Africa.

Both England and Wales had a week or so to get ready for their meeting in the semi-final, but it soon became apparent that Wales's clash with Western Samoa had taken far more out of them than England's much easier final group game against South Africa.

According to Mike Nicholas, he and Clive Griffiths were called up to Manchester a couple days before the semi-final at which point the Welsh recovery stalled. Instead of focusing on recovery, the squad apparently continued to party a little too hard and it cost them dear. Jonathan Davies was one of seven Welsh rugby union caps in the starting line-up with three more on the bench.

Saturday 21 October 1995: England 25 Wales 10
Manchester, 30,042

Old Trafford, the iconic home of Manchester United, had become the regular venue for many of rugby league's most important matches and it was chosen to host the semi-final on 21 October. Due to redevelopment work, one side of the stadium was closed reducing the capacity to around 31,000. Such was the interest in the match, that even though it was to be shown live on television, the attendance very nearly reached capacity. Live television coverage did not deter an estimated 10,000 Welsh supporters from making the trip to Manchester on Saturday 21 October. In fine voice, the Welsh national anthem *Hen Wlad Fy Nhadau* (*Land of my Fathers*) echoed around the stadium before kick-off. Throughout the match they formed a vocal part of what was the largest crowd ever to watch a Welsh XIII.

There was a boost for Wales when John Devereux and Scott Gibbs passed late fitness tests. Wigan's protracted dominance of the domestic game meant that England fielded a team heavily populated with their players. There were seven directly from the Wigan side and two who had recently taken their leave to chase honours in the newly expanded Australian competitions. A knee infection kept one Wiganer, Shaun Edwards, out of the England line up. Phil Larder chose Edwards's former club-mate Denis Betts to take over as captain.

Nearly halfway through the first half, Wales opened the scoring through a Jonathan Davies penalty goal. England's greater power was soon apparent and they replied with two tries from Paul Newlove and Tony Smith plus a penalty goal from Andy Farrell and a drop-goal from Bobbie Goulding. All Wales could muster in response was a second penalty goal from Jonathan Davies which left them trailing 11–4 at half time.

Almost immediately after the break, Paul Moriarty was sin-binned and while he was off the field Martin Offiah crossed for another England try. Offiah got another one 15 minutes later to open a 15 point gap between the sides. Soon after coming on to the field, substitute Rowland Phillips played the ball to himself after a tackle and plunged over the line to grab the first Welsh try. Jonathan Davies converted to leave Wales trailing by nine points with 14 minutes left. That try energised the Welsh XIII and there was a chance that the gap might have been narrowed further as Anthony Sullivan found space, but Kris Radlinski tackled him into touch. There just time for a final England try by Phil Clarke, converted by Bobbie Goulding to make the score 25–10.

England's victory sent them on their way to a re-match with Australia in the final at Wembley. Defeat at Old Trafford brought Wales a standing ovation as they left the field. For Graham Thomas, writing in the *South Wales Echo*, there was more to the day than just the score for Wales had "won nothing but pride and new admirers".

Old Trafford marked the end of an era in terms of the relationship between rugby league and rugby union in Wales. Radical change had and was happening in the world of rugby union and things would never be the same again for either game.

13. A new dawn in Wales

Not for 100 years had the British rugby union season opened more dramatically than it did in the autumn of 1995. Like the fall of the Berlin Wall, the end of a fully amateur game came quickly and unexpectedly. Even when rugby union's International Rugby Board (IRB) met on 14 March 1995, it still had the arrogance to rule that while former rugby league professionals could be allowed to play rugby union, that could only be after an interval of three years away from the 'rebel' game. The confidence behind that statement disappeared rapidly as rising fears about the global intentions of Rupert Murdoch's media empire took hold.

Against a background of stories, only some of which were speculative, that Murdoch planned to grab control and create a hybrid game merging elements of union and league, the IRB met in Paris over the weekend of 26 and 27 August 1995. The IRB's decision to repeal the amateur regulations and make rugby union an 'open' game threw all Britain's leading players and officials into uncharted territory. Almost a century to the day after the 'split' with the NU had occurred, the WRU faced up to the loss of all its 'amateur' certainties. Much was thought to ride on the ability of union officials to strike the right balance and lead their game forward. Time was not on their side as the owners of the senior clubs dashed to secure as many talented players as they could.

Certainly, the officials had a lot of adjustments to make. Their top priority was to consign all the abuse that had been heaped on professionalism – and its emphasis on money and winning – over the years to the dustbin. New attitudes had to be fostered to celebrate professionalism and the attractive and successful teams it would produce. No longer could senior rugby union claim that it was a sport, not a business, and that any slide towards the latter would see sportsmanship automatically sacrificed.

No longer could professionalism be blamed for anything and everything bad in the world of rugby union. From this point onwards professionalism was simply a contractual issue and all implications of moral weakness were supposedly forgotten.

Everyone expected that the IRB's decision would lead to a change of attitude, but it did not happen overnight. When the Rugby League World Cup was underway, the WRU was free to take an advantage of the game's new openness, but it chose instead to deny the Welsh XIII the use of the National Stadium.

Free to operate professionally at last, the most ambitious Welsh clubs went on the hunt, determined to add some of the very best players to their rosters. Many were shocked when, almost overnight, what had been a one-way street heading north reversed direction. A number of players who had previously switched from rugby union were offered the chance to end their involvement with rugby league and return in triumph to their roots. Within days of that semi-final defeat at Old Trafford, Jonathan Davies became the first to take the road home, making the ground-breaking move from Warrington to Cardiff RUFC once the 'Blue and Blacks' had managed to raise the asking price, thought to be around £100,000.

The last hurrah

Rugby league entered its second century with its radical spirit intact. To avail itself of a major sponsorship with Sky Sports, the RFL had taken the revolutionary step of moving the professional game to a summer season. The old First Division of the NRL had morphed into the Super League and most of its members had been rebranded with the addition of new animalistic marketing monikers. Most of the players in Super League were now full-time professionals.

There was a chance for Wales to defend its European champion's title. Having beaten the French earlier in the month in Carcassonne, the Welsh then heard the news that England had annihilated the French at Gateshead the following Sunday. All that was left was for the two victors to meet in Cardiff on the evening of 26 June 1996. For the first time the WRU allowed its own headquarters, the National Rugby Stadium, the predecessor of today's Principality Stadium, to host the match. Clive Griffiths, now coaching the newly established South Wales club, and Keighley Cougars' Phil Larder were once again appointed as the respective coaches. It was decided that no match fees were to be paid.

Wednesday 26 June 1996: Wales 12 England 26
Cardiff, 5,245

The Welsh management had problems. Long-term injuries ruled out John Devereux and Scott Gibbs. Scott Quinnell had negotiated a move back to rugby union and had played his last league match for Wigan the previous Friday. Salford Reds' David Young and St Helens' Anthony Sullivan could not get fit in time and they were replaced by Neil Cowie and Diccon Edwards. There was some good news. Kevin Ellis and Allan Bateman were both out in Australia, but the latter secured the approval of his club to fly back from Sydney for the match, paying his own fare if necessary. Also, since playing for England in 1992, Jason Critchley had checked his family tree, found the necessary Celtic connection, and was included on Wales's wing.

The two weeks rest after the French match allowed England to bring back several key players who had been nursing injuries. Daryl Powell returned in place of Steve Blakeley, Andy Farrell returned at loose-forward pushing Paul Sculthorpe into the second row in place of Steve McNamara, Nathan McAvoy replaced Paul Newlove who was ill and Bobbie Goulding having recovered from a fractured collarbone got a place on the bench. Andy Farrell led out England and by so doing wrote himself into the game's record books. At 21, Farrell became the youngest captain in the history of international rugby league.

Fittingly the match provided the chance for two more players to join the list of dual internationals – John Bentley appearing for England and Richard Webster for Wales. They entered the record books as the 12th and 80th dual international for their respective countries.

Wales took the lead on nine minutes through a Chris Morley try, converted by Iestyn Harris. Bobbie Goulding was brought off the bench after 20 minutes and soon put points on the scoreboard with a penalty goal. A Chris Joynt try followed, converted by Goulding, to give England a two point lead which they held until the interval.

The match remained close early in the second half; a Goulding try and conversion being matched by a Jason Critchley try, converted by Harris, to keep England's lead at two points. It was only in the last quarter-of-an-hour that England managed to pull away. Shaun Edwards went over for a try which Goulding converted. Then, with just four minutes remaining Steve Prescott found space and went 80 yards to add another England try which Goulding again converted to ensure the victory, 26–12.

The attendance of 5,425 was considered reasonable as the semi-final of soccer's Euro96 competition between England and Germany was being broadcast live from Wembley Stadium that evening. Defeat meant Wales finished as the runner-up in the Championship table to England.

Farewell but not goodbye

Nearly all the big-name converts from Welsh rugby union still playing rugby league returned to their former game after the first summer season was over. They were welcomed home with open arms. Slurs forgiven if not forgotten, Scott Gibbs was once again exchanging one St Helens for another and in doing so became the first former rugby league professional to make an appearance in the Welsh XV. He played against Italy in October. Gibbs and the other returnees, sharpened and hardened by the rigours of the professional game, had an immediate impact on Welsh rugby union and over the next couple of months Jonathan Davies, Allan Bateman, David Young and Scott Quinnell all answered the WRU selectors call.

Those losses left the Welsh rugby league team decimated. For 85 years, the team had battled tenaciously for recognition and honours, but as the WRU finally embraced open professionalism its future was in doubt like never before. It was a development that meant that the rugby league team would not in future be built around big-name professional signings from Welsh rugby union. Fundamental changes would have to be made as part of a new departure for the rugby league game in Wales. New leaders and a new approach would be needed.

Scott Gibbs, shown here with the Super League Trophy during his time at St Helens, was one of the lats high profile rugby union players to switch to rugby league in the 'amateur' era.
(Courtesy Alex Service)

A selection of Welsh legends

This selection is obviously a personal choice but I hope the individuals selected reflect the huge contribution made by Welshmen to the game of rugby league over the years both on- and-off the field.

Bill McCutcheon
Born: Swansea 21 June 1870
Died: Oldham 3 July 1949

For one young Welsh winger, the evolving rugby game in the north of England offered new and exciting opportunities. The uncapped William M McCutcheon, then in his late teens, moved from Swansea to Oldham for better clerical employment in December 1888.

McCutcheon was appointed as Oldham's captain for his first full season, 1889–90, when the club decided to adopt the four-threequarter-system that was being pioneered in South Wales. The following season he made his debut for Wales against Scotland.

He did much to reshape Oldham's style of play in the 1890s when the club became the first northern club to regularly use that radical, exciting threequarter formation. Success was not long in coming and it was McCutcheon who led Oldham to the Lancashire Club Championship title in 1893–94. His play also brought a seventh and final Welsh cap against England in January 1894.

He is often referred to in Welsh rugby histories as being a Swansea player when he won those caps, but his true allegiance by then was to Oldham and Lancashire, making 19 appearances for the latter prior to the split.

After Oldham joined the NU, McCutcheon played on for a couple more seasons. When his playing days were over, he took on other roles for the club. In 1907 it was recorded that he was serving as Oldham's trainer. By then, McCutcheon was active in the affairs of the club. As Oldham's representative on the NU committee, he had played a crucial part in the reshaping of the rugby game in the north of England in 1906. He was also a leading referee, officiating at the 1906 NU Cup Final and the NRL Championship Finals of 1913 and 1914. By then he had become the only Welshman to officiate at the NU's England versus Wales matches, which he did on three occasions. McCutcheon held the office of President from 1924 to 1926 and by the time he retired from the club's management he had served Oldham continuously for 38 years.

Ben Gronow
Born: Bridgend 10 March 1887
Died: Huddersfield 24 November 1967

When Bridgend's Ben Gronow, an apprentice stonemason who had appeared in the Welsh pack in all four home international matches in 1910, was first approached about turning professional it was by the Ebbw Vale NU club. Their offer of £25 and a job was nowhere near enough to convince young Gronow that his future lay in Wales. Luckily for him, Huddersfield's football committee was also on the hunt for talent in South Wales. After the season had ended, serious contact was made and the club's representatives convinced the 23-year-old Gronow to sign for Huddersfield for £120 in mid-May.

Gronow stood out as a modern forward. He was a fine scrummager who was also an enthusiastic tackler and could give and take a pass. After appearing in the first practice match on 20 August 1910, Gronow made his NU debut at Fartown in the opening league fixture against Ebbw Vale on 3 September.

With all contracts and arrangements in place, the 1914–15 season went ahead as planned. A run of big wins, beginning at the start of December 1914, saw Gronow take over from the injured Major Holland as goalkicker. He showed a rare aptitude and by the end of the season he had broken Major Holland's total to set a new Huddersfield record of 140 goals. Drafted in 1916, Gronow joined the ranks of the Army Service Corps for the rest of the First World War.

In 1919–20 he raised his own record for goalkicking to 148 and his points total to 332. A member of Huddersfield's famed 'team of all the talents', Gronow won all the domestic game's honours and toured Australasia in 1920 and again in 1924. That second tour brought the curtain down on his representative career, leaving him with seven Great Britain caps and eight Wales caps. Gronow remained at Fartown until June 1925 when he emigrated to Australia where he spent two seasons as player-coach at Grenfell in NSW. After a spell in the Huddersfield reserves in 1927–28, he signed for Batley in September in 1928 and was soon elected captain. Later he joined Featherstone Rovers as player-coach where he remained until he retired as a player in November 1929.

To try and improve their team's performance Bradford Northern's directors appointed Gronow as trainer-coach in 1933. Early in his first season with Northern he inspired his team to give the touring Australians a real test. A strong Kangaroo team was expected to overrun Northern, but on a very wet day in October 1933, the home side sneaked a surprise win. Shocked by that defeat the tourists' management requested a rematch and the RFL agreed. Nearly three weeks later the Kangaroos were back and a crowd three times bigger was there to see the visitors achieve a narrow victory. A request for a deciding third match was turned down by the tourists' management who insisted that no suitable dates could be found on their itinerary. Those two matches were crucial in reviving the fortunes of a practically moribund club. Gronow continued as trainer-coach the following season, the club's first at Odsal Stadium, but that was his last.

From then on he would confine his coaching activities to various Rugby Union clubs in west Yorkshire while serving on the football committee of the Huddersfield club for many years. Gronow was made an Honorary Life Member of the club he served so well shortly before he died.

Jim Sullivan
Born: Cardiff 2 December 1903
Died: Wigan 14 September 1977

It was Cardiff that first recognised the potential of a local youngster, Jim Sullivan, and gave him his chance in senior rugby. Sullivan's first full season in senior rugby, 1920–21, brought him many plaudits, an appearance for the Barbarians and had taken him to the verge of international honours. But, in the summer of 1921 he was a 17-year-old apprentice boilermaker worried about his chances of future employment. There was also significant family pressure for the youngster to contribute towards the household's bills as soon as possible.

That summer Sullivan asked Cardiff RUFC for help, but he was told by club officials that anything like a job on the ground would professionalise him. Desperate to retain Sullivan, the situation was reconsidered and Cardiff made Sullivan an offer of a painting and cleaning job at the Arms Park. It was too late for that. The day before Sullivan had agreed to 'go north'.

Wanting a large fee, Sullivan spurned offers from the likes of Huddersfield and Wakefield Trinity considering them too low, before signing a 12-year contract with Wigan in July 1921. The contract provided a fee of £750 plus match fees worth £5 for a win, £4/15 (£4.75) for a draw and £4/10 (£4.50) for a defeat. Sullivan's fee was said to equal the previous highest, paid to Wickham Powell, also of Cardiff, by Rochdale Hornets 12 months earlier.

Impressive accuracy and range enabled Jim Sullivan to set new goal scoring records. He broke Ben Gronow's records in 1922–23 with 161 goals and 349 points. In 1933–34 he established long-standing records with 194 goals and 406 points. His career statistics over his time at Wigan are truly remarkable. Prior to wartime he always kicked at least 100 goals a season for the club. Recognising his knowledge of the game, he held the post of player-coach at Wigan from 3 October 1932 onwards. Over a two decade career with Wigan, he was on the winning side in two Challenge Cup finals, three Lancashire Cup finals and four NRL Championship finals. He was also a member of four Lancashire League winning teams.

He made his debut for Wales against Australia in 1921 and would go on to captain the side on 12 occasions. Sullivan first toured Australasia in 1928 and was appointed captain, the first Welshman to be asked to lead the party, for his second tour four years later. During the Second World War, Sullivan assisted Wigan and on occasion Bradford Northern, Dewsbury and Keighley before rejoining Wigan in 1945. In 1944 he officially announced his retirement from playing, but did make a few appearances in 1945–46, his last league start being at Batley on 23 February. Sullivan retired as the club's record points' scorer knowing that the records he set would endure for a long, long time.

After that, as manager-coach he concentrated solely on preparing the team. A great student of the game, the team he unleashed on peacetime rugby league was one of the most influential ever, revolutionising many aspects of play. That team, almost entirely homegrown, had matured in reserved occupations during the war years and was ready and waiting to explode onto the peacetime stage.

Over the next seven seasons, Sullivan's team never finished outside the top two places in the NRL table and on four occasions were its leaders. Wigan's trophy cabinet had major silverware on its shelves every season. Four times the NRL Championship found its way to Central Park. The Challenge Cup arrived there twice. The Lancashire Cup sat there five times and the Lancashire League trophy four. It was a rich harvest of honours and was testimony to the skills of a coach at the height of his powers.

However, success on the field was not enough for Sullivan. Unhappy with his pay at Wigan, Sullivan pushed for an increase. With all options exhausted Sullivan quit on Saturday 28 June 1952 after 31 years at Central Park. Wigan's loss proved to be St Helens' gain as Sullivan immediately accepted a seven-year contract to replace Emlyn Jenkins at his old club's keenest rivals. As if to confirm he was the master coach Sullivan worked his magic once more at Knowsley Road, fashioning a Saints team from the one that had finished the previous season 21st in the NRL and £2,500 in debt.

Almost immediately the Saints were transformed into a trophy-winning outfit. Once again, his high regard for fitness and pace paid dividends on the field. Although the honours' haul was lower it was still an impressive achievement. Over six seasons Sullivan's men won the NRL Championship twice and the Challenge Cup, the Lancashire Cup and Lancashire League once. His last season, 1958/59, showed what a talented team Sullivan had built for the future.

St Helens became the first club to pass 1,000 points (1,005) in a league season of 38 matches, and went on to finish as champions.

Having spent two seasons at Rochdale Hornets – 1959 to 1961 – Jim Sullivan was convinced to return to Central Park. However, only one week into his new job, he was taken ill with pneumonia followed by a stroke after which he had to resign and call time on his coaching career.

Dai Rees
Born: Abertillery 16 September 1897
Died: Halifax 23 May 1975

Dai Rees was an uncapped centre when he joined Halifax from his home town club, Abertillery RUFC, on 22 July 1921. A job on the ground-staff at Thrum Hall was also on offer which was what he wanted the most; it enabled him to get out of coal mining. Within a year he had been converted from a centre to a second-row forward. He gained honours in representative rugby, playing six times for the Wales XIII, touring 'down-under' in 1924 and made one appearance for Great Britain against New Zealand in October 1926. Club honours were much harder to come by. The only honour, but the big one, came his way in May 1931 when he led Halifax to victory at Wembley.

His splendid leadership in the Cup campaign led to him being made player-coach for 1931–32. Sadly, a knee injury forced Rees to retire in January 1932. He was then employed as Halifax's first team trainer-coach until it was announced, on 17 July 1936, that Bradford Northern had secured his services as trainer-coach. Later he became manager-coach.

The team Dai Rees built at Odsal enjoyed great success despite the onset of the Second World War. That was in large part due to Rees being astute about the game, having a shrewd analytical eye and being a good man-manager. He was widely recognised as someone who could work out innovative tactical plans and weld players into very formidable teams. Rees was seen as an excellent strategist who was capable of giving his men a sound tactical appreciation of their opponents.

These were qualities that would bring him a place in the history books. With the 1947 Test series against New Zealand poised at one win apiece, the Great Britain selectors decided that something extra was needed to ensure that the third Test was won. To increase the chances of a win the selectors decided to employ the services of a coach. When the British team for the third Test was announced on Monday 8 December, there was an extra name on the list. Dai Rees was named as the British coach for the first ever Test match at Odsal Stadium. It was also announced that for the first time in the series the team would get together in Leeds on the Wednesday beforehand and that Rees would organise training at Odsal the following day. Britain played brilliantly to win the match and the series.

After Rees's success the previous year it seemed that the selectors had decided that a coach might be also useful to have around in non-emergency situations. When the selectors met on Wednesday 22 September 1948 to choose the team to meet Australia in the first Test, they agreed that they would once again ask Dai Rees to act as coach. The news broke on Monday 4 October, only six days before the first Test, that Rees had declined to take up his appointment to coach the Test team. In a letter to Bill Fallowfield, Rees explained that he would only accept if the appointment was for the whole series and not on a match-by-match basis. As the selectors would not agree to that, Rees refused the offer. He did not get another chance.

109

Left: Bill McCutcheon; right: Ben Gronow

Jim Sullivan (All photos courtesy Robert Gate)

Left: Dai Rees; right: Gus Risman (Courtesy Robert Gate)

Trevor Foster, Ernest Ward, Roy Francis and Jim Stott in London in January 1944 before playing for the Army rugby union team against the RAF at Richmond. (Courtesy Simon Foster)

Top: Cliff Evans and Clive Sullivan; Bottom left: Davud Watkins (All courtesy Robert Gate)
Bottom right: Jonathan Davies (rlphotos.com)

The team Dai Rees built at Odsal enjoyed great success despite the onset of the Second World War. All told, Northern enjoyed 15 very successful years. Rees's team won the NRL Championship once, the Challenge Cup three times, the Yorkshire Cup four times and the Yorkshire League three times. There was always a Welsh flavour to Rees's teams and on two occasions in April 1949 Bradford Northern fielded a team containing eight Welsh players. Although a place in the NRL play-offs proved beyond them, Northern did reach Wembley for the third consecutive time the following month. Victory at Wembley brought the season to a close on a high for Rees's men. For Rees there would also be further recognition. A meeting of Abertillery Council decided to send him a message of congratulations on Northern's Cup win at the end of the month.

Dai Rees was made a director of Bradford Northern in 1949, but the flow of trophies would come to an abrupt end after the Yorkshire Cup was won at the end of October 1953. No more trophies would find their way to Odsal Stadium for 14 years.

Sadly, Northern went into decline and Rees was eventually removed as manager-coach on 23 March 1960, having held the position for nearly 24 years. Briefly he took over the job of stadium manager. Some critics supported the move believing that Rees's ideas and tactics were outdated. After a short time as stadium manager Rees resigned, having accepted an invitation to join the Halifax board of directors.

Augustus 'Gus' Risman
Born: Cardiff 23 March 1911
Died: Workington 17 October 1994

Augustus, or Gus as he was better known, Risman, then an unemployed teenager, had travelled to Stroud where he was to make his debut for Cardiff Scottish. As he walked to the ground, a well-known agent, Frank Young, introduced himself and asked if he had ever considered playing rugby league. There was not time for the discussion to go much further, but Young made contact again a few days later at Risman's home in Barry. This time Young put an offer on the table – would Risman be willing to play in a trial for Leeds? Risman said he would and although Leeds withdrew their interest, a trial was arranged at Salford. Risman stayed with Salford for two months and played in the 'A' team. When the season ended, he went home for the summer of 1929. The news he had been hoping for came at the start of the new season. Salford wanted him to join them – and offered a fee of £52 (payable at £1 per week) plus match terms of £3 for a win and 35/- (£1.75) for a draw or a defeat. A job in the offices at Shell-Mex was also arranged. Later, he would become a cinema manager.

During his time with Salford, he represented Great Britain 17 times and Wales 18 times, captaining his country on five occasions. His captaincy of the stylish and successful Salford team from 1935–36 onwards led to an invitation to produce the first guide to playing rugby league. Entitled *How to Play Rugby League Football*, it was published as part of the well-established Foulsham's Sports Library around 1938. For the first time rugby league had marked out its claim to be a separate game when it came to coaching.

Once Salford suspended activities in December 1940, Risman made the most of his freedom playing and winning trophies at various times with Bradford Northern, Dewsbury and Leeds while serving at various times in the military police, the Parachute Regiment and the Army's PE Corps. His play for Wales during the conflict was highly praised, but the undoubted high point of his international career came at the end of the War when he became the second Welshman to lead the Great Britain tour party that became known s 'The Indomitables' to Australia and New Zealand in 1946. It was a gruelling trip from start to finish, but the party battled through to retain the Ashes before losing the final Test to New Zealand.

Prior to his departure for the south-seas, Risman had been approached and subsequently agreed to join Workington Town as player-manager upon his return. Town was then coming towards the end of its first NRL season and the young club wanted a big-name to take it forward. Many thought that Risman, by then aged 36 and almost beyond the veteran stage, would be keen to hang up his boots. He, however, was keen to carry on playing and made his debut for Town at the start of October 1946.

Gus Risman through his work as player-manager brought pride to Workington and the crowds grew as success came to west Cumbria. And success did come with both the NRL Championship and the Challenge Cup finding their way to Workington at the start of the 1950s. Risman resigned in the summer of 1954 after a disagreement with Town's directors over the signing of a replacement full-back. He played briefly for Batley at the end of 1954 before announcing his retirement at the ripe old age of 43.

His experience and knowledge of the game meant he could not be left on the sidelines for long. He returned to the game, succeeding Jimmy Douglas as Salford's coach-manager in February 1956. Risman held the job for the next four years with limited success. The methods that had brought success at Workington had not worked as well, although he was thought to have not had the best of luck while at Salford. He then took over as team-manager at Oldham in 1960 and held the job for two seasons. His next and final opportunity came in Bradford after the re-born club got back into action. Risman took over as Northern's manager-coach on 3 October 1964. In his second season success in the Yorkshire Cup was a clear indication that Northern was on the way back. Believing that his job at the now revitalised club was done, Risman resigned on 28 April 1967.

Trevor Foster MBE

Born: Newport 3 December 1914
Died: Bradford 2 April 2005

In his biography, Trevor Foster recounts that while he was still at the start of his senior career, playing for Pill Harriers, a rugby league scout had paid a visit to his parents' house in Newport representing Wigan. Foster was offered a trial which he declined, still having his eyes firmly fixed on winning a Welsh rugby union cap. On 13 November 1937, two Wigan directors approached him as he walked home from Rodney Parade after the match against Cardiff. They asked if they could talk further at his parents' home. He cautiously agreed and once inside they offered him £300, which once again he declined.

An Easter visit from two Bradford Northern representatives, who cautioned him about the effect injuries might have on their offer, began to change his mind. Just when Northern thought that they had his signature Foster hesitated. With the family urging him to sign and Harry Hornby, Northern's chairman, telling him that with the money on offer he could buy a cap or two, he gave in. He signed for £400 in September 1938 and like many others before him never looked back.

The outbreak of the Second World War 12 months later inevitably disrupted Foster's integration into the new game. Foster had soon enlisted and saw service as an Army PTI (a colleague on the PTI training was Roy Francis) while continuing to gain honours with Bradford

114

Northern. Through the war years and beyond he played 16 times for the Welsh XIII (seven as captain), toured 'down-under' as a member of the 'Indomitables' party in 1946 during which he won the first three of his Great Britain caps.

In mid-January 1949, Trevor Foster, with the agreement of Bradford Northern, was appointed as Rugby League's first official national coach. With support from a couple of other professionals, Foster put together a show, *Focus on Rugby*, organised a summer camp for youth and prepared a strategic review, *A basis for a development plan for Rugby League Football* before he resigned in November 1950.

When he finally ceased playing in April 1955, he became Dai Rees's assistant coach and took over as Bradford Northern's coach when Rees was sidelined on 23 March 1960. As Northern's affairs deteriorated more and more, Foster, resigned on 7 December 1960. After nearly a year out of the game, Trevor Foster succeeded Dai Prosser as Leeds coach on 4 December 1961. Foster was given sole responsibility for coaching, training and selection.

After Roy Francis took over as coach in October 1963, Foster continued as 'A' team coach at Headingley until October 1966. During that time, he played a crucial role in reforming a new Bradford Northern after financial problems had caused the old club to close down and resign from the NRL in January 1964. Thanks to his efforts Northern would be able to successfully return to league action the following autumn.

In time Trevor Foster would return to Odsal Stadium and the rejuvenated Bradford Northern where he organised an under-17 colts' team, which finished as champions of the Leeds and District League in 1969–70. An under-19 team would follow to further boost Northern's prospects. He was awarded the MBE in the New Year's Honours List in 2001 for services to the Community in Bradford.

Roy Francis

Born: Port Talbot 20 January 1919
Died: Leeds 6 April 1989

Roy Francis, after a disrupted playing career, would go on to bring a new dimension to rugby league coaching. Francis had joined Wigan from Brynmawr in November 1936. With very limited chances to demonstrate his talents, he found himself moved on to Barrow in January 1939. His opportunities there were also limited as war service as a PTI got in the way. Finally, recognition came his way and his appearance against New Zealand for the third Test in December 1947 wrote him into the record books as Great Britain's first black player.

After guest appearances for Dewsbury during the war, he returned to Barrow and then moved onto Warrington in July 1948. In his only full season at Wilderspool he was second highest try-scorer behind Brian Bevan. His final move as a player was to Hull in November 1949 aged 30. Francis was appointed player-coach at Hull in 1951 where he helped develop the modern forward style further by emphasising the role of fast-moving forwards. He played his last match for Hull on Boxing Day 1955. The end of his playing career brought Francis new responsibility as stepped up to become the first black coach of an English professional football club.

That emphasis on pace proved a success as his mighty pack carried Hull to the NRL Championship in 1956 and 1958 (runner-up in 1957) and to two defeats at Wembley in 1959 and 1960, along with appearances in the Yorkshire Cup final. That team was already starting to break up by the time it was defeated by St Helens in the Challenge Cup semi-final at Odsal in April 1961. Finding adequate forward replacements proved difficult and Francis was probably rethinking his tactics as the team slipped down the table and new opportunities arose.

When Roy Francis arrived at Headingley in October 1963 a once great Leeds team was beginning to break up. The era of the legendary Lewis Jones (last match March 1964) and other stalwarts like Don Robinson (moved on in summer 1964) was over and its close provided him with both the opportunity and the necessity to draft in new blood.

From the start he pioneered modern coaching methods and brought a new and unique style of play to Leeds. A fitness fanatic, Francis put the emphasis on speed and regularly organised sprint training with his players wearing spikes. He was ahead of his time in that he coached both the individual player and the team. Building his team around 13 athletes who could use the full width of the pitch, Francis sought to end the mindset that the pack had to gain dominance before play could be opened out. Instead, he gave his backs the freedom to attack from the start and take control of the match.

Although there was no game-plan as we would know it today, Francis expected each of his players to have all the basic skills to fulfil what were to him interchangeable roles between forwards and backs. Besides the specific skill of scrummaging, Francis expected his forwards to cover the pitch alongside his backs. The introduction of the limited tackle law, which meant the pack could no longer confine its activities to the centre of the field, was just what Francis had been waiting for. His young team was ready for the big-time by 1966. For the next two seasons they finished as leaders of the NRL and twice captured the Yorkshire League trophy and then the Challenge Cup in 1968.

With only one win to their credit the North Sydney Bears' committee invited Roy Francis over for a spell of six weeks in summer 1968. Francis rapidly proved his worth as the Bears turned in three wins from six matches while he was there which lifted them off the bottom. Once Francis left the Bears reverted to their old form and failed to win another match. North Sydney's committee was impressed and it led to Francis's Headingley contract being finished prematurely so he could leave Leeds in the autumn of 1968 with the offer of a three-year contract as full-time manager-coach in Sydney.

His second spell found him struggling to turn the club around and with Bears staying determinedly in mid-table his relationship with the committee soured. Feeling unwanted, Francis asked to be released from his contract and he returned home in March 1971. It was an experience that seemed to deflate and disorient him.

Once back in England he took some time off before returning to The Boulevard for a brief coaching stint in 1972–73. After another year out he returned to Headingley for 1974–75, winning the Premiership, reaching the Challenge Cup semi-final and finishing third in the league before being sacked by Leeds.

Finally, he coached Bradford Northern where he spent almost all of 1975–76 and 1976–77. After that he retired.

Cliff Evans

Born: Resolven 14 July 1913
Died: Wiltshire 17 July 1982

Cliff Evans, an uncapped half-back, had accepted a fee of £600 and left his native Neath for Salford in October 1933. With Billy Watkins barring his way to a place in the first team, he agreed a move to Leeds for £700 in October 1936. Evans played regularly for the first team but his position varied depending on the vagaries of Leeds extravagant recruitment policy.

The outbreak of the Second World War saw him guest for Salford for a while. Evans joined the services and became a parachute instructor at Manchester Ringway.

Evans ended his playing days at Headingley in September 1946. He became coach at Leeds in early the following year, but resigned in September 1948 due to difficulties reaching a balance with his teaching responsibilities in Salford. Within a year he had relocated to California. After working at a variety of jobs around Los Angeles and getting involved with a high-profile group attempting to launch rugby league on the West Coast Evans packed his bags and came back to England in the summer of 1954. He once again became a schoolmaster in Salford and took over as coach at Swinton, a club in need of reviving.

Initially, under Evans' direction, Swinton showed little signs of progress, The directors, however, appreciated his work and gave him a five-year contract during 1955–56. Evans brought advanced training techniques and a unique vision of the game to his role. There were a number of talented young players already at the club when Evans arrived and he added to them by building an effective youth policy, recruiting players both locally and across south Lancashire. His first team squad had an average of only 22 in 1957–58. Evans's approach brought steady progress and put honours back on the club's agenda by the end of the decade.

In 1960–61, Swinton reached the Lancashire Cup final, the club's first appearance in a final for over 20 years, and won the Lancashire League. There was room for further improvement and a Swinton team playing some exciting attacking rugby finished as NRL champions in both 1962–63 and 1963–64. Staying at the top proved to be more difficult.

With the team in decline and problems growing between the board and the supporters, Evans resigned, "for personal reasons", as Swinton's coach in the autumn of 1967.

In January 1968 he was appointed as St Helens new coach. In two seasons at Knowsley Road his team won the Lancashire Cup and the Lancashire League. Citing travelling difficulties from his school in Salford, Evans resigned a week before the second season's end.

Evans replaced another Welshman, Griff Jenkins, as Salford's coach in May 1970 with the job of harnessing the many talented players signed by Brian Snape, the club chairman. The club's first major silverware for 33 years, the Lancashire Cup, arrived at The Willows in October 1972 and the prospects for more looked good.

Sadly, poor health forced Evans to stand down in December 1973 just when his work was about to come to fruition. That season finished with Salford as NRL champions.

Clive Sullivan MBE
Born: Cardiff 9 April 1943
Died: Hull 8 October 1985

Cardiff-born Clive Sullivan lost interest in rugby once his school-years were over, but re-found the game after enlisting in the Army aged 17. While based at Catterick Camp with the Royal Signals, Sullivan came to the notice of rugby league scouts. He played a trial with Bradford Northern's 'A' team, but was not signed on. One of the touch judges officiating at that match recognised the young winger's potential and recommended him to Hull FC. In December 1961 Roy Francis invited Sullivan for a trial and this time the outcome was much better. A contract was offered and Sullivan signed.

Clive Sullivan had become a professional rugby player, but the early years would be hard. Having undergone specialist training, the Army refused to allow him to leave for a number of years. A serious car crash in 1963 left him with serious injuries that threatened both his life and his career. He not only survived, but recovered sufficiently well to return to rugby at the highest level. Four years later there was another career-threatening injury. A torn thigh muscle required surgery and Sullivan suffered severe muscle wastage before the doctors had done with him. Once again his strength and tenacity carried him through and soon he was back on the rugby field.

His love of the game ran deep and his career was a long one. Sullivan played professionally for over two decades and eventually made over 600 appearances. He began with Hull FC in December 1961 and while he accumulated few honours, he grew in stature and eventually became player-coach in February 1973. Following a dispute with the board he resigned in March the following year. The club's record try-scorer then made the short, but significant, journey eastwards to join Hull KR in August.

He remained with the Robins for six years, finishing his time with them after collecting a Challenge Cup winner's medal at Wembley. A brief spell at Oldham ended in some acrimony in December 1980. Then, The Boulevard beckoned again. He returned as Hull FC's 'A' team coach. Injuries saw him briefly back in first team action for Hull in 1981–82. This meant he was directly involved in a memorable season which ended with him collecting a second Challenge Cup winner's medal.

With the Welsh XIII in abeyance in the early part of his career, Clive Sullivan made only seven appearances for Wales and undoubtedly missed out on captaining his country. He made the first of his 17 appearances for Great Britain in January 1967. Sullivan is best remembered for becoming captain of Great Britain at the 1972 World Cup tournament in France when he would make history by becoming the first black man to lead a British sports team. Having led his team to victory in France he would retain the captaincy against the Kangaroos the following autumn. Clive Sullivan was awarded the MBE in January 1974.

His playing days over, Sullivan still had more to give to the game. When lowly Doncaster offered the chance to get into coaching, he joined them as player-coach in March 1983, staying until the close-season of 1984. Any coaching ambitions he harboured were derailed when he was diagnosed with cancer. No further involvement with the game would be possible and he died aged just forty-two in October 1985. There are many tributes to his memory in Hull, and the main road into the city from the M62 motorway is called Clive Sullivan Way.

David Watkins MBE

Born: Christchurch, Caerleon 5 March 1942
Died: 3 September 2023

After rejecting many previous approaches from rugby league, Watkins was approached by his former Welsh rugby union teammate, John Mantle, in the club house after a sevens tournament at Davenport RUFC. Mantle checked on Watkins' interest and suggested that he phone the Salford chairman, Brian Snape, who had been in the crowd watching him play. Contact was made and a deal that was too good to refuse was hammered out. Having collected 21 Wales rugby union caps and captained his country in the last three matches of 1967, toured Australasia in 1966 with the British Lions and captained Newport from 1964 to 1967, Watkins signed for Salford on 19 October 1967.

It was a mark of his standing in Welsh rugby and of the changing times that his departure for Salford brought a letter from Bill Clement, the secretary on behalf of the WRU. No one had received such a letter before, stating as it did "I now express to you my appreciation and thanks for your tremendous contribution to Welsh rugby in recent years. You have been a credit to Wales both on and off the field, and our loss is the professional game's gain." In future years a select few who made the switch would also receive similar letters.

Being highly rewarded to take up the professional game led to envy getting the better of some of his opponents and he was on the receiving end of some rough treatment. The courage with which he handled himself and his situation was remarkable. In an article published in the *Western Mail* on 13 February 1975, three days before the Welsh XIII versus France match at Swansea, Stuart Perrott made it known that "David Watkins says he was immediately a marked man on League pitches, breaking his arm, jaw, his nose broken four times in his first two years. Most of the injuries were from late and illegal tackles." It was not the sort of publicity the League game would have sought in South Wales, but it made the paper's readers aware of how hard Watkins had worked to survive and prosper in his adopted game.

After that rough start Watkins would prove remarkably adept and resilient. In April 1971 he began a period in his playing career which showed his durability; between then and April 1974 he would rack up 140 consecutive appearances. After Cliff Evans took over as Salford's coach in 1970, Watkins would receive some focused coaching, successfully converting to centre, a position that proved far more suitable, and he would discover his abilities as a goalkicker. In 1972–73 Watkins set a new world record of 221 goals, but fell three points short of Lewis Jones' srecord aggregate of 496 set in 1956–57.

Planning ahead for his retirement, Watkins accepted a job as manager of the Merthyr Tydfil branch of a finance company and returned home in 1976. Despite the arduous car journey north for matches he kept on playing. Living back home he became an ambassador for the northern game in South Wales. It was a role that suited him and when interviewed by Tom Lyons of the *Daily Mirror* for the Wales versus England programme in May 1978, Watkins humbly noted the changing times. "I can honestly say I have met no antagonism in Wales. I have always tried to do my best for Wales and my clubs – at both codes. I can do no more than that."

Watkins stayed with Salford playing in various positions until April 1979, when, after amassing 407 appearances for the Red Devils (two as substitute), he played a final season with Swinton. While with Salford two League titles and a Lancashire Cup winner's medal had come his way along with 16 Welsh and six Great Britain rugby league caps. After serving as joint-coach with Wales, Watkins was appointed as Great Britain's coach for the 1977 World Cup, the first Welsh coach to be tasked with preparing a British team 'down-under'. Later he was the managing director and at one time coach of the Cardiff Blue Dragons. David Watkins was awarded the MBE in January 1986 for services to Rugby League. Sadly, he died while this book was being produced.

Jonathan Davies OBE
Born: Trimsaran 24 October 1962

Jonathan Davies's leadership qualities were recognised early on and he was appointed captain of Neath in both 1985–86 and 1986–87. By 1987 rumours of League interest were fuelling speculation and Neath's management demanded assurances about his future plans. When none were forthcoming Davies was cut from Neath's squad. Fortunately, Llanelli had a place for him in their team. Davies had made the first of his 32 appearances for the Welsh Rugby Union XV in 1985 and captained them on three occasions – the last two times against Western Samoa and Romania in autumn 1988.

Following negotiations with Doug Laughton and Jim Mills, the 26-year-old Jonathan Davies signed for Widnes in January 1989 for a record fee of £150,000. It was a sign of his standing in the rugby world that the press conference held to announce his signing was mobbed by journalists. Those who doubted whether such a slightly built stand-off had the build to survive in rugby league in the bulked-up 1990s would be left in no doubt of his ability or toughness. Like David Watkins he converted from stand-off to centre where he proved a great success.

Laughton had begun to assemble a special team at some cost in the bid for the game's major honours, but only the Premiership and the Lancashire Cup were won before financial problems threatened the club's very existence. Needing to reduce expenditure fast, Widnes allowed Davies to join Warrington on a free transfer in July 1993. He also spent one off-season with the Sydney-based Canterbury-Bankstown Bulldogs in 1991 and then the North Queensland Cowboys four years later. He made 13 appearances for the Great Britain rugby league team and seven for the Welsh XIII.

In his book, Bill Samuel maintains that Davies always believed he was going to finish his playing days in Welsh Rugby Union. At the time that seemed highly unlikely, but Davies would be the first to prove that the return journey could be made. Rugby Union going open sadly brought his Rugby League career to an abrupt halt after six seasons. Professionalism was no longer terminal and Davies was soon donning Cardiff's blue-and-black shirt. As his playing career inevitably drew to a close Davies would make four more international appearances in the red shirt of the Welsh XV in 1997.

Once his playing days were over Davies embarked on a new career as a commentator and analyst on both codes of rugby for the BBC and also as a chat-show host for S4C. It proved to be a great move for him and his new career would keep him busy for many years to come. He would, however, find some time to take on the role of President as the Celtic Crusaders fought hard to establish a Super League club in South Wales in the first decade of the 21st century.

Davies was awarded the MBE for services to Rugby League football in the 1995 New Year's Honours List and elevated to the OBE 20 years later for his charitable work in South Wales.

Off the record: the Welsh team that wasn't Wales

1920–21

Saturday 5 February 1921: England 33 Other Nationalities (Wales) 16
Workington, 10,000, £730

To promote the Northern Union game in west Cumberland, England met an Other Nationalities XIII at Workington's Lonsdale Park on Saturday 5 February 1921. The England team showed one change – Harold Wagstaff coming in for Albert Ackroyd – from the one that had faced Wales three weeks earlier at Headingley. The Other Nationalities team contained eight of the Welsh team that had faced England that day. The five newcomers were – Wickham Powell, Wyndham Emery, Willie Davies, Johnny Rogers and Percy Coldrick. All those newcomers were Welsh so, for the only time in its colourful existence, the Other Nationalities' team would be composed of a single nationality. Being all Welsh meant that many considered the meeting at Workington to be a return match. Both teams travelled to Carlisle and stayed overnight before making their way south along the coast to Workington the next morning.

The match showed signs of being a close, hard-fought encounter but then once again, as at Headingley, injury struck. This time it was the Other Nationalities who lost a man, Jack Beames being forced to leave the field with a dislocated shoulder after 15 minutes. England took advantage to run in four tries – a pair from Stone, Rhodes and Clark – to two from Wales – Gronow and Rogers – to lead 18-8 at the break. While England added three more tries in the second half, the one from Jimmy Owen coming after a spectacular 50-yard sprint, the Other Nationalities had to rely solely on the boot of Ben Gronow. Altogether Gronow would have eight penalty attempts at goal, of which he would be successful with four. Thanks to Gronow's eight point contribution the final score was 33–16 to England but the main news of the afternoon was the presence of a NU county record crowd of 10,000.

England: W Rhodes (Dewsbury); WJ Stone (Hull), H Wagstaff (Huddersfield) captain, W Batten (Hull), J Owen (St Helens Rec); J Brittain (Leeds), J Parkin (Wakefield T); J Cartwright (Leigh), W Cunliffe (Warrington), R Marlor (Oldham), H Hilton (Oldham), D Clark (Huddersfield), E Shaw (Wigan).
Tries: Stone (2), Wagstaff, Owen, Rhodes, Brittain, Clark;
Goals: Rhodes (6)

Other Nationalities: WG Thomas (Huddersfield) captain; W Powell (Rochdale H), CW Emery (Leigh), WA Davies (Leeds), B Williams (Batley); JH Rogers (Huddersfield), SG Jerram (Wigan); F Willis (Batley), B Gould (Leeds), AP Coldrick (Wigan), JR Beames (Halifax), B Gronow (Huddersfield), H Whitney (Salford).
Tries: Rogers, Gronow;
Goals: Gronow (5)

Referee: A Hesford (Broughton)

Appendices

Teams and scorers

1907–08

Monday 20 April 1908: Wales 35 England 18
Tonypandy, 12,000

Wales: TE Jenkins (Ebbw Vale); L Treharne (Wigan), TB Jenkins (Wigan), P Thomas (Leeds), D Thomas (Halifax); R Rees (Merthyr Tydfil), J Thomas (Wigan); A Buckler (Salford), G Ruddick (Broughton R), D Jones (Merthyr Tydfil), DB Davies (Merthyr Tydfil), O Burgham (Ebbw Vale), WJ Saunders (Ebbw Vale).
Tries: Treharne (2), TB Jenkins (2), Ruddick, Burgham, D Thomas; Goals: J Thomas (7)

England: WH Taylor (Hull) capt; J Fish (Warrington), G Dickenson (Warrington), A Hogg (Broughton R), W Batten (Hunslet); J Jolley (Runcorn), T White (Oldham); J Spencer (Salford), W Holder (Hull), JW Birch (Leeds), R Padbury (Runcorn), A Robinson (Halifax), S Warwick (Salford).
Tries: Fish (2), Spencer, Birch; Goals: Fish (2), Jolley

Referee: R Robinson (Bradford)

1908–09

Monday 28 December 1908: England 31 Wales 7
Broughton, 4,000

England: H Gifford (Barrow); W Batten (Hunslet), G Dickenson (Warrington), J Lomas (Salford) capt, G Tyson (Oldham); E Brookes (Warrington), JH Hilton (Halifax); W Jukes (Hunslet), JW Higson (Hunslet), A Smith (Oldham), W Longworth (Oldham), A Robinson (Halifax), A Mann (Bradford N).
Tries: Longworth (2), Mann (2) Brookes, Lomas, Robinson; Goals: Lomas (5)

Wales: TJ Paddison (Merthyr Tydfil); D Thomas (Halifax), T Llewellyn (Oldham), TB Jenkins (Wigan), WJ Williams (Halifax); J Thomas (Wigan), W Hopkins (Aberdare); G Ruddick (Broughton R), J Foley (Ebbw Vale), DB Davies (Merthyr Tydfil), D Rees (Salford), W O'Neill (Warrington), WH Dowell (Warrington).
Try: D Thomas; Goals: J Thomas (2)

Referee: W McCutcheon (Oldham)

1909–10

Saturday 4 December 1909: England 19 Wales 13
Wakefield, 4,000, £90

England: H Place (Hunslet); G Tyson (Oldham), J Lomas (Salford), FW Oliver (York), W Batten (Hunslet); F Smith (Hunslet), TH Newbould (Wakefield T); J Ferguson (Oldham) capt, F Boylen (Hull), W Jukes (Hunslet), R Padbury (Runcorn), JL Clampitt (Broughton R), F Hill (Batley).
Tries: Lomas, Batten, Newbould, Ferguson, Clampitt; Goals: Lomas (2)

Wales: WF Young (Leeds); WJ Williams (Halifax), P Thomas (Hull KR), TB Jenkins (Wigan) capt, WT Davies (Batley); E Jenkins (Warrington), J Davies (Huddersfield); DB Davies (Merthyr Tydfil), H de Francis (Wigan), D Galloway (Treherbert), FH Shugars (Warrington), W O'Neill (Warrington), J Foley (Ebbw Vale).
Tries: WT Davies, de Francis, Foley; Goals: Young (2)

Referee: W McCutcheon (Oldham)

Saturday 9 April 1910: Wales 39 England 18
Ebbw Vale, 4,000, £181

Wales: WF Young (Leeds); WJ Williams (Halifax), TE Jenkins (Ebbw Vale) capt, TB Jenkins (Wigan), LJ Llewellyn (Ebbw Vale); R Rees (Merthyr Tydfil), J Thomas (Wigan); DB Davies (Merthyr Tydfil), G Ruddick (Broughton R), D Galloway (Treherbert), FH Shugars (Warrington), J Foley (Ebbw Vale), D Lewis (Merthyr Tydfil).
Tries: Williams (3), TE Jenkins (2), Llewellyn (2), TB Jenkins, J Thomas; Goals: Young (3), J Thomas (3)

England: J Sharrock (Wigan); J Leytham (Wigan), J Lomas (Salford), Joe Riley (Halifax), W Batten (Hunslet); F Smith (Hunslet), T White (Oldham); AE Avery (Oldham), F Webster (Leeds), F Boylen (Hull), W Jukes (Hunslet), W Ward (Leeds), R Ramsdale (Wigan).
Tries: Leytham, Lomas, Smith, Jukes; Goals: Lomas (2), Leytham

Referee: JH Smith (Widnes)

1910–11

Saturday 10 December 1910: England 39 Wales 13
Coventry, 4,500, £126

England: E Clarkson (Hull); J Miller (Wigan), H Wagstaff (Huddersfield), W Lynch (Wakefield T), J Leytham (Wigan) capt; T White (Oldham), F Smith (Hunslet); W Jukes (Hunslet), F Webster (Leeds), W Winstanley (Leigh), AE Avery (Oldham), H Kershaw (Wakefield T), J Tomes (Coventry).
Tries: Miller (2), Leytham (2), White (2), Wagstaff, Jukes, Kershaw; Goals: Leytham (4), Wagstaff (2)

Wales: TE Jenkins (Ebbw Vale); LJ Llewellyn (Ebbw Vale), P Thomas (Hull KR), TB Jenkins (Wigan) capt, WJ Williams (Halifax); DB Davies (Swinton), J Davies (Huddersfield); FH Shugars (Warrington), JH Blackmore (Hull KR), J Foley (Ebbw Vale), DB Davies (Swinton), B Gronow (Huddersfield), E Jenkins (Rochdale H).
Tries: Llewellyn, Foley, Davies; Goals: Gronow (2)

Referee: EH Smirk (Wigan)

Saturday 1 April 1911: Wales 8 England 27
Ebbw Vale, 4,000

Wales: TE Jenkins (Ebbw Vale); LJ Llewellyn (Ebbw Vale), WS Thomas (Salford), TB Jenkins (Wigan), WT Davies (Halifax); TH Grey (Huddersfield), J Thomas (Wigan); FH Shugars (Warrington), JH Blackmore (Hull KR), J Foley (Ebbw Vale), DB Davies (Swinton), EJ Thomas (Salford), E Jenkins (Rochdale H).
Tries: Llewellyn, TB Jenkins; Goal: J Thomas

England: E Clarkson (Hull); WF Kitchen (Huddersfield), J Lomas (Oldham), H Wagstaff (Huddersfield), J Miller (Wigan); F Smith (Hunslet), T White (Oldham); JL Clampitt (Broughton R), F Webster (Leeds), W Winstanley (Leigh), AE Avery (Oldham), H Kershaw (Wakefield T), A Kennedy (Runcorn).
Tries: Kitchen (2), Miller (2), Wagstaff, Smith, Avery;
Goals: Lomas (2), Wagstaff

Referee: BR Ennion (Wigan)

1911–12

Saturday 20 January 1912: England 31 Wales 5
Oldham, 8,000

England: E Clarkson (Hull); S Moorhouse (Huddersfield), H Wagstaff (Huddersfield), W Batten (Hunslet), A Jenkinson (Hunslet); JR Hilton (Halifax), F Smith (Hunslet); T Woods (Rochdale H) capt, F Harrison (Leeds), D Clark (Huddersfield), JL Clampitt (Broughton R), R Padbury (Runcorn), W Winstanley (Wigan).
Tries: Moorhouse (2), Jenkinson (2), Clark (2), Wagstaff, Batten, Padbury; Goals: Batten, Hilton

Wales: TE Jenkins (Ebbw Vale); WT Davies (Halifax), TB Jenkins (Wigan) capt, E Davies (Oldham), LJ Llewellyn (Ebbw Vale); J Davies (Huddersfield), TH Grey (Huddersfield); WG Thomas (Warrington), W Sandham (Hull KR), E Jenkins (Rochdale H), FH Shugars (Warrington), C Rees (Salford), WG Evans (Leeds).
Try: WT Davies; Goal: Thomas

Referee: W McCutcheon (Oldham)

1912–13

Saturday 15 February 1913: England 40 Wales 16
Plymouth, 7,500, £250

England: A Carmichael (Hull KR); S Moorhouse (Huddersfield), H Wagstaff (Huddersfield), W Batten (Hunslet) capt, A Jenkinson (Hunslet); F Gleave (Wigan), EW Jones (Rochdale H); D Clark (Huddersfield), JL Clampitt (Broughton R), T Woods (Rochdale H), R Ramsdale (Wigan), A Moore (Hull KR), F Harrison (Leeds).
Tries: Moorhouse (4), Clampitt (2), Wagstaff, Jenkinson, Jones, Woods; Goals: Carmichael (5)

Wales: WD John (Salford); TJ Williams (Oldham), E Davies (Oldham), TB Jenkins (Wigan), AJ Francis (Hull); J Thomas (Wigan) capt, E Jones (Broughton R); J Chilcott (Huddersfield), WG Evans (Leeds), AP Coldrick (Wigan), JA Merry (Hull), DB Davies (Oldham), BW Fredericks (Oldham).
Tries: Williams, Jones, Chilcott, DB Davies; Goals: Thomas (2)

Referee: JF May (St Helens)

1913–14

Saturday 14 February 1914: England 16 Wales 12
St Helens, 10,000, £282

England: AE Wood (Oldham); S Moorhouse (Huddersfield), H Wagstaff (Huddersfield) capt, W Hall (Oldham), W Reid (Widnes); T Milner (Dewsbury), EW Jones (Rochdale H); JL Clampitt (Broughton R),

F Longstaff (Huddersfield), R Ramsdale (Wigan), WJ Roman (Rochdale H), A Johnson (Widnes), D Clark (Huddersfield).
Tries: Moorhouse, Wagstaff, Reid, Milner; Goals: Wood (2)

Wales: WG Thomas (Wigan); F Williams (Halifax), TB Jenkins (Wigan), WA Davies (Leeds), AJ Francis (Hull); JH Rogers (Huddersfield), J Thomas (Wigan) capt; R Richards (Wigan), EJ Thomas (Salford), JR Beames (Halifax), B Gronow (Huddersfield), AP Coldrick (Wigan), J Chilcott (Huddersfield).
Tries: Williams (2), Francis, Coldrick

Referee: JF May (St Helens)

1920–21

Wednesday 19 January 1921: England 35 Wales 9
Leeds, 13,000, £1,636

England: W Rhodes (Dewsbury); WJ Stone (Hull), AW Akroyd (Halifax), W Batten (Hull), J Owen (St Helens Rec); J Brittain (Leeds), J Parkin (Wakefield T); J Cartwright (Leigh), W Cunliffe (Warrington), R Marlor (Oldham), H Hilton (Oldham), D Clark (Huddersfield), E Shaw (Wigan).
Tries: Parkin (2), Stone, Owen, Brittain, Hilton, Clark; Goals: Rhodes (7)

Wales: WG Thomas (Huddersfield) capt; JA Bacon (Leeds), D Hurcombe (Wigan), T Howley (Wigan), B Williams (Batley); R Lloyd (Halifax), SG Jerram (Wigan); F Willis (Batley), B Gould (Leeds), FL Roffey (Wigan), JR Beames (Halifax), B Gronow (Huddersfield), H Whitney (Salford).
Try: Williams; Goals: Gronow (3)

Referee: F Renton (Hunslet)

1922–23

Monday 11 December 1922: England 12 Wales 7
London, 3,000, £250

England: T Clarkson (Leigh); WJ Stone (Hull), W Batten (Hull), J Tranter (Warrington), W Bentham (Broughton R); J Parkin (Wakefield T) capt, J Brittain (Leeds); W Cunliffe (Warrington), GA Skelhorne (Warrington), J Cartwright (Leigh), R Taylor (Hull), J Darwell (Leigh), J Price (Wigan).
Tries: Stone (2), Parkin, Taylor

Wales: J Sullivan (Wigan); JA Bacon (Leeds), J Shea (Wigan), CW Emery (Leigh), B Williams (Batley); E Caswell (Hull), JH Rogers (Huddersfield); B Gronow (Huddersfield) capt, B Gould (Wakefield T), G Oliver (Hull), T Woods (Wigan), W Hodder (Wigan), DE Morgan (Hull).
Try: Morgan; Goals: Sullivan (2)

Referee: RA Jones (Widnes)

Wednesday 7 February 1923: England 2 Wales 13
Wigan, 12,000

England: T Clarkson (Leigh); J Owen (St Helens Rec), H Wagstaff (Huddersfield), W Batten (Hull), WJ Stone (Hull); J Greenall (St Helens Rec), J Parkin (Wakefield T) capt; W Cunliffe (Warrington), J Cartwright (Leigh), GA Skelhorne (Warrington), R Taylor (Hull), J Darwell (Leigh), L Marshall (Bramley).
Goal: Stone

Wales: J Sullivan (Wigan); E Thomas (Oldham), JA Bacon (Leeds), J Shea (Wigan), D Hurcombe (Wigan); G Owens (Wigan), SG Jerram (Wigan); B Gronow (Huddersfield) capt, B Gould (Wakefield T), F Brown (Oldham), T Woods (Wigan), D Edwards (Rochdale H), D Rees (Halifax).
Tries: Hurcombe (2), Brown; Goals: Sullivan (2)

Referee: A Brown (Wakefield)

1923–24

Monday 1 October 1923: England 18 Wales 11
Huddersfield, 11,066, £761

England: SO Walmsley (Leeds); WJ Stone (Hull), J Hirst (Featherstone R), J Tranter (Warrington), J Owen (St Helens Rec); F Todd (Halifax), J Greenall (St Helens Rec); W Burgess (Barrow), J Cartwright (Leigh), W Cunliffe (Warrington), R Sloman (Oldham), J Darwell (Leigh), F Gallagher (Batley).
Tries: Owen (2), Stone, Todd; Goals: Walmsley (2), Burgess

Wales: J Sullivan (Wigan); D Hurcombe (Wigan), E Davies (Oldham), HR Rees (Batley), JA Corsi (Oldham); G Owens (Wigan), SG Jerram (Wigan); F Brown (Oldham), B Gronow (Huddersfield), B Gould (Wakefield T), JF Thompson (Leeds), DE Morgan (Hull), D Rees (Halifax).
Tries: Hurcombe (2), HR Rees; Goal: Thompson

Referee: F Mills (Oldham)

1924–25

Saturday 7 Feb 1925: England 27 Wales 22
Workington, 14,000, £700

England: E Knapman (Oldham); S Rix (Oldham), CW Carr (Barrow), E Evans (Swinton), H Young (Widnes); J Parkin (Wakefield T) capt, L Fairclough (St Helens); W Burgess (Barrow), J Bennett (Rochdale H), W Cunliffe (Warrington), D Clark (Huddersfield), R Taylor (Hull), F Gallagher (Batley).
Tries: Carr (2), Taylor (2), Evans, Young, Clark; Goals: Knapman (3)

Wales: J Sullivan (Wigan); J Ring (Wigan), T Howley (Wigan), HR Rees (Batley), F Evans (Swinton); SG Jerram (Wigan), D Hurcombe (Wigan) capt; DE Morgan (Hull), W Hodder (Wigan), C Sage (Hunslet), JF Thompson (Leeds), A Baker (Oldham), D Rees (Halifax).
Tries: Ring (2), Evans (2), Howley, Thompson; Goals: Sullivan (2)

Referee: F Mills (Oldham)

1925–26

Wednesday 30 September 1925: England 18 Wales 14
Wigan, 12,000

England: L Osborne (Hull KR); S Langshaw (Rochdale H), CW Carr (Barrow), E Evans (Swinton), J Wallace (St Helens Rec); G Hesketh (Oldham), L Fairclough (St Helens); W Cunliffe (Warrington), JA Peacock (Warrington), W Burgess (Barrow), R Sloman (Oldham), R Taylor (Hull), F Gallagher (Batley) capt.
Tries: Carr (2), Fairclough, Burgess; Goals: Osborne (3)

Wales: J Sullivan (Wigan); F Evans (Swinton), JA Bacon (Leeds), T Howley (Wigan), J Ring (Wigan); SG Jerram (Wigan), D Hurcombe (Wigan) capt; W Hodder (Wigan), C Sage (Hunslet), D Edwards (Rochdale H), JF Thompson (Leeds), J Hennessey (Rochdale H), D Rees (Halifax).
Tries: Evans, Howley, Ring, Rees; Goal: Sullivan

Referee: A Brown (Wakefield)

Monday 12 April 1926: Wales 22 England 30
Pontypridd, 23,000, £2,306

Wales: J Sullivan (Wigan) capt; F Evans (Swinton), MA Rosser (Leeds), J Jones (Leeds), JA Bacon (Leeds); IJ Fowler (Batley), W Rees (Swinton); W Hodder (Wigan), DE Morgan (Hull), FL Roffey (St Helens), JF Thompson (Leeds), D Rees (Halifax), B Phillips (Huddersfield).
Tries: Sullivan, Evans, Rosser, Bacon, Fowler, Morgan; Goals: Sullivan (2)

England: JW Brough (Leeds); S Rix (Oldham), CW Carr (Barrow), E Evans (Swinton), W Bentham (Broughton R); J Parkin (Wakefield T) capt, L Fairclough (St Helens); W Burgess (Barrow), J Bennett (Wigan), W Cunliffe (Warrington), R Taylor (Hull), R Sloman (Oldham), F Gallagher (Batley).
Tries: Carr (2), Taylor (2), Rix, Bentham, Burgess, Gallagher; Goals: Burgess (3)

Referee: Rev FH Chambers (Dewsbury)

1926–27

Wednesday 6 April 1927: England 11 Wales 8
Broughton, 6,000, £420

England: L Osborne (Hull KR); A Ellaby (St Helens), CW Carr (Barrow), A Frodsham (St Helens), C Brockbank (Swinton); L Fairclough (St Helens), J Parkin (Wakefield T) capt; H Bowman (Hull), H Smith (Halifax), L Houghton (St Helens), A Fildes (St Helens Rec), EC Haines (Salford), F Gallagher (Batley).
Tries: Ellaby, Carr, Fairclough; Goal: Osborne

Wales: J Sullivan (Wigan) capt; J Ring (Wigan), G Lewis (St Helens), JA Bacon (Leeds), F Evans (Swinton); E Caswell (Hull), W Rees (Swinton); G Oliver (Pontypridd), TA Green (Pontypridd), DM Jenkins (Hunslet), E Watkins (Leeds), TP Davies (Pontypridd), JH Gore (Salford).
Tries: Ring, Bacon; Goal: Sullivan

Referee: J Eddon (Swinton)

1927–28

Wednesday 11 January 1928: England 20 Wales 12
Wigan, 12,000

England: T Dingsdale (St Helens Rec); A Ellaby (St Helens), J Oliver (Batley), E Evans (Swinton), TE Holliday (Oldham); L Fairclough (St Helens), J Parkin (Wakefield T) capt; H Bowman (Hull), N Bentham (Wigan H), J Miller (Warrington), B Halfpenny (St Helens), M Hodgson (Swinton), H Young (Bradford N).
Tries: Ellaby (3), Oliver, Evans, Halfpenny; Goal: Dingsdale

Wales: J Sullivan (Wigan) capt; F Evans (Swinton), G Parker (Huddersfield), AJ Higgs (Oldham), J Ring (Wigan); W Rees (Swinton), DM Davies (Warrington); JF Thompson (Leeds), LL White (Pontypridd), TP Davies (Warrington), F Stephens (Wigan), A Baker (Oldham), JH Gore (Salford).
Tries: Parker, Gore; Goals: Sullivan (3)

Referee: F Peel (Bradford)

1928–29

Wednesday 14 November 1928: Wales 15 England 39
Cardiff, 15,000

Wales: J Sullivan (Wigan) capt; TE Gwynne (Hull), G Lewis (St Helens), T Parker (Wigan), J Ring (Wigan); W Rees (Swinton), E Williams (Huddersfield); W Hodder (Wigan), LL White (Hunslet), F Stephens (Wigan), DM Jenkins (Hunslet), AC Evans (Halifax), D Maidment (Wakefield T).
Tries: Ring, Jenkins, Maidment: Goals: Sullivan (3);

England: JW Brough (Leeds); A Ellaby (St Helens), CW Carr (Barrow), W Dingsdale (Warrington), A Frodsham (St Helens); J Parkin (Wakefield T) capt, L Fairclough (St Helens); H Bowman (Hull), N Bentham (Wigan H), W Burgess (Barrow), W Horton (Wakefield T), R Sloman (Oldham), F Gallagher (Leeds).
Tries: Ellaby (3), Dingsdale (2), Brough, Carr, Frodsham, Parkin; Goals: Parkin (4), Brough (2)

Referee: Not known

1930–31

Wednesday 18 March 1931: England 23 Wales 18
Huddersfield, 6,000, £348

England: JC Walkington (Hunslet); S Smith (Leeds), W Dingsdale (Warrington), A Atkinson (Castleford), A Ellaby (St Helens) capt; L Fairclough (St Helens), L Adams (Leeds); L Houghton (Wigan), SC Halliday (Huddersfield), AG Thomas (Leeds), AG Middleton (Salford), T Banks (Huddersfield), H Young (Huddersfield).
Tries: Ellaby (2), Dingsdale (2), Banks; Goals: Walkington (4)

Wales: J Sullivan (Wigan) capt; AC Lloyd (York), AJF Risman (Salford), MA Rosser (York), G Parker (Huddersfield); W Thomas (York), T Flynn (Warrington); JF Thompson (Leeds), LL White (Hunslet), DM Jenkins (Hunslet), D Rees (Halifax), AC Evans (Castleford), R Hathway (Oldham).
Tries: Risman, Rosser, Parker, Thompson; Goals: Sullivan (3)

Referee: AE Harding (Manchester)

1931–32

Wednesday 27 January 1932: England 19 Wales 2
Salford, 8,000, £420

England: LC Bowkett (Huddersfield); A Ellaby (St Helens), S Brogden (Huddersfield), W Dingsdale (Warrington), S Smith (Leeds); B Evans (Swinton) capt, E Pollard (Wakefield T); J Wright (Swinton), J Lowe (Leeds), N Silcock (Widnes), W Horton (Wakefield T), M Hodgson (Swinton), J Feetham (Salford).
Tries: Ellaby, Brogden, Dingsdale, Smith, Pollard; Goals: Bowkett, Pollard

128

Wales: J Sullivan (Wigan) capt; W Jones (Keighley), AJF Risman (Salford), EG Davies (Wigan), G Parker (Huddersfield); IA Towill (Huddersfield), W Watkins (Salford); WA Williams (Salford), LL White (Hunslet), WC Morgan (Wigan), R Hathway (Oldham), WT Thomas (Oldham), N Fender (York).
Goal: Sullivan
Referee: J Eddon (Swinton)

1932–33

Wednesday 30 November 1932: England 14 Wales 13
Leeds, 4,000, £184

England: JW Brough (Leeds); A Ellaby (St Helens), A Atkinson (Castleford) S Brogden (Huddersfield), S Smith (Leeds); B Evans (Swinton) capt, E Pollard (Wakefield T); N Silcock (Widnes), O Dolan (St Helens Rec), L Higson (Wakefield T), M Hodgson (Swinton), GH Exley (Wakefield T), F Butters (Swinton).
Tries: Smith (2), Atkinson, Silcock; Goal: Hodgson

Wales: J Sullivan (Wigan) capt; JC Morley (Wigan), EG Davies (Wigan), MA Rosser (York), S Ray (Warrington); W Watkins (Salford), E Jenkins (Salford); JF Thompson (Leeds), LL White (Hunslet), DM Jenkins (Leeds), A Casewell (Salford), WT Thomas (Oldham), N Fender (York).
Tries: Morley, Rosser, White; Goals: Sullivan (2)

Referee: A Holbrook (Warrington)

1934–35 International Championship

Wednesday 10 April 1935: England 24 Wales 11
Liverpool, 7,100, £462

England: JW Brough (Leeds); S Smith (Leeds), W Belshaw (Liverpool S), S Brogden (Leeds), B Hudson (Salford); G Todd (Hunslet), T McCue (Widnes); JH Woods (Liverpool S), T Armitt (Swinton), N Silcock (Widnes), W Dalton (Salford), LA Troup (Barrow), H Beverley (Hunslet).
Tries: Silcock (2), Smith, Brogden, Hudson, Beverley; Goals: Belshaw (3)

Wales: T Scourfield (Huddersfield); I Davies (St Helens), EG Davies (Wigan), SJ Mountain (Huddersfield), L Orchard (Keighley); E Jenkins (Salford), W Watkins (Salford); L Rees (Oldham), HC Day (Salford), H Edwards (Wigan), N Pugh (Oldham), F Talbot (Huddersfield), OT Griffiths (St Helens).
Tries: EG Davies, Orchard, Griffiths; Goal: I Davies

Referee: P Cowell (Warrington)

1935–36 International Championship

Saturday 1 February 1936: England 14 Wales 17
Hull, 17,000, £880

England: JW Brough (Leeds) capt; B Hudson (Salford), T Kenny (Salford), S Brogden (Leeds), J Oliver (Hull); G Todd (Hunslet), L Adams (Castleford); N Silcock (Widnes), T Armitt (Swinton), W Horton (Wakefield T), LA Troup (Barrow), M Hodgson (Swinton), W Dalton (Salford).
Tries: Hudson, Brogden; Goals: Hodgson (4)

Wales: J Sullivan (Wigan) capt; JC Morley (Wigan), D Madden (Huddersfield), AJF Risman (Salford), AS Edwards (Salford); GH Bennett (Wigan), W Watkins (Salford); H Jones (Keighley), HC Day (Salford), L Rees (Oldham), N Pugh (Oldham), N Fender (York), OT Griffiths (Halifax).
Tries: Bennett (2), Madden; Goals: Sullivan (4)

Referee: L Thorpe (Wakefield)

1936–37 International Championship

Saturday 7 November 1936: Wales 3 England 2
Pontypridd, 12,000, £650

Wales: J Sullivan (Wigan) capt; D Madden (Huddersfield), G Gummer (Barrow), AJF Risman (Salford), AS Edwards (Salford); E Jenkins (Salford), W Watkins (Salford); DR Prosser (York), AM Meek (Halifax), DM Evans (Huddersfield), N Fender (York), N Pugh (Oldham), A Givvons (Oldham).
Try: Edwards

England: W Belshaw (Liverpool S); SV Pepperell (Huddersfield), W Stott (Broughton R), AJ Croston (Castleford), S Brogden (Leeds); J Garvey (Broughton R), E Thompson (Broughton R); A Higgins (Widnes), T Armitt (Swinton), J Miller (Warrington), M Hodgson (Swinton) capt, J Arkwright (Warrington), H Beverley (Hunslet).
Goal: Hodgson

Referee: AE Harding (Manchester)

1937–38 International Championship

Saturday 29 January 1938: England 6 Wales 7
Bradford, 8,637, £495

England: JC Walkington (Hunslet) capt; B Hudson (Salford), S Brogden (Leeds), AJ Croston (Castleford), JH Cumberbatch (Newcastle); T Shannon (Widnes), T McCue (Widnes); A Higgins (Widnes), T Armitt (Swinton), H Irving (Halifax), RH Ayres (Barrow), C Booth (Hull), H Beverley (Halifax).
Tries: Hudson, Cumberbatch

Wales: J Sullivan (Wigan) capt; WH Johnson (Huddersfield), CH Evans (Leeds), AJF Risman (Salford), AS Edwards (Salford); O Morris (Hunslet), D Jenkins (Leeds); DR Prosser (Leeds), CD Murphy (Leeds), L Rees (Oldham), G Morgan (Dewsbury), N Fender (York), A Givvons (Oldham).
Try: Evans; Goals: Sullivan (2)

Referee: F Fairhurst (Wigan)

1938–39 International Championship
Saturday 5 November 1938: Wales 17 England 9
Llanelli, 15,000, £890

Wales: J Sullivan (Wigan) capt; D Case (Bradford N), D Madden (Huddersfield), AJF Risman (Salford), AS Edwards (Salford); CH Evans (Leeds), D Jenkins (Leeds); FW Whitcombe (Broughton R), CD Murphy (Leeds), G Hughes (Swinton), HW Thomas (Salford), E Hughes (Huddersfield), A Givvons (Oldham).
Tries: Case, Risman, Edwards; Goals: Sullivan (3), Risman

England: W Belshaw (Warrington); E Batten (Hunslet), C Morrell (Hunslet), AJ Croston (Castleford), S Brogden (Hull) capt; T Shannon (Widnes), T McCue (Widnes); L Thacker (Hull), T Armitt (Swinton), A Higgins (Widnes), K Jubb (Leeds), C Booth (Hull), A Watson (Leeds).
Try: Shannon; Goals: Belshaw (3)

Referee: P Cowell (Warrington)

Wartime Internationals

1939–40

Saturday 23 December 1939: England 3 Wales 16
Bradford, 15,257, £850

England: W Belshaw (Warrington); E Batten (Hunslet), AJ Croston (Castleford), JH Lawrenson (Wigan), O Peake (Warrington); T Kenny (Salford), H Goodfellow (Wakefield T); FStC Gregory (Warrington), T Armitt (Swinton), H Dyer (Leeds), R Roberts (Widnes), C Booth (Hull), EH Sadler (Castleford).
Try: Batten

Wales: J Sullivan (Wigan) capt; A Bassett (Halifax), CH Evans (Leeds), AJF Risman (Salford), AS Edwards (Salford); WTH Davies (Bradford N), D Jenkins (Leeds); FW Whitcombe (Bradford N), CD Murphy (Leeds), DM Davies (Salford), TJF Foster (Bradford N), EJ Orford (Wakefield T), A Givvons (Oldham).
Tries: Davies, Foster; Goals: Sullivan (5)

Referee: P Cowell (Warrington)

1940–41

Saturday 9 November 1940: England 8 Wales 5
Oldham, 5,000, £234

England: W Belshaw (Warrington); E Batten (Hunslet), J Waring (St Helens), JH Lawrenson (Wigan), O Peake (Warrington); F Tracey (St Helens), T McCue (Widnes); R Roberts (Widnes), E Brooks (Oldham), H Irving (Halifax), E Tattersfield (Leeds), G Bunter (Broughton R), JD Moore (Bradford N).
Tries: Batten, Moore; Goal: Belshaw

Wales: J Jones (Wigan); E Walters (Bradford N), AJF Risman (Salford) capt, CH Evans (Leeds), SA Williams (Salford); O Morris (Leeds), D Jenkins (Leeds); FW Whitcombe (Bradford N), CD Murphy (Leeds), G Hughes (Swinton), WT Thomas (Wigan), EJ Orford (Wakefield T), TJF Foster (Bradford N).
Try: Foster; Goal: Jones

Referee: GS Phillips (Widnes)

1941–42

Saturday 18 October 1941: England 9 Wales 9
Bradford, 4,339, £287

England: W Belshaw (Warrington) capt; E Batten (Hunslet), JH Lawrenson (Wigan), E Ward (Bradford N), O Peake (Warrington); S Brogden (Hull), TA Johnson (Hull); L Higson (Bradford N), E Brooks (Oldham), L Thacker (Hull), H Irving (Halifax), K Jubb (Leeds), E Tattersfield (Leeds).
Try: Lawrenson; Goals: Belshaw (3)

Wales: J Jones (Wigan); E Walters (Bradford N), CH Evans (Leeds), AJF Risman (Salford) capt, AS Edwards (Salford); O Morris (Leeds), D Jenkins (Leeds); DR Prosser (Leeds), CD Murphy (Leeds), FW Whitcombe (Bradford N), E Watkins (Wigan), EJ Orford (Wakefield T), TJF Foster (Bradford N).
Try: Edwards; Goals: Risman (3)

Referee: Not known

1942–43

Saturday 27 February 1943: England 15 Wales 9
Wigan, 17,000, £1,020

England: W Belshaw (Warrington) capt; E Batten (Hunslet), J Stott (St Helens), S Brogden (Hull), GA Aspinall (Liverpool S); M Ryan (Wigan), W Thornton (Hunslet); K Gee (Wigan), J Egan (Wigan), H Wilkinson (Wakefield T), K Jubb (Leeds), H Irving (Halifax), E Tattersfield (Leeds).
Tries: Aspinall, Ryan, Jubb; Goals: Belshaw (3)

Wales: A Davies (Huddersfield); E Walters (Bradford N), J Jones (Wigan), SA Williams (Salford), AS Edwards (Salford); WT Davies (Huddersfield), D Jenkins (Leeds); FW Whitcombe (Bradford N), CD Murphy (Leeds), DR Prosser (Leeds), E Watkins (Wigan), TJF Foster (Bradford N) capt, WG Chapman (Warrington).
Try: Jones; Goals: A Davies (3)

Referee: F Fairhurst (Wigan)

1943–44

Saturday 26 February 1944: England 9 Wales 9
Wigan, 16,028, £1,277

England: JC Walkington (Hunslet); E Batten (Bradford N), B Knowelden (Barrow), J Robinson (Castleford), AE Johnson (Warrington); SV Pepperell (Huddersfield), T Bradshaw (Wigan); H Wilkinson (Wakefield T), J Egan (Wigan), K Gee (Wigan), W Hutchinson (Bradford N), H Millington (Widnes), E Tattersfield (Leeds).
Try: Knowelden; Goals: Pepperell (2), Gee

Wales: J Jones (Barrow); E Walters (Bradford N), WT Davies (Huddersfield), AJF Risman (Salford) capt, AS Edwards (Salford); WTH Davies (Bradford N), D Jenkins (Leeds); DR Prosser (Leeds), CD Murphy (Leeds), FW Whitcombe (Bradford N), EJ Orford (Wakefield T), TJF Foster (Bradford N), WG Chapman (Warrington).
Tries: Edwards (2), Jones

Referee: E Devine (Leeds)

1944–45

Saturday 10 March 1945: England 18 Wales 8

Wigan, 23,500, £1,880

England: W Belshaw (Warrington) capt; E Batten (Bradford N), E Ward (Bradford N), B Knowelden (Barrow), AE Johnson (Warrington); W Horne (Barrow), T Bradshaw (Wigan); H Wilkinson (Wakefield T), J Egan (Wigan), C Stansfield (Hunslet), RH Ayres (Barrow), GS Brown (Batley), W Hutchinson (Bradford N).
Tries: Batten (3), Horne; Goals: Ward (2), Belshaw

Wales: J Jones (Barrow); S Powell (St Helens), DI Davies (Leeds), AJF Risman (Salford) capt, AS Edwards (Salford); WTH Davies (Bradford N), M de Lloyd (Warrington); WF Hughes (Barrow), HC Day (Salford), E Evans (Salford), BJ Bowen (Wigan), E Watkins (Wigan), IA Owens (Leeds).
Tries: Edwards (2); Goal: Powell

Referee: GS Phillips (Widnes)

1945–46 International Championship

Saturday 24 November 1945: Wales 11 England 3
Swansea, 30,000, £4,100

Wales: J Jones (Barrow); A Bassett (Halifax), G Price (Leeds), AJF Risman (Salford) capt, AS Edwards (Salford); WTH Davies (Bradford N), D Jenkins (Leeds); FW Whitcombe (Bradford N), CD Murphy (Leeds), WF Hughes (Barrow), DV Phillips (Oldham), DM Davies (Salford), IA Owens (Leeds).
Tries: Price (2), Owens; Goal: Risman

England: M Ryan (Wigan); E Batten (Bradford N), J Kitching (Bradford N), E Ward (Bradford N), AE Johnson (Warrington); W Horne (Barrow), T McCue (Widnes) capt; TL Taylor (Castleford), J Egan (Wigan), T Rostron (Oldham), R Nicholson (Huddersfield), F Higgins (Widnes), L Bratley (Wakefield T).
Try: Nicholson

Referee: GS Phillips (Widnes)

1946–47 International Championship

Saturday 12 October 1946: England 10 Wales 13
Swinton, 20,213, £2,547

England: E Ward (Bradford N) capt; J Kitching (Bradford N), JH Lawrenson (Wigan), EJ Ashcroft (Wigan), AE Johnson (Warrington); W Horne (Barrow), T McCue (Widnes) capt; K Gee (Wigan), J Egan (Wigan), G Curran (Salford), L White (York), H Murphy (Wakefield T), A Dockar (Hull KR).
Tries: White, Dockar; Goals: Lawrenson (2)

Wales: T Griffiths (Hunslet); RL Francis (Barrow), G Price (Leeds), WT Davies (Huddersfield), RW Lloyd (Castleford); WTH Davies (Bradford N), D Jenkins (Leeds); FW Whitcombe (Bradford N), AM Meek (Halifax), DM Davies (Salford), TJF Foster (Bradford N) capt, DV Phillips (Oldham), IA Owens (Leeds).
Tries: Francis, WT Davies, Lloyd; Goals: WT Davies (2)

Referee: R Kendall (Keighley)

Saturday 16 November 1946: Wales 5 England 19
Swansea, 25,000, £4,180

133

Wales: J Jones (Barrow); A Bassett (Halifax), G Price (Leeds), WT Davies (Huddersfield), RW Lloyd (Castleford); WTH Davies (Bradford N), D Jenkins (Leeds); FW Whitcombe (Bradford N), AM Meek (Halifax), DM Davies (Salford), TJF Foster (Bradford N) capt, DV Phillips (Oldham), IA Owens (Leeds).
Try: Jenkins; Goal: WT Davies
England: M Ryan (Wigan); E Batten (Bradford N), E Ward (Bradford N) capt, JH Lawrenson (Wigan), AE Johnson (Warrington); W Horne (Barrow), T Bradshaw (Wigan); K Gee (Wigan), J Egan (Wigan), G Curran (Salford), L White (York), W Hudson (Batley), A Dockar (Hull KR).
Tries: Johnson (3), Lawrenson (2); Goals: Lawrenson (2)

Referee: P Cowell (Warrington)

1947–48 International Championship

Saturday 20 September 1947: England 8 Wales 10
Wigan, 27,000, £3,100

England: M Ryan (Wigan); WG Ratcliffe (Wigan), J Kitching (Bradford N), E Ward (Bradford N) capt, A Bowers (Hull); R Rylance (Wakefield T), T Bradshaw (Wigan); K Gee (Wigan), J Egan (Wigan), R Nicholson (Huddersfield), L White (Wigan), L Aston (St Helens), A Dockar (Hull KR).
Tries: Ratcliffe, White; Goal: Rylance

Wales: J Jones (Barrow); E Walters (Bradford N), EH Ward (Wigan) capt, G Price (Leeds), SA Williams (Salford); WTH Davies (Bradford N), WG Morgan (Huddersfield); DEJ Harris (Castleford), AM Meek (Halifax), E Gwyther (Belle Vue R), BV Goldswain (Hull KR), LM Thomas (Oldham), TEH Evans (Bradford N).
Tries: Thomas (2); Goals: Ward (2)

Referee: GS Phillips (Widnes)

Saturday 6 December 1947: Wales 7 England 18
Swansea, 10,000, £1,257

Wales: J Jones (Barrow); RL Francis (Barrow), EH Ward (Wigan) capt, N Harris (Oldham), RW Lloyd (Castleford); RL Williams (Leeds), D Jenkins (Leeds); WRT Jones (Swinton), AM Meek (Halifax), E Gwyther (Belle Vue R), TJF Foster (Bradford N), LM Thomas (Oldham), IA Owens (Leeds).
Try: Foster; Goals: Ward (2)

England: M Ryan (Wigan); A Bowers (Hull), EJ Ashcroft (Wigan), GR Pepperell (Huddersfield), AE Johnson (Warrington); W Horne (Barrow), T Bradshaw (Wigan); W Derbyshire (Warrington), J Egan (Wigan) capt, G Curran (Salford), L White (Wigan), H Palin (Warrington), D Clarkson (Hunslet).
Tries: Bowers (2), Ashcroft, Pepperell; Goals: Horne (2), Palin

Referee: P Cowell (Warrington)

1948–49 International Championship

Wednesday 22 September 1948: England 11 Wales 5
Wigan, 12,638, £1,423

England: JA Ledgard (Leigh); JH Lawrenson (Wigan), GR Pepperell (Huddersfield), AJ Pimblett (Warrington), S McCormick (Belle Vue R); J Fleming (Warrington), GJ Helme (Warrington); K Gee

(Wigan), J Egan (Wigan), G Curran (Salford), H Murphy (Wakefield T), L White (Wigan), H Palin (Warrington).
Tries; Pimblett, McCormick, Helme; Goal: Palin

Wales: J Jones (Barrow); SM Llewellyn (St Helens), EH Ward (Wigan), JB Mahoney (Oldham), AS Edwards (Bradford N); L Constance (St Helens), D Jenkins (Leeds) capt; DM Davies (Salford), AM Meek (Huddersfield), E Gwyther (Belle Vue R), C Staines (Castleford), WJD Howes (Wakefield T), IA Owens (Leeds).
Try: Mahoney; Goal: Ward

Referee: CF Appleton (Warrington)

Saturday 5 February 1949: Wales 14 England 10
Swansea, 9,553, £1,429

Wales: J Jones (Barrow); AH Daniels (Halifax), EH Ward (Wigan) capt, N Harris (Oldham), DJ Boocker (Wakefield T); RL Williams (Leeds), WM Banks (Huddersfield); AM Meek (Huddersfield), FF Osmond (Swinton), E Hawkins (Salford), DV Phillips (Belle Vue R), G Parsons (St Helens), IA Owens (Huddersfield).
Tries: Daniels, Phillips; Goals: Ward (4)

England: M Ryan (Wigan); JH Lawrenson (Wigan), AJ Pimblett (Warrington), E Ward (Bradford N) capt, S McCormick (St Helens); J Fleming (Warrington), GJ Helme (Warrington); K Gee (Wigan), J Egan (Wigan), G Curran (Salford), R Nicholson (Huddersfield), JJ Featherstone (Warrington), WH Ivison (Workington T).
Tries: Lawrenson, McCormick; Goals: Ward (2)

Referee: AS Dobson (Featherstone)

1949–50 International Championship

Wednesday 1 March 1950: England 11 Wales 6
Wigan, 27,500, £3,322

England: M Ryan (Wigan); R Pollard (Dewsbury), E Ward (Bradford N) capt, T Danby (Salford), J Hilton (Wigan); J Cunliffe (Wigan), T Bradshaw (Wigan); K Gee (Wigan), J Egan (Wigan), JJ Featherstone (Warrington), J Barraclough (Hull KR), F Higgins (Widnes), H Street (Dewsbury).
Tries: Hilton (3); Goal: Ward

Wales: DR Morgan (Swinton); AH Daniels (Halifax), JB Mahoney (Dewsbury), WLT Williams (Hunslet), SM Llewellyn (St Helens); RL Williams (Leeds), WM Banks (Huddersfield); T Danter (Hull), FF Osmond (Swinton), E Hawkins (Salford), TJF Foster (Bradford N) capt, WJD Howes (Wakefield T), BV Goldswain (Oldham).
Tries: Daniels, Williams

Referee: CF Appleton (Warrington)

1950–51 International Championship

Saturday 14 Octo0ber 1950: Wales 4 England 22
Abertillery, 8,000, £1,000

Wales: JD Evans (Hunslet); R Lambert (Neath), D Gullick (St Helens), JB Mahoney (Dewsbury), DJ Boocker (Wakefield T); RL Williams (Leeds) capt, WM Banks (Huddersfield); T Danter (Hull), FF Osmond (Swinton), E Gwyther (Belle Vue R), G Parsons (St Helens), BV Goldswain (Oldham), G James (Hunslet). Goals: Goldswain (2)

England: E Ward (Bradford N) capt; JH Lawrenson (Workington T), J Broome (Wigan), EJ Ashcroft (Wigan), T Danby (Salford); J Cunliffe (Wigan), T Bradshaw (Wigan); JJ Featherstone (Warrington), J Egan (Leigh), AG Prescott (St Helens), F Higgins (Widnes), E Slevin (Wigan), H Street (Dewsbury). Tries: Lawrenson, Broome, Bradshaw, Street; Goals: Ward (5)

Referee: AS Dobson: (Pontefract)

1951–52 International Championship

Wednesday 19 September 1951: England 35 Wales 11
St Helens, 20,918, £2,259

England: JA Ledgard (Leigh) capt; G Tullock (Hull KR), E Gibson (Workington T), EJ Ashcroft (Wigan), S McCormick (St Helens); J Cunliffe (Wigan), A Burnell (Hunslet); K Gee (Wigan), VM McKeating (Workington T), M Scott (Hull), L White (Halifax), CH Pawsey (Leigh), W Blan (Wigan). Tries: Burnell (2), Blan (2), Tullock, Gibson, White; Goals: Gee (7)

Wales: JD Evans (Hunslet); AH Daniels (Halifax), WLT Williams (Hunslet), VJG Harrison (St Helens), R Lambert (Dewsbury); RL Williams (Leeds) capt, WM Banks (Huddersfield); LO Phillips (Swinton), FF Osmond (Swinton), E Gwyther (Belle Vue R), DV Phillips (Belle Vue R), G Parsons (St Helens), WR Cale (St Helens). Tries: Daniels, Williams, Lambert; Goal: Harrison

Referee: CF Appleton: (Warrington)

1952–53 International Championship

Wednesday 17 September 1952: England 19 Wales 8
Wigan, 13,503, £1,810

England: JA Ledgard (Leigh); T O'Grady (Oldham), D Greenall (St Helens), E Ward (Bradford N), F Castle (Barrow); W Horne (Barrow) capt, A Burnell (Hunslet); AG Prescott (St Helens), A Ackerley (Halifax), JJ Featherstone (Warrington), CH Pawsey (Leigh), D Schofield (Rochdale H), H Street (Wigan). Tries: Burnell (2), Greenall, Ward, Pawsey; Goals: Ledgard (2)

Wales: SA Williams (Salford); AH Daniels (Halifax), WLT Williams (Hunslet), D Gullick (St Helens), R Lambert (Warrington); HR Price (Belle Vue R), WM Banks (Huddersfield); M Condon (Halifax), PT Harris (Hull), B Day (Oldham), G Parsons (St Helens), B Radford (Bradford N), BV Goldswain (Oldham) capt. Tries: Lambert, Price; Goal: Goldswain

Referee: CF Appleton (Warrington)

1953–54 International Championship

Wednesday 16 September 1953: England 24 Wales 5
St Helens, 19,357, £2,520

England: JA Ledgard (Leigh); R Cracknell (Huddersfield), D Greenall (St Helens), A Davies (Oldham), S McCormick (St Helens); W Horne (Barrow) capt, S Kielty (Halifax); M Scott (Hull), A Ackerley (Halifax), JB Henderson (Workington T), CH Pawsey (Leigh), N Silcock (Wigan), K Traill (Bradford N).
Tries: Davies (2), Ledgard, Greenall, McCormick, Horne; Goals: Ledgard (3)

Wales: JD Evans (Hunslet) capt; AH Daniels (Halifax), WLT Williams (Hunslet), D Gullick (St Helens), DR Bevan (Wigan); HR Price (Warrington), WM Banks (Huddersfield); LO Phillips (Swinton), PT Harris (Hull), E Gwyther (Leeds), G Parsons (St Helens), CH Winslade (Oldham), BV Goldswain (Oldham).
Try: Daniels; Goal: Evans

Referee GS Phillips (Widnes)

1968–69

Thursday 7 November 1968: England 17 Wales 24
Salford, 6,002, £1,461

England: B Jefferson (Keighley); MA Smith (Leeds), W Benyon (St Helens), C Hesketh (Salford) JB Atkinson (Leeds); DW Davies (Swinton), MD Shoebottom (Leeds); D Hartley (Castleford), K Taylor (Oldham), CH Watson (St Helens) capt, A Morgan (Featherstone R), K Parr (Warrington), R Batten (Leeds); A Buckley (Swinton) replaced Shoebottom.
Tries: Smith (2), Atkinson, Taylor, Watson; Goal: Jefferson

Wales: TG Price (Bradford N); FH Wilson (St Helens), A Kersey-Brown (Huddersfield), DE Jones (Halifax), CA Sullivan (Hull); D Watkins (Salford), WR Prosser (Salford); DJ Warlow (St Helens), A Fisher (Bradford N), GT Rees (St Helens), CJ Dixon (Halifax), J Mantle (St Helens) capt, TK Coslett (St Helens); R Wanbon (St Helens) replaced Rees.
Tries: Sullivan, Watkins, Rees, Dixon; Goals: Price (6)

Referee: WH Thompson (Huddersfield)

1969–70 European Championship

Saturday 18 October 1969: England 40 Wales 23
Leeds, 8,355, £2,345

England: A Keegan (Hull); W Burgess (Salford), S Hynes (Leeds), C Hesketh (Salford), JB Atkinson (Leeds); R Millward (Hull KR), AJ Murphy (Leigh) capt; JR Stephens (Wigan), P Flanagan (Hull KR), J Ward (Castleford), D Robinson (Swinton), R Haigh (Wakefield T), R Batten (Leeds); CH Watson (St Helens) replaced Robinson.
Tries: Hynes (2), Batten (2), Millward, Murphy, Haigh, Watson; Goals: Millward (7), Murphy

Wales: TG Price (Bradford N); CA Sullivan (Hull), DE Jones (Halifax), PH Rowe (Wigan), FH Wilson (St Helens); PJ Morgan (Hunslet), WR Prosser (Salford); J Mills (Bradford N), A Fisher (Bradford N), GT Rees (St Helens), R Wanbon (St Helens), CJ Dixon (Salford), J Mantle (St Helens) capt.
Tries: Sullivan, Jones, Rowe, Morgan, Dixon; Goals: Price (4)

Referee: E Clay (Rothwell)

Tuesday 24 February 1970: Wales 7 England 26
Leeds, 9,393, £2,670

Wales: S Ferguson (Leigh); CA Sullivan (Hull), GH Lewis (Leigh) capt, KS Jarrett (Barrow), FH Wilson (St Helens); PJ Morgan (Hunslet), C Williams (Hunslet); J Mills (Bradford N), A Fisher (Bradford N), R Wanbon (St Helens), GT Rees (St Helens), C Standing (Oldham), TK Coslett (St Helens); D Willicombe (Halifax) replaced Lewis.
Try: Jarrett; Goals: Ferguson (2)

England: RF Dutton (Widnes); MA Smith (Leeds), S Hynes (Leeds), W Benyon (St Helens), JB Atkinson (Leeds); MD Shoebottom (Leeds), B Seabourne (Leeds) capt; M Dixon (Featherstone R), P Flanagan (Hull KR), CH Watson (St Helens), P Lowe (Hull KR), R Haigh (Wakefield T), MJ Reilly (Castleford); R Millward (Hull KR) replaced Shoebottom.
Tries: Hynes (2), Smith, Atkinson, Shoebottom, Lowe; Goals: Dutton (4)

Referee: RL Thomas (Oldham)

1974–75 European Championship

Tuesday 25 February 1975: England 12 Wales 8
Salford, 8,494, £3,711

England: L Sheard (Wakefield T); G Dunn (Hull KR), D Noonan (Warrington), LP Dyl (Leeds), JB Atkinson (Leeds); K Gill (Salford), R Millward (Hull KR) capt; MJ Coulman (Salford), JD Gray (Wigan), P Jackson (Bradford N), T Martyn (Warrington), J Cunningham (Barrow), M Morgan (Wakefield T); D Chisnall (Warrington) replaced Morgan.
Tries: Noonan, Atkinson; Goals: Gray (3)

Wales: WL Francis (Wigan); R Mathias (St Helens), D Willicombe (Wigan), FH Wilson (St Helens), JC Bevan (Warrington); D Watkins (Salford) capt, P Banner (Salford); J Mills (Widnes), RP Evans (Swinton), J Mantle (St Helens), S Gallacher (Keighley), CJ Dixon (Salford), TK Coslett (St Helens); G Turner (Hull KR) replaced Bevan, MJ Nicholas (Warrington) replaced Coslett.
Try: Watkins; Goals: Watkins, Coslett; Drop-goal: Watkins

Referee: S Wall (Leigh)

1975 World Championship

Tuesday 10 June 1975: England 7 Wales 12
Brisbane, 6,000, $11,891

England: GA Fairbairn (Hull KR); KJ Fielding (Salford), D Noonan (Warrington), LP Dyl (Leeds), JB Atkinson (Leeds); R Millward (Hull KR) capt, S Nash (Featherstone R); D Chisnall (Warrington), M Morgan (Wakefield T), MJ Coulman (Salford), E Chisnall (St Helens), G Nicholls (St Helens), S Norton (Castleford); K Gill (Salford) replaced Millward, T Martyn (Warrington) replaced Coulman.
Try: Fairbairn; Goals: Fairbairn (2)

Wales: WL Francis (Wigan); CA Sullivan (Hull KR), D Willicombe (Wigan), D Watkins (Salford) capt, R Mathias (St Helens); D Treasure (Oldham), P Banner (Salford); J Mills (Widnes), A Fisher (Leeds), R Wanbon (Warrington), E Cunningham (St Helens), CJ Dixon (Salford), TK Coslett (St Helens); FH Wilson (St Helens) replaced Banner, J Mantle (St Helens) replaced Dixon.
Tries: Watkins, Treasure; Goals: Watkins (3)

Referee: D Lancaster (Australia)

Saturday 20 September 1975: England 22 Wales 16
Warrington, 5,034, £3,684

Wales: WL Francis (Wigan); CA Sullivan (Hull KR), D Watkins (Salford) capt, FH Wilson (St Helens), JC Bevan (Warrington); D Treasure (Oldham), P Banner (Salford); J Mantle (St Helens), A Fisher (Leeds), M James (St Helens), B Gregory (Wigan), E Cunningham (St Helens), TK Coslett (St Helens); G Turner (Hull KR) replaced Treasure, PH Rowe (Blackpool B) replaced Gregory.
Tries: Banner, Coslett; Goals: Watkins (5)

England: GA Fairbairn (Wigan); KJ Fielding (Salford), E Hughes (Widnes), JS Holmes (Leeds), JB Atkinson (Leeds); K Gill (Salford), R Millward (Hull KR) capt; JB Hogan (Wigan), JH Bridges (Featherstone R), C Forsyth (Bradford N), RA Irving (Wigan), J Grayshon (Dewsbury), S Norton (Castleford); D Eckersley (St Helens) replaced Holmes, G Nicholls (St Helens) replaced Gill.
Tries: Fielding, Hughes, Holmes;
Goals: Fairbairn (6); Drop-goal: Bridges

Referee: M Caillol (France)

1976–77 European Championship

Saturday 29 January 1977: England 2 Wales 6
Leeds, 6,472, £4,142

England: GA Fairbairn (Wigan); S Wright (Widnes), JS Holmes (Leeds), LP Dyl (Leeds), L Jones (St Helens); K Gill (Salford), R Millward (Hull KR) capt; JB Hogan (Wigan), JH Bridges (Featherstone R), J Thompson (Featherstone R), J Grayshon (Dewsbury), L Gorley (Workington T), CD Laughton (Widnes); D Eckersley (Widnes) replaced Gill, MJ Reilly (Castleford) replaced Gorley.
Goal: Fairbairn

Wales: D Watkins (Salford) capt; R Mathias (St Helens), JC Bevan (Warrington), E Cunningham (St Helens), MCR Richards (Salford); WL Francis (Wigan), P Woods (Widnes); J Mills (Workington T), A Fisher (Leeds), J Mantle (Salford), MJ Nicholas (Warrington), CJ Dixon (Salford), PH Rowe (Huddersfield); R Wilkins (Workington T) replaced Watkins
Try: Cunningham; Goal: Woods; Drop-goal: Rowe

Referee: WH Thompson (Huddersfield)

1977–78 European Championship

Sunday 28 May 1978: England 60 Wales 13
St Helens, 9,759, £6,921

England: G Pimblett (St Helens); S Wright (Widnes), E Hughes (Widnes), LP Dyl (Leeds), JB Atkinson (Leeds); R Millward (Hull KR) capt, S Nash (Salford); M Harrison (Leeds), K Elwell (Widnes), G Nicholls (St Helens), P Rose (Hull KR), L Casey (Hull KR), S Norton (Hull); D Eckersley (Widnes) replaced Millward, J Thompson (Bradford N) replaced Nicholls.
Tries: Wright (4), Hughes (2), Atkinson (2), Pimblett, Dyl, Millward, Nash, Casey, Norton; Goals: Pimblett (9)

Wales: D Watkins (Salford); R Mathias (St Helens), G Turner (Hull), D Willicombe (Wigan), CA Sullivan (Hull KR); WL Francis (St Helens) capt, P Woods (Widnes); J Mills (Widnes), RP Evans (Salford), M

139

James (St Helens), F Davies (New Hunslet), J Mantle (Leigh), E Cunningham (St Helens); G Pritchard (Barrow) replaced Turner, C Jones (Leigh) replaced Mantle.
Tries: Willicombe, Sullivan, James; Goals: Watkins, Woods

Referee: GF Lindop (Wakefield)

1978–79 European Championship

Friday 16 March 1979: England 15 Wales 7
Widnes, 5,099, £4,475

England: K Mumby (Bradford N); S Wright (Widnes), P Glynn (St Helens), K Smith (Wakefield T), E Hughes (Widnes); K Kelly (Warrington), G Stephens (Castleford); HG Beverley (Workington T), G Liptrot (St Helens), B Lockwood (Hull KR) capt, T Martyn (Warrington), J Grayshon (Bradford N), M Adams (Widnes); J Woods (Leigh) replaced Stephens, D Watkinson (Hull KR) replaced Beverley.
Tries: Mumby, Smith, Woods; Goal: Woods (2), Mumby

Wales: H Box (Featherstone R); CA Sullivan (Hull KR), J Risman (Workington T), JC Bevan (Warrington), BJ Juliff (Wakefield T); WL Francis (St Helens) capt, P Woods (Rochdale H); J Mills (Widnes), T Cunningham (Warrington), M James (St Helens), T. Skerrett (Wakefield T), P.H. Rowe (Huddersfield), R Mathias (St Helens); MJ Nicholas (Warrington) replaced Cunningham, P Prendiville (Hull) replaced Nicholas.
Try: Box; Goals: Box (2)

Referee: R Campbell (Widnes)

1979–80 European Championship

Friday 29 February 1980: England 26 Wales 9
Hull, 7,557, £7,950

England: GA Fairbairn (Wigan); S Wright (Widnes), JD Joyner (Castleford), M Smith (Hull KR), DL Drummond (Leigh); S Evans (Featherstone R), N Holding (St Helens); R Holdstock (Hull KR), DJ Ward (Leeds) capt, Keith Rayne (Wakefield T), L Casey (Hull KR), P Gorley (St Helens), H Pinner (St Helens); J Woods (Leigh) replaced Drummond, J Grayshon (Bradford N) replaced Smith.
Tries: Joyner, Holdstock, Keith Rayne, Fairbairn; Goals: Fairbairn (6); Drop-goals: Pinner (2)

Wales: H Box (Featherstone R); P Prendiville (Hull), G Walters (Hull), WL Francis (Oldham) capt, BJ Juliff (Wakefield T); P Woods (Hull), N Flowers (Wigan); M James (St Helens), D Parry (Blackpool B), G Shaw (Widnes), C Seldon (St Helens), JC Bevan (Warrington), R Mathias (St Helens); S Diamond (Wakefield T) replaced Box.
Try: Juliff; Goals: Woods (3)

Referee: R Campbell (Widnes)

1980–81 European Championship
Wednesday 18 March 1981: England 17 Wales 4
Hull, 4,786

England: GA Fairbairn (Wigan) capt; T Richardson (Castleford), JD Joyner (Castleford), M Smith (Hull KR), S Fenton (Castleford); K Kelly (Warrington), S Nash (Salford); R Holdstock (Hull KR), DJ Ward

(Leeds), L Casey (Hull KR), I Potter (Warrington), WK Pattinson (Workington T), S Norton (Hull); J Woods (Leigh) replaced Kelly, M Adams (Widnes) replaced Smith.
Tries: Joyner, Kelly, Woods; Goals: Fairbairn (4)

Wales: S Rule (Salford); A Cambriani (Fulham), G Walters (Hull), JC Bevan (Warrington) capt, BJ Juliff (Wakefield T); DJ Wilson (Swinton), P Woods (Hull); M James (St Helens), D Parry (Blackpool B), G Owen (Oldham), T Skerrett (Hull), CJ Dixon (Hull KR), R Mathias (St Helens); M Herdman (Fulham) replaced Dixon. Goals: Rule (2)

Referee: J Holdsworth (Leeds)

1981–82

Sunday 8 November 1981: Wales 15 England 20
Cardiff, 13,173

Wales: G Pritchard (Cardiff City BD); A Cambriani (Fulham), S Bayliss (St Helens), SP Fenwick (Cardiff City BD), JC Bevan (Warrington) capt; DJ Wilson (Swinton), N Flowers (Wigan); M James (St Helens), D Parry (Blackpool B), TP David (Cardiff City BD), M Herdman (Fulham), G Shaw (Widnes), P Ringer (Cardiff City BD); R Owen (St Helens) replaced David, P Prendiville (Hull) replaced Ringer.
Tries: Flowers, Prendiville; Goals: Fenwick (4); Drop-goal: Wilson

England: GA Fairbairn (Wigan); DL Drummond (Leigh), M Smith (Hull KR), LP Dyl (Leeds), HC Gill (Wigan); J Woods (Leigh), S Nash (Salford); J Grayshon (Bradford N), DJ Ward (Leeds) capt, J Millington (Hull KR), P Lowe (Hull KR), P Gorley (St Helens), S Norton (Hull); L Gorley (Widnes) replaced Lowe.
Tries: Drummond, P. Gorley, Grayshon, Gill; Goals: Woods (3), Fairbairn

Referee: DG Kershaw (York)

1984–85

Sunday 14 October 1984: Wales 9 England 28
Ebbw Vale, 2,111

Wales: L Hallet (Bridgend BD); C Camilleri (Bridgend BD), P Prendiville (Hull), M Davies (Bridgend BD), P Ford (Warrington); DJ Wilson (Swinton), N Flowers (Bridgend BD); T Skerrett (Hull) capt, C Preece (Bradford N), G Shaw (Wigan), M McJennett (Barrow), C O'Brien (Bridgend BD), BJ Juliff (Wigan); G Johns (Blackpool B) replaced Juliff, G Walters (Bridgend BD) replaced Flowers.
Try: Wilson; Goals: Hallet (2); Drop-goal: Wilson

England: M Burke (Widnes); DL Drummond (Leigh), GE Schofield (Leeds), EC Hanley (Bradford N), G Clark (Hull KR); S Donlan (Leigh) capt, DS Cairns (Barrow); D Hobbs (Featherstone R), K Beardmore (Castleford), H Waddell (Blackpool B), A Kelly (Hull KR), AI Goodway (Oldham), M Huddart (Whitehaven); B Ledger (St Helens) replaced Clark, C Arkwright (St Helens) replaced Hobbs.
Tries: Clark (3), Hanley, Burke; Goals: Burke (4)

Referee: D Fox (Wakefield)

1992–93

Friday 27 November 1992: Wales 11 England 36
Swansea, 10,243

Wales: P Ford (Salford); G Cordle (Bradford N), AG Bateman (Warrington), JA Devereux (Widnes), AC Sullivan (St Helens); JL Griffiths (St Helens), K Ellis (Warrington); M Jones (Hull), DJ Bishop (London C), D Young (Salford) capt, WP Moriarty (Widnes), I Marlow (Hull), RA Ackerman (Salford); AM Hadley (Widnes), RD Phillips (Warrington), PG Pearce (Ryedale-York), M Moran (Leigh).
Tries: Griffiths, Jones; Goal: Devereux; Drop-goal: Ellis

England: S Spruce (Widnes); A Hunte (St Helens), GJ Connolly (St Helens), P Newlove (Featherstone R), MN Offiah (Wigan); GE Schofield (Leeds) capt, MA Ford (Castleford); L Crooks (Castleford), L Jackson (Sheffield E), SJ Molloy (Leeds), RA Eyres (Widnes), P Clarke (Wigan), EC Hanley (Leeds); DA Powell (Sheffield E), CM Joynt (St Helens), J Critchley (Salford), D Busby (Hull).
Tries: Offiah (2), Crooks, Hanley, Newlove, Schofield, Spruce; Goals: Crooks (4)

Referee: A Sablayrolles (France)

1994–95 European Championship

Wednesday 1 February 1995: Wales 18 England 16
Cardiff, 6,232

Wales: P Atcheson (Wigan); P Ford (Salford), AG Bateman (Warrington), IR Harris (Warrington), AC Sullivan (St Helens); JD Davies (Warrington) capt, K Ellis (Workington T); K Skerrett (Wigan), M Hall (Wigan), D Young (Salford), WP Moriarty (Halifax), M Perrett (Halifax), RA Eyres (Leeds); D Powell (Wakefield T), AM Hadley (Widnes), RD Phillips (Workington T), N Cowie (Wigan).
Tries: Ellis (2); Goals: Davies (4); Drop-goals: Davies (2)

England: R Gay (Hull); JT Robinson (Wigan), DA Powell (Sheffield E), P Newlove (Bradford N), I Butt (Featherstone R); GE Schofield (Leeds), JD Fox (Bradford N); K Harrison (Halifax), R Russell (Castleford), H Howard (Leeds), A Farrell (Sheffield E), S Nickle (St Helens), P Clarke (Wigan) capt; S Baldwin (Halifax), MD Cassidy (Wigan), SS McNamara (Hull), S McCurrie (Widnes).
Tries: Gay, Fox, Robinson; Goals: Schofield (2)

Referee: R Smith (Castleford)

1995 World Cup

Saturday 21 October 1995: England 25 Wales 10
Manchester, 30,042

England: K Radlinski (Wigan); JT Robinson (Wigan), N Pinkney (Keighley C), P Newlove (Bradford B), MN Offiah (Wigan); A Smith (Castleford), R Goulding (St Helens); K Harrison (Halifax), L Jackson (Sheffield E), A Platt (Auckland W–Widnes), DC Betts (Auckland W) capt, P Clarke (Sydney City R), AD Farrell (Wigan); B-J Mather (Wigan), MD Cassidy (Wigan), SJ Haughton (Wigan), D Sampson (Castleford).
Tries: Offiah (2), Newlove, Betts, Clarke; Goals: Goulding, Farrell; Drop-goal: Goulding

Wales: IR Harris (Warrington); JA Devereux (Widnes), AG Bateman (Warrington), IS Gibbs (St Helens), AC Sullivan (St Helens); JD Davies (Warrington) capt, K Ellis (Warrington); K Skerrett (Wigan), M Hall

(Wigan), D Young (Salford), WP Moriarty (Halifax), LS Quinnell (Wigan), RA Eyres (Leeds); M Jones (Warrington), K Cunningham (St Helens), RD Phillips (Workington T), AM Hadley (Widnes).
Try: Phillips; Goals: Davies (3)

Referee: E Ward (Australia)

1996 European Championship

Wednesday 26 June 1996: Wales 12 England 26
Cardiff, 5,425

Wales: P Atcheson (Oldham B); D Edwards (Castleford T), AG Bateman (Cronulla-Sutherland S), G Davies (Warrington W), J Critchley (Keighley C); IR Harris (Warrington W), I Watson (Salford R); M Jones (Warrington W), K Cunningham (St Helens), N Cowie (Wigan W), WP Moriarty (South Wales) capt, M Perrett (Halifax BS), C Morley (St Helens); M Hall (Wigan W), RE Webster (Salford R), RD Phillips (Workington T), G Stephens (Hull).
Tries: Morley, Critchley; Goals: Harris (2)

England: S Prescott (St Helens); JT Robinson (Wigan W), GJ Connolly (Wigan W), N McAvoy (Salford R), J Bentley (Halifax BS); DA Powell (Keighley C), S Edwards (Wigan W); P Broadbent (Sheffield E), J Lawless (Sheffield E), SJ Molloy (Featherstone R), CM Joynt (St Helens), P Sculthorpe (Warrington W), AD Farrell (Wigan W) capt; B Goulding (St Helens), S Blakeley (Salford R), B McDermott (Leeds R), MD Cassidy (Wigan W).
Tries: Prescott, Edwards, Joynt, Goulding; Goals: Goulding (5)

Referee: W Harrigan (Australia)

England versus Wales 1908 to 1996 summary

Matches in Wales: Wales 8 wins England 9 wins
Matches in England: England 35 wins, Wales 7 wins, 2 drawn
Matches on neutral ground: Wales 1 win
Overall record: England 44 wins, Wales 16 wins, 2 drawn
Scoring records: England 1,209 points – Wales 728 points
Biggest England victory: 60-13 on 28 May 1978 at St Helens
Biggest Wales victory: 35-18 on 20 April 1908 at Tonypandy

Individual records
England
Most tries in a match: 4 Stan Moorhouse (Huddersfield) at Plymouth 19 Feb 1913; Stuart Wright (Widnes) at St Helens 28 May 1978
Most goals in a match: 9 Geoff Pimblett (St Helens) at St Helens 28 May 1978
Most appearances against Wales: 12 by Joe Egan

Wales
Most tries in a match: 3 Billy Williams (Halifax) at Ebbw Vale 9 April 1910
Most goals in a match: 7 Johnny Thomas (Wigan) at Tonypandy 20 April 1908
Most appearances against England: 17 by Jim Sullivan

English appearances against Wales: 1908 to 1996

+ denotes a substitute appearance
A name in bold type indicates an English Rugby Union international

Name	Rugby League club & dates of matches
Ackerley, Alvin	Halifax Sep-52, Sep-53
Adams, Leslie 'Juicy'	Leeds Mar-31 Castleford Feb-36
Adams, Mick	Widnes Mar-79, +Mar-81
Akroyd, Albert W	Halifax Jan-21
Arkwright, Chris	St Helens Oct-84
Arkwright, Jack	Warrington Nov-36
Armitt, Thomas	Swinton Apr-35, Feb-36, Nov-36, Jan-38, Nov-38, Dec-39
Aspinall, George A	Liverpool S Feb-43
Ashcroft, Ernest J	Wigan Oct-46, Dec-47, Oct-50, Sep-51
Aston, Leonard	St Helens Sep-47
Atkinson, Arthur	Castleford Mar-31, Nov-32
Atkinson, John B	Leeds Nov-68, Oct-69, Feb-70, Feb-75, Jun-75, Sep-75, May-78
Avery, Albert E	Oldham Apr-10, Dec-10, Apr-11
Ayres, Robert H 'Bobby'	Barrow Jan-38, Mar-45
Baldwin, Simon	Halifax Feb-95
Banks, Thomas	Huddersfield Mar-31
Barraclough, James	Hull KR Mar-50
Batten, William 'Billy'	Hunslet Apr-08, Dec-08, Dec-09, Apr-10, Jan-12, Feb-13 Hull Jan-21, Dec-22, Feb-23
Batten, Eric	Hunslet Nov-38, Dec-39, Nov-40, Oct-41, Feb-43 Bradford N Feb-44, Mar-45, Nov-45, Nov-46
Batten, Raymond	Leeds Nov-68, Oct-69
Beardmore, Kevin	Castleford Oct-84
Belshaw, William	Liverpool S Apr-35, Nov-36, Warrington Nov-38, Dec-39, Nov-40, Oct-41, Feb-43, Mar-45
Bennett, Jack	Rochdale H Feb-25, Wigan Apr-26
Bentham, Nathaniel	Wigan H Jan-28, Nov-28
Bentham, William	Broughton R Dec-22, Apr-26
Bentley, John	Halifax Jun-96
Benyon, William	St Helens Nov-68, Feb-70
Betts, Denis C	Auckland W Oct-95
Beverley, Harry	Hunslet Apr-35, Nov-36 Halifax Jan-38
Beverley, Harry G	Workington T Mar-79
Birch, James W	Leeds Apr-08
Blakeley, Steve	Salford Jun-96
Blan, William	Wigan Sep-51
Booth, Charles	Hull Jan-38, Nov-38, Dec-39
Bowkett, Leonard C	Huddersfield Jan-32
Bowman, Harold	Hull Apr-27, Jan-28, Nov-28
Bowers, Albert	Hull Sep-47, Dec-47
Boylen, Francis	Hull Dec-09, Apr-10
Bradshaw, Thomas	Wigan Feb-44, Mar-45, Nov-46, Sep-47, Dec-47, Mar-50, Oct-50
Bratley, Len	Wakefield T Nov-45

Bridges, JH 'Keith'	Featherstone R Sep-75, Jan-77
Brittain, Joseph	Leeds Jan-21, Dec-22
Broadbent, Paul	Sheffield E Jun-96
Brockbank, Christopher	Swinton Apr-27
Brogden, Stanley	Huddersfield Jan-32, Nov-32, Leeds Apr-35, Feb-36, Nov-36, Jan-38 Hull Nov-38, Oct-41, Feb-43
Brookes, Ernest	Warrington Dec-08
Brooks, Edgar	Oldham Nov-40, Oct-41
Broome, Jack	Wigan Oct-50
Brough, James W	Leeds Apr-26, Nov-28, Nov-32, Apr-35, Feb-36
Brown, George S	Batley Mar-45
Buckley, Alan	Swinton +Nov-68
Bunter, George	Broughton R Nov-40
Burgess, William	Barrow Oct-23, Feb-25, Sep-25, Apr-26, Nov-28
Burgess, William	Salford Oct-69
Burke, Mick	Widnes Oct-84
Burnell, Alfred	Hunslet Sep-51, Sep-52
Busby, Dean	Hull Nov-92
Butt, Ikram	Featherstone R Feb-95
Butters, Fred	Swinton Nov-32
Cairns, David S	Barrow Oct-84
Carmichael, Alfred	Hull KR Feb-13
Carr, Charles W	Barrow Feb-25, Sep-25, Apr-26, Apr-27, Nov-28
Cartwright, Joseph	Leigh Jan-21, Dec-22, Feb-23, Oct-23
Casey, Len	Hull KR May-78, Feb-80, Mar-81
Cassidy, Michael D	Wigan Feb-95, Oct-95, Jun-96
Castle, Frank	Barrow Sep-52
Chisnall, David	Warrington Feb-75, Jun-75
Chisnall, Eric	St Helens Jun-75
Clampitt, James L	Broughton R Dec-09, Apr-11, Jan-12, Feb-13, Feb-14
Clark, Douglas	Huddersfield Jan-12, Feb-13, Feb-14, Jan-21, Feb-25
Clark, Garry	Hull KR Oct-84
Clarke, Philip	Wigan Nov-92, Feb-95 Sydney City R Oct-95
Clarkson, Des	Hunslet Dec-47
Clarkson, Ellis	Hull Dec-10, Apr-11, Jan-12
Clarkson, Thomas	Leigh Dec-22, Feb 23
Connolly, Gary J	St Helens Nov-92 Wigan Jun-96
Coulman, Michael J	Salford Feb-75, Jun-75
Cracknell, Richard	Huddersfield Sep-53
Critchley, Jason	Salford Nov-92
Crooks, Lee	Castleford Nov-92
Croston, A James	Castleford Nov-36, Jan-38, Nov-38, Dec-39
Cumberbatch, James H	Newcastle Jan-38
Cunliffe, Jack	Wigan Mar-50, Oct-50, Sep-51
Cunliffe, William	Warrington Jan-21, Dec-22, Feb-23, Oct-23, Feb-25, Sep-25, Apr-26
Cunningham, John	Barrow Feb-75
Curran, George	Salford Oct-46, Nov-46, Dec-47, Sep-48, Feb-49
Dalton, W 'Paddy'	Salford Apr-35, Feb-36
Danby, Thomas	Salford Mar-50, Oct-50

Darwell, Joseph	Leigh Dec-22, Feb-23, Oct-23
Davies, Alan	Oldham Sep-53
Davies, D William	Swinton Nov-68
Derbyshire, William	Warrington Dec-47
Dickenson, George	Warrington Apr -08, Dec-08
Dingsdale, Thomas	St Helens Rec Jan-28
Dingsdale, William	Warrington Nov-28, Mar-31, Jan-32
Dixon, Malcolm	Featherstone R Feb-70
Dockar, Alec	Hull KR Oct-46, Nov-46, Sep-47
Dolan, Oliver	St Helens Rec Nov-32
Donlan, Steve	Leigh Oct-84
Drummond, Desmond L	Leigh Feb-80, Nov-81, Oct-84
Dunn, Gerald 'Ged'	Hull KR Feb-75
Dutton, Raymond F	Widnes Feb-70
Dyer, Harry	Leeds Dec-39
Dyl, Leslie P	Leeds Feb-75, Jun-75, Jan-77, May-78, Nov-81
Eckersley, David	St Helens +Sep-75, +Jan-77, +May-78
Edwards, Shaun	Wigan Jun-96
Egan, Joseph	Wigan Feb-43, Feb-44, Mar-45, Nov-45, Oct-46, Nov-46, Sep-47, Dec-47, Sep-48, Feb-49, Mar-50, Oct-50
Ellaby, Alfred	St Helens Apr-27, Jan-28, Nov-28, Mar-31, Jan-32, Nov-32
Elwell, Keith	Widnes May-78
Evans, Bryn	Swinton Jan-32, Nov-32
Evans, E 'Jack'	Swinton Feb-25, Sep-25, Apr-26, Jan-28
Evans, Steve	Featherstone R Feb-80
Exley, GH 'Mick'	Wakefield T Nov-32
Eyres, Richard A	Widnes Nov-92
Fairbairn, George A	Hull KR Jun-75 Wigan Sep-75, Jan-77, Feb-80, Mar-81, Nov-81
Fairclough, Leslie	St Helens Feb-25, Sep-25, Apr-26, Apr-27, Jan-28, Nov-28, Mar-31
Farrell, Andrew D	Wigan Oct-95, Jun-96
Farrell, Anthony	Sheffield E Feb-95
Featherstone, James J	Warrington Feb-49, Mar-50, Oct-50, Sep-52
Feetham, Jack	Salford Jan-32
Fenton, Steve	Castleford Mar-81
Ferguson, Joseph	Oldham Dec-09
Fildes, Albert	St Helens Rec Apr-27
Fielding, Keith J	Salford Jun-75, Sep-75
Fish, Jack	Warrington Apr-08
Flanagan, Peter	Hull KR Oct-69, Feb-70
Fleming, Jackie	Warrington Sep-48, Feb-49
Ford, Michael A	Castleford Nov-92
Forsyth, Colin	Bradford N Sep-75
Fox, J Deryck	Bradford N Feb-95
Frodsham, Alfred	St Helens Apr-27, Nov-28
Gallagher, Frank	Batley Oct-23, Feb-25, Sep-25, Apr-26, Apr-27 Leeds Nov-28
Garvey, Jack	Broughton R Nov-36
Gay, Richard	Hull Feb-95
Gee, Kenneth	Wigan Feb-43, Feb-44, Oct-46, Nov-46, Sep-47, Sep-48, Feb-49, Mar-50, Sep-51
Gibson, Edward 'Eppie'	Workington T Sep-51

Gifford, Harry	Barrow Dec-08
Gill, Henderson C	Wigan Nov-81
Gill, Ken	Salford Feb-75, +Jun-75, Sep-75, Jan-77
Gleave, Fred	Wigan Feb-13
Glynn, Peter	St Helens Mar-79
Goodfellow, Herbert	Wakefield T Dec-39
Goodway, Andrew I	Oldham Oct-84
Gorley, Leslie	Workington T Jan-77, +Nov-81
Gorley, Peter	St Helens Feb-80, Nov-81
Goulding, R 'Bobbie'	St Helens Oct-95, Jun-96
Gray, John D	Wigan Feb-75
Grayshon, Jeff	Dewsbury Sep-75, Jan-77, Mar-79 Bradford N +Feb-80, Nov-81
Greenall, Douglas	St Helens Sep-52, Sep-53
Greenall, Johnny	St Helens Rec Feb-23, Oct-23
Gregory, Francis St C	Warrington Dec-39
Haigh, Robert	Wakefield T Oct-69, Feb-70
Haines, Edward C	Salford Apr-27
Halfpenny, Ben	St Helens Jan-28
Hall, William	Oldham Feb-14
Hanley, Ellery C	Bradford N Oct-84 Leeds Nov-92
Halliday, S Cyril	Huddersfield Mar-31
Harrison, Fred	Leeds Jan-12, Feb-13
Harrison, Karl	Halifax Feb-95, Oct-95
Harrison, Michael	Leeds May-78
Hartley, Dennis	Castleford Nov-68
Haughton, Simon J	Wigan Oct-95
Helme, Gerry	Warrington Sep-48, Feb-49
Henderson, John B	Workington T Sep-53
Hesketh, Christopher	Salford Nov-68, Oct-69
Hesketh, George	Oldham Sep-25
Higgins, Alec	Widnes Nov-36, Jan-38, Nov-38
Higgins, Fred	Widnes Nov-45, Mar-50, Oct-50
Higson, John William	Hunslet Dec-08
Higson, Len	Wakefield T Nov-32, Oct-41
Hill, Fred	Batley Dec-09
Hilton, Herman	Oldham Jan-21
Hilton, James H	Halifax Dec-08, Jan-12
Hilton, Jack	Wigan Mar-50
Hirst, Jack	Featherstone R Oct-23
Hobbs, David	Featherstone R Oct-84
Hodgson, Martin	Swinton Jan-28, Jan-32, Nov-32, Feb-36, Nov-36
Hogan, J Brian	Wigan Sep-75, Jan-77
Hogg, Andrew	Broughton R Apr-08
Holder, William	Hull Apr-08
Holding, Neil	St Helens Feb-80
Holdstock, Roy	Hull KR Feb-80, Mar-81
Holliday, Thomas E	Oldham Jan-28
Holmes, John S	Leeds Sep-75, Jan-77
Horne, William	Barrow Mar-45, Nov-45, Oct-46, Nov-46, Dec-47, Sep-52, Sep-53
Horton, William	Wakefield T Nov-28, Jan-32, Feb-36

Houghton, Lou	St Helens Apr-27 Wigan Mar-31
Howard, Harvey	Leeds Feb-95
Huddart, Milton	Whitehaven Oct-84
Hudson, Bernard 'Barney'	Salford Apr-35, Feb-36, Jan-38
Hudson, William	Batley Nov-46
Hughes, Eric	Widnes Sep-75, May-78, Mar-79
Hunte, Alan	St Helens Nov-92
Hutchinson, William	Bradford N Feb-44, Mar-45
Hynes, Sydney	Leeds Oct-69, Feb-70
Irving, Hudson	Halifax Jan-38, Nov-40, Oct-41, Feb-43
Irving, Robert A	Wigan Sep-75
Ivison, William H	Workington T Feb-49
Jackson, Lee	Sheffield E Nov-92, Oct-95
Jackson, Philip	Bradford N Feb-75
Jefferson, Brian	Keighley Nov-68
Jenkinson, Albert	Hunslet Jan-12, Feb-13
Johnson, Arthur	Widnes Feb-14
Johnson, Albert E	Warrington Feb-44, Mar-45, Nov-45, Oct-46, Nov-46, Dec-47
Johnson, Thomas A	Hull Oct-41
Jolley, James	Runcorn Apr-08
Jones, Ernest W	Rochdale H Feb-13, Feb-14
Jones, Les	St Helens Jan-77
Joyner, John D	Castleford Feb-80, Mar-81
Joynt, Christopher M	St Helens Nov-92, Jun-96
Jubb, Kenneth	Leeds Nov-38, Oct-41, Feb-43
Jukes, William	Hunslet Dec-08, Dec-09, Apr-10, Dec-10
Keegan, Arthur	Hull Oct-69
Kelly, Andrew	Hull KR Oct-84
Kelly, Ken	Warrington Mar-79, Mar-81
Kennedy, Alfred	Runcorn Apr-11
Kenny, Thomas	Salford Feb-36, Dec-39
Kershaw, Herbert	Wakefield T Dec-10, Apr-11
Kielty, Stanley	Halifax Sep-53
Kitchin, William F	Huddersfield Apr-11
Kitching, Jack	Bradford N Nov-45, Oct-46, Sep-47
Knapman, Ernest	Oldham Feb-25
Knowelden, Brindle 'Bryn'	Barrow Feb-44, Mar-45
Langshaw, Stanley	Rochdale H Sep 25
Laughton, C Douglas	Widnes Jan-77
Lawless, John	Sheffield E Jun-96
Lawrenson, John H	Wigan Dec-39, Nov-40, Oct-41, Oct-46, Nov-46, Sep-48, Feb-49 Workington T Oct-50
Ledgard, James A	Leigh Sep-48, Sep-51, Sep-52, Sep-53
Ledger, Barrie	St Helens Oct-84
Leytham, James	Wigan Apr-10, Dec-10
Liptrot, Graham	St Helens Mar-79
Lockwood, Brian	Hull KR Mar-79
Lomas, James	Salford Dec-08, Dec-09, Apr-10 Oldham Apr-11
Longstaff, Fred	Huddersfield Feb-14
Longworth, William	Oldham Dec-08

Lowe, John	Leeds Jan-32
Lowe, Philip	Hull KR Feb-70, Nov-81
Lynch, William	Wakefield T Dec-10
Mann, Alfred	Bradford N Dec-08
Marlor, Rothwell	Oldham Jan-21
Marshall, Lou	Bramley Feb-23
Martyn, Thomas	Warrington Feb-75, +Jun-75, Mar-79
Mather, Barrie-Jon	Wigan Oct-95
McAvoy, Nathan	Salford Jun-96
McCormick, Stanley	Belle Vue R Sep-48 St Helens Feb-49, Sep-51, Sep-53
McCue, Thomas	Widnes Apr-35, Jan-38, Nov-38, Nov-40, Nov-45, Oct-46
McCurrie, Steven	Widnes Feb-95
McDermott, Barrie	Leeds Jun-96
McKeating, Vincent M	Workington T Sep-51
McNamara, Steven S	Hull Feb-95
Middleton, Alfred G	Salford Mar-31
Miller, Joseph	Wigan Dec-10, Apr-11
Miller, Jack 'Cod'	Warrington Jan-28, Nov-36
Millington, Harry	Widnes Feb-44
Millington, John	Hull KR Nov-81
Milner, Thomas	Dewsbury Feb-14
Millward, Roger	Hull KR Oct-69, +Feb-70, Feb-75, Jun-75, Sep-75, Jan-77, May-78
Molloy, Steve J	Leeds Nov-92 Featherstone R Jun-96
Moore, Arthur	Hull KR Feb-13
Moore, Jack D	Bradford N Nov-40
Moorhouse, Stanley	Huddersfield Jan-12, Feb-13, Feb-14
Morrell, Cyril	Hunslet Nov-38
Morgan, Arnold	Featherstone R Nov-68
Morgan, Mick	Wakefield T Feb-75, Jun-75
Mumby, Keith	Bradford N Mar-79
Murphy, Alexander J	Leigh Oct-69
Murphy, Harry	Wakefield T Oct-46, Sep-48
Nash, Steve	Featherstone R Jun-75, May-78 Salford Mar-81, Nov-81
Newbould, Thomas H	Wakefield T Dec-09
Newlove, Paul	Featherstone R Nov-92 Bradford N Feb-95 Bradford B Oct-95
Nicholls, George	St Helens Jun-75, +Sep-75, May-78
Nicholson, Robert	Huddersfield Nov-45, Sep-47, Feb-49
Nickle, Sonny	St Helens Feb-95
Noonan, Derek	Warrington Feb-75, Jun-75
Norton, Steven	Castleford Jun-75, Sep-75, May-78, Mar-81, Nov-81
O'Grady, Terry	Oldham Sep-52
Offiah, Martin N	Wigan Nov-92, Oct-95
Oliver, FW	York Dec-09
Oliver, Joseph	Batley Jan-28 Hull Feb-36
Osborne, Lawrie	Hull KR Sep-25, Apr-27
Owen, James	St Helens Rec Jan-21, Feb-23, Oct-23
Padbury, Richard	Runcorn Apr-08, Dec-09, Jan-12
Palin, Herbert	Warrington Dec-47, Sep-48
Parkin, Jonathan 'Jonty'	Wakefield T Jan-21, Dec-22, Feb-23, Feb-25, Apr-26, Apr-27, Jan-28, Nov-28

Parr, Kenneth	Warrington Nov-68
Pattinson, William K	Workington T Mar-81
Pawsey, Charles H	Leigh Sep-51, Sep-52, Sep-53
Peacock, J Alfred	Warrington Sep-25
Peake, Oswald 'Ossie'	Warrington Dec-39, Nov-40, Oct-41
Pepperell, G Russell	Huddersfield Dec-47, Sep-48
Pepperell, Stanley V	Huddersfield Nov-36, Feb-44
Pimblett, Albert J	Warrington Sep-48, Feb-49
Pimblett, Geoff	St Helens May-78
Pinkney, Nick	Keighley C Oct-95
Pinner, Harry	St Helens Feb-80
Place, Herbert	Hunslet Dec-09
Platt, Andrew	Widnes Oct-95
Pollard, Ernest	Wakefield T Jan-32, Nov-32
Pollard, Roy	Dewsbury Mar-50
Potter, Ian	Warrington Mar-81
Powell, Daryl A	Sheffield E Nov-92, Feb-95 Keighley C Jun-96
Prescott, Alan G	St Helens Oct-50, Sep-52
Prescott, Stephen	St Helens Jun-96
Price, Jack	Wigan Dec-22
Radlinski, Kris	Wigan Oct-95
Ramsdale, Richard	Wigan Apr-10, Feb-13, Feb-14
Ratcliffe, W Gordon	Wigan Sep-47
Rayne, Keith	Wakefield T Feb-80
Reid, William	Widnes Feb-14
Reilly, Malcolm J	Castleford Feb-70, +Jan-77
Rix, Sidney	Oldham Feb-25, Apr-26
Rhodes, William	Dewsbury Jan-21
Richardson, Terry	Castleford Mar-81
Riley, Joseph	Halifax Apr-10
Roberts, Robert	Widnes Dec-39, Nov-40
Robinson, Asa	Halifax Apr-08, Dec-08
Robinson, David	Swinton Oct-69
Robinson, James	Castleford Feb-44
Robinson, Jason T	Wigan Feb-95, Oct-95, Jun-96
Roman, Walter J	Rochdale H Feb-14
Rose, Paul	Hull KR May-78
Rostron, Thomas	Oldham Nov-45
Russell, Richard	Castleford Feb-95
Ryan, Martin	Wigan Feb-43, Nov-45, Nov-46, Sep-47, Dec-47, Feb-49, Mar-50
Rylance, Ronald	Wakefield T Sep-47
Sadler, Edward H	Castleford Dec-39
Sampson, Dean	Castleford Oct-95
Schofield, Derrick	Rochdale H Sep-52
Schofield, Garry E	Leeds Oct-84, Nov-92, Feb-95
Scott, Michael	Hull Sep-51, Sep-53
Sculthorpe, Paul	Warrington Jun-96
Seabourne, Barry	Leeds Feb-70
Shannon, Thomas	Widnes Jan-38, Nov-38
Sharrock, James	Wigan Apr-10

Shaw, Ernest	Wigan Jan-21
Sheard, Leslie	Wakefield T Feb-75
Shoebottom, Michael D	Leeds Nov-68, Feb-70
Silcock, Nathan	Widnes Jan-32, Nov-32, Apr-35, Feb-36
Silcock, Nat	Wigan Sep-53
Skelhorne, G Arthur	Warrington Dec-22, Feb-23
Slevin, Edward 'Ted'	Wigan Oct-50
Sloman, Robert	Oldham Oct-23, Sep-25, Apr-26, Nov-28
Smith, Arthur	Oldham Dec-08
Smith, Fred	Hunslet Dec-09, Apr-10, Dec-10, Apr-11, Jan-12
Smith, Herbert	Halifax Apr-27
Smith, Keith	Wakefield T Mar-79
Smith, M Alan	Leeds Nov-68, Feb-70
Smith, Michael	Hull KR Feb-80, Mar-81, Nov-81
Smith, Stanley	Leeds Mar-31, Jan-32, Nov-32, Apr-35
Smith, Anthony	Castleford Oct-95
Spencer, Jack	Salford Apr-08
Spruce, Stuart	Widnes Nov-92
Stansfield, Colin	Hunslet Mar-45
Stephens, Gary	Castleford Mar-79
Stephens, John R	Wigan Oct-69
Stone, William J	Hull Jan-21, Dec-22, Feb-23, Oct-23
Stott, Jimmy	St Helens Feb-43
Stott, William	Broughton R Nov-36
Street, Harry	Dewsbury Mar-50, Oct-50 Wigan Sep-52
Tattersfield, Edward	Leeds Nov-40, Oct-41, Feb-43, Feb-44
Taylor, Kevin	Oldham Nov-68
Taylor, Thomas L	Castleford Nov-45
Taylor, Robert	Hull Dec-22, Feb-23, Feb-25, Sep-25, Apr-26
Taylor, W Harry	Hull Apr-08
Thacker, Laurie	Hull Nov-38, Oct-41
Thomas, Arthur G	Leeds Mar-31
Thompson, Ernest	Broughton R Nov-36
Thompson, James	Featherstone R Jan-77 Bradford N +May-78
Thornton, William	Hunslet Feb-43
Todd, Frank	Halifax Oct-23
Todd, George	Hunslet Apr-35, Feb-36
Tomes, Jack	Coventry Dec-10
Tranter, James	Warrington Dec-22, Oct-23
Tracey, Frank	St Helens Nov-40
Trail, Kenneth	Bradford N Sep-53
Troup, Lancelot A 'Alec'	Barrow Apr-35, Feb-36
Tullock, Geoffrey	Hull KR Sep-51
Tyson, George	Oldham Dec-08, Dec-09
Waddell, Hugh	Blackpool B Oct-84
Wagstaff, Harold	Huddersfield Dec-10, Apr-11, Jan-12, Feb-13, Feb-14, Feb-23
Walkington, Jack C	Hunslet Mar-31, Jan-38, Feb-44
Wallace, John	St Helens Rec Sep-25
Walmsley, Sydney O	Leeds Oct-23

Ward, Ernest	Bradford N Oct-41, Mar-45, Nov-45, Oct-46, Nov-46, Sep-47, Feb-49, Mar-50, Oct-50, Sep-52
Ward, David J	Leeds Feb-80, Mar-81, Nov-81
Ward, John	Castleford Oct-69
Ward, William	Leeds Apr-10
Waring, Jack	St Helens Nov-40
Warwick, Silas	Salford Apr-08
Watkinson, David	Hull KR +Mar-79
Watson, Alfred	Leeds Nov-38
Watson, Clifford H	St Helens Nov-68, +Oct-69, Feb-70
Webster, Fred	Leeds Apr-10, Dec-10, Apr-11
White, Les	York Oct-46, Nov-46 Wigan Sep-47, Dec-47, Sep-48 Halifax Sep-51
White, Thomas	Oldham Apr-08, Apr-10, Dec-10, Apr-11
Wilkinson, Harry	Wakefield T Feb-43, Feb-44, Mar-45
Winstanley, William	Leigh Dec-10, Apr-11 Wigan Jan-12
Wood, Alfred E	Oldham Feb-14
Woods, John	Leigh +Mar-79, +Feb-80, +Mar-81, Nov-81
Woods, J Harry	Liverpool S Apr-35
Woods, Thomas	Rochdale H Jan-12, Feb-13
Wright, Joseph	Swinton Jan-32
Wright, Stuart	Widnes Jan-77, May-78, Mar-79, Feb-80
Young, Harold	Widnes Feb-25
Young, Harold	Bradford N Jan-28, Huddersfield Mar-31

Welsh appearances against England: 1908 to 1996

+ denotes a substitute appearance
A name in bold type indicates a Welsh Rugby Union international
A name underlined indicates an English Rugby Union international
A name in italics indicates an appearance for Wales in a victory international in 1945/46
The player's last Welsh club has been included where known and applicable

Name	Welsh club	Rugby League club and appearances (month-year)
Ackerman, Robert A	London Welsh	Salford Nov-92
Atcheson, Paul		Wigan Feb-95, Oldham Jun-96
Bacon, James A 'Jim'	Cross Keys	Leeds Jan-21, Dec-22, Feb-23, Sep-25, Apr-26, Apr-27
Baker, Ambrose	Neath	Oldham Feb-25, Jan-28
Banks, William M 'Billy'	Maesteg	Huddersfield Feb-49, Mar-50, Oct-50, Sep-51, Sep-52, Sep-53
Banner, Peter		Salford Feb-75, Jun-75, Sep-75
Bassett, Arthur	Cardiff	Halifax Dec-39, Nov-45, Nov-46
Bateman, Allan G	Neath	Warrington Nov-92, Feb-95, Oct-95, Cronulla Sutherland S Jun-96
Bayliss, Steve	Ystradgynlais	St Helens Nov-81
Beames, John R 'Jack'	Newport	Halifax Feb-14, Jan-21
Bennett, George H	Risca	Wigan Feb-36
Bevan, David R 'Dai'		Wigan Sep-53
Bevan, John C	Cardiff	Warrington Feb-75, Sep-75, Jan-77, Mar-79, Feb-80, Mar-81, Nov-81
Bishop, David J	Pontypool	London C Nov-92
Blackmore, Jacob H 'Jake'	Abertillery	Hull KR Dec-10, Apr-11
Boocker, Dennis J		Wakefield T Feb-49, Oct-50
Bowen, B 'Jack'	Llanelli	Wigan Mar-45
Box, Harold		Featherstone R Mar-79, Feb-80
Brown, Fred	Pontypridd	Oldham Feb-23, Oct-23
Buckler, Arthur	Pill Harriers	Salford Apr-08
Burgham, Oliver	Abertillery	Ebbw Vale Apr-08
Cale, W Raymond	Pontypool	St Helens Sep-51
Cambriani, Adrian	Swansea	Fulham Mar-81, Nov-81
Camilleri, Chris	Cardiff	Bridgend BD Oct-84
Case, Desmond J	Newport	Bradford N Nov-38
Casewell, J Aubrey		Salford Nov-32
Caswell, Edward	Cardiff	Hull Dec-22, Apr-27
Chapman, William G	Bridgend	Warrington Feb-43, Feb-44
Chilcott, John 'Jack'	Cross Keys	Huddersfield Feb-13, Feb-14
Coldrick, A Percy	Newport	Wigan Feb-13, Feb-14
Condon, Mike	Army	Halifax Sep-52
Constance, Leonard	Pontypool	St Helens Sep-48
Cordle, Gerald	Cardiff	Bradford N Nov-92
Corsi, Joseph A	Crumlin	Oldham Oct-23
Coslett, T Kelvin 'Kel'	Aberavon	St Helens Nov-68, Feb-70, Feb-75, Jun-75, Sep-75

Cowie, Neil		Wigan Feb-95, Jun-96
Critchley, Jason		Keighley C Jun-96
Cunningham, Eddie		St Helens Jun-75, Sep-75, Jan-77, May-78
Cunningham, Keiron		St Helens Oct-95, Jun-96
Cunningham, Tommy		Warrington Mar-79
Daniels, Arthur H	Pontyberem	Halifax Feb-49, Mar-50, Sep-51, Sep-52, Sep-53
Danter, Thomas	Bridgend	Hull Mar-50, Oct-50
David, Thomas	Pontypridd	Cardiff City BD Nov-81
Davies, Alban	Cardiff	Huddersfield Feb-43
Davies, Dai	Llanelli	Swinton Dec-10
Davies, David B	Merthyr	Merthyr Tydfil Apr-08, Dec-08, Dec-09, Apr-10 Swinton Dec-10, Apr-11 Oldham Feb-13
Davies, Dai M	Neath	Warrington Jan-28
Davies, Dai M	Talywain	Salford Dec-39, Nov-45, Oct-46, Nov-46, Sep-48
Davies, Evan	Llanelli	Oldham Jan-12, Feb-13, Oct-23
Davies, E Gwyn	Cardiff	Wigan Jan-32, Nov-32, Apr-35
Davies, Frank		New Hunslet May-78
Davies, Gareth		Warrington Jun-96
Davies, Islwyn	Swansea	St Helens Apr-35
Davies, D Idwal	Swansea	Leeds Mar-45
Davies, Jim	Swansea	Huddersfield Dec-09, Dec-10, Jan-12
Davies, Jonathan D	Llanelli	Warrington Feb-95, Oct-95
Davies, Mike	Fairwater	Bridgend BD Oct-84
Davies, T Percy 'Ponty'	Pontypridd	Pontypridd Apr-27 Warrington Jan-28
Davies, William 'Avon'	Swansea	Leeds Feb-14
Davies, William T	Tredegar	Batley Dec-09, Halifax Apr-11, Jan-12
Davies, William T	Neath	Huddersfield Feb-43, Feb-44, Oct-46, Nov-46
Davies, WTH 'Billy'	Swansea	Bradford N Dec-39, Feb-44, Mar-45, Nov-45, Oct-46, Nov-46, Sep-47
Day, Bryn	Bridgend	Oldham Sep-52
Day, Hubert C 'Bert'	Newport	Salford Apr-35, Feb-36, Mar-45
De Francis, Howell	Llanelli	Wigan Dec-09
De Lloyd, Melville	Llanelli	Warrington Mar-45
Devereux, John A	Bridgend	Widnes Nov-92, Oct-95
Diamond, Steve	Newbridge	Wakefield T +Feb-80
Dixon, Colin J	Cardiff Youth	Halifax Nov-68 Salford Oct-69, Feb-75, Jun-75, Jan-77 Hull KR Mar-81
Dowell, William H	Pontypool	Warrington Dec-08
Edwards, Alan S	Aberavon	Salford Feb-36, Nov-36, Jan-38, Nov-38, Dec-39, Oct-41, Feb-43, Feb-44, Mar-45, Nov-45 Bradford N Sep-48
Edwards, David	Glynneath	Rochdale H Feb-23, Sep-25
Edwards, Diccon		Castleford Jun-96
Edwards, Harold	Abertillery / Edgware	Wigan Apr-35
Ellis, Kevin	Bridgend	Warrington Nov-92 Workington T Feb-95 Warrington Oct-95
Emery, Wyndham C	Bridgend	Leigh Dec-22
Evans, Arthur C 'Candy'	Pontypool	Halifax Nov-28 Castleford Mar-31

Evans, Clifford H	Neath	Leeds Jan-38, Nov-38, Dec-39, Nov-40, Oct-41
Evans, Dai M	Neath	Huddersfield Nov-36
Evans, Emrys	Llanelli	Salford Mar-45
Evans, Frank	Llanelli	Swinton Feb-25, Sep-25, Apr-26, Apr-27, Jan-28
Evans, TE Hagen	Llanelli	Bradford N Sep-47
Evans, JD 'Jack'	Newport	Hunslet Oct-50, Sep-51, Sep-53
Evans, Richard P 'Dick'		Swinton Feb-75 Salford May-78
Evans, William G	Brynmawr	Leeds Jan-12, Feb-13
Eyres, Richard A		Leeds Feb-95, Oct-95
Fender, Norman	Cardiff	York Jan-32, Nov-32, Feb-36, Nov-36, Jan-38
Fenwick, Steve P	Bridgend	Cardiff City BD Nov-81
Ferguson, Stewart	Swansea	Leigh Feb-70
Fisher, Anthony	RAF	Bradford N Nov-68, Oct-69, Feb-70 Leeds Jun-75, Sep-75, Jan-77
Flowers, Ness	Neath	Wigan Feb-80, Nov-81 Bridgend BD Oct-84
Flynn, Tommy	Talywain	Warrington Mar-31
Foley, Jack	Brynmawr	Ebbw Vale Dec-08, Dec-09, Apr-10, Dec-10, Apr-11
Ford, Phil	Cardiff	Warrington Oct-84 Salford Nov-92, Feb-95
Foster, Trevor	Newport	Bradford N Dec-39, Nov-40, Oct-41, Feb-43, Feb-44, Oct-46, Nov-46, Dec-47, Mar-50
Fowler, Isaac J	Llanelli	Batley Apr-26
Francis, Alf J	Treherbert NU	Hull Feb-13, Feb-14
Francis, Roy L	Brynmawr	Barrow Oct-46, Dec-47
Francis, WL 'Bill'		Wigan Feb-75, Jun-75, Sep-75, Jan-77 St Helens May-78, Mar-79 Oldham Feb-80
Fredericks, Bernard W	Newport	Oldham Feb-13
Gallacher, I Stuart	Llanelli	Keighley Feb-75
Galloway, David	Treherbert	Treherbert Dec-09, Apr-10
Gibbs, I Scott	Swansea	St Helens Oct-95
Givvons, Alex	Cross Keys	Oldham Nov-36, Jan-38, Nov-38, Dec-39
Goldswain, Bryn V	RAF / Abercrave	Hull KR Sep-47, Mar-50, Oct-50, Sep-52, Sep-53
Gore, John H 'Jack'	Blaina	Salford Apr-27, Jan-28
Gould, Bernard J	Aberavon	Leeds Jan-21 Wakefield T Dec-22, Feb-23, Oct-23
Green, T Albert	Cross Keys	Pontypridd Apr-27
Gregory, Brian		Wigan Sep-75
Grey, Thomas H	Swansea	Huddersfield Apr-11, Jan-12
Griffiths, Jonathan L	Llanelli	St Helens Nov-92
Griffiths, Oswald T 'Ossie'	Aberavon	St Helens Apr-35 Halifax Feb-36
Griffiths, Tyssul 'Tuss'	Newport	Hunslet Oct-46
Gronow, Benjamin	Bridgend	Huddersfield Dec-10, Feb-14, Jan-21, Dec-22, Feb-23, Oct-23
Gullick, Don	Pontypool	St Helens Oct-50, Sep-52, Sep-53
Gummer, George	Pontypridd	Barrow Nov-36
Gwynne, T Emlyn	Mountain Ash	Hull Nov-28
Gwyther, Elwyn	Llanelli	Belle Vue R Sep-47, Dec-47, Sep-48, Oct-50, Sep-51 Leeds Sep-53
Hadley, Adrian M	Cardiff	Widnes Nov-92, Feb-95, Oct-95

Hall, Martin		Wigan Feb-95, Oct-95, Jun-96
Hallett, Lynn	Bridgend	Bridgend BD Oct-84
Harris, Dilwyn EJ 'Dyl'	Maesteg	Castleford Sep-47
Harris, Iestyn R		Warrington Feb-95, Oct-95, Jun-96
Harris, Norman	Cross Keys	Oldham Dec-47, Feb-49
Harris, P Tommy	Newbridge	Hull Sep-52, Sep-53
Harrison, Vivian JG	London Welsh	St Helens Sep-51
Hathway, Reginald	Newport	Oldham Mar-31, Jan-32
Hawkins, Eynon	Bridgend	Salford Feb-49, Mar-50
Hennessey, John	Glynneath	Rochdale H Sep-25
Herdman, Martin		Fulham +Mar-81, Nov-81
Higgs, Alfred J	Blaenavon	Oldham Jan-28
Hodder, Wilfred	Pontypool	Wigan Dec-22, Feb-25, Sep-25, Apr-26, Nov28
Hopkins, William	Bridgend	Aberdare Dec-08
Howes, WJ Derek	Llanelli	Wakefield T Sep-48, Mar-50
Howley, Tommy	Ebbw Vale	Wigan Jan-21, Feb-25, Sep-25
Hughes, Emlyn	Llanelli	Huddersfield Nov-38
Hughes, W Fred	Llanelli / Cheltenham	Barrow Mar-45, Nov-45
Hughes, Gomer	Penarth	Swinton Nov-38, Nov-40
Hurcombe, Danny	Talywain	Wigan Jan-21, Feb-23, Oct-23, Feb-25, Sep-25
James, Granville	Newbridge	Hunslet Oct-50
James, Mel	Swansea	St Helens Sep-75, May-78, Mar-79, Feb-80, Mar-81, Nov-81
Jarrett, Keith S	Newport	Barrow Feb-70
Jenkins, Dai	Cardiff	Leeds Jan-38, Nov-38, Dec-39, Nov-40, Oct-41, Feb-43, Feb-44, Nov-45, Oct-46, Nov-46, Dec-47, Sep-48
Jenkins, David M	Treorchy	Hunslet Apr-27, Nov-28, Mar-31 Leeds Nov-32
Jenkins, E 'Jack'	Llwynypia	Warrington Dec-09, Jan-12
Jenkins, Ernest	Newport	Rochdale H Dec-10, Apr-11, Jan-12
Jenkins, Emlyn	Cardiff	Salford Nov-32, Apr-35, Nov-36
Jenkins, T Bertram 'Bert'	Mountain Ash	Wigan Apr-08, Dec-08, Dec-09, Apr-10, Dec-10, Apr-11, Jan-12, Feb-13, Feb-14
Jenkins, TE 'Chick'	Pontypool	Ebbw Vale Apr-08, Apr-10, Dec-10, Apr-11, Jan-12
Jerram, Sidney G	Swansea	Wigan Jan-21, Feb-23, Oct-23, Feb-25, Sep-25
John, W Dai	Penygraig	Salford Feb-13
Johns, Graeme	University	Blackpool B Oct-84
Johnson, William H	Newport	Huddersfield Jan-38
Jones, Clive	Aberavon	Leigh +May-78
Jones, David 'Tarw'	Aberdare	Merthyr Tydfil Apr-08
Jones, David E	Maesteg	Halifax Nov-68, Oct-69
Jones, E 'Ned'	Maesteg	Broughton R Feb-13
Jones, Harold 'Hal'	Cardiff	Keighley Feb-36
Jones, Joseph	Swansea	Leeds Apr-26
Jones, Joseph	Cilfynydd	Wigan Nov-40, Oct-41, Feb-43, Feb-44 Barrow Mar-45, Nov-45, Nov-46, Sep-47, Dec-47, Sep-48, Feb-49
Jones, Mark	Neath	Hull Nov-92 Warrington Oct-95, Jun-96
Jones, Wyndham	Mountain Ash	Keighley Jan-32
Jones, WRT 'Dickie'	Aberavon	Swinton Dec-47
Juliff, Brian J	Pontypridd	Wakefield T Mar-79, Feb-80, Mar-81 Wigan Oct-84

Kersey-Brown, Alex	London Welsh	Huddersfield Nov-68,
Lambert, Roy	Resolven	Neath Oct-50 Dewsbury Sep-51 Warrington Sep-52
Lewis, Daniel	Cardiff	Merthyr Tydfil Apr-10
Lewis, George	Pontypool	St Helens Apr-27, Nov-28
Lewis, Gordon H	Swansea	Leigh Feb-70
Llewellyn, Lew J	Pill Harriers	Ebbw Vale Apr-10, Dec-10, Apr-11, Jan-12
Llewellyn, Stewart M 'Steve'	Abertillery	St Helens Sep-48, Mar-50
Llewellyn, Tom	Cardiff	Oldham Dec-08
Lloyd, Arthur C	Penarth	York Mar-31
Lloyd, Robert	Pontypool	Halifax Jan-21
Lloyd, Reginald W	Resolven	Castleford Oct-46, Nov-46, Dec-47
Madden, Dennis	Aberavon	Huddersfield Feb-36, Nov-36, Nov-38
Mahoney, Joe B	Cardiff	Oldham Sep-48 Dewsbury Mar-50, Oct-50
Maidment, David J	Ebbw Vale	Wakefield T Nov-28
McJennett, Mark J	Newport	Barrow Oct-84
Mantle, John T	Newport	St Helens Nov-68, Oct-69, Feb-75, +Jun-75, Sep-75 Salford Jan-77 Leigh May-78
Marlow, Ian		Hull Nov-92
Mathias, Roy	Llanelli	St Helens Feb-75, Jun-75, Jan-77, May-78, Mar-79, Feb-80, Mar-81
Meek, A Melville	Abertillery	Halifax Nov-36, Oct-46, Nov-46, Sep-47, Dec-47, Sep-48, Feb-49
Merry, J Augustus	Pill Harriers	Hull Feb-13
Mills, Jim	Cardiff	Bradford N Oct-69, Feb-70 Widnes Feb-75, Jun-75 Workington T Jan-77 Widnes May-78, Mar-79
Moran, Mark		Leigh Nov-92
Morgan, D Ralph	Newport	Swinton Mar-50
Morgan, D Edgar	Llanelli	Hull Dec-22, Oct-23, Feb-25, Apr-26
Morgan, Gill	Abertillery	Dewsbury Jan-38
Morgan, Philip	Cardiff	Hunslet Oct-69, Feb-70
Morgan, WC 'Bill'	Newport	Wigan Jan-32
Morgan, W Glyn	Cardiff	Huddersfield Sep-47
Moriarty, W Paul	Swansea	Widnes Nov-92, Halifax Feb-95, Oct-95 South Wales Jun-96
Morley, Chris		St Helens Jun-96
Morley, Jack C	Newport	Wigan Nov-32, Feb-36
Morris, Oliver	Pontypridd	Hunslet Jan-38, Leeds Nov-40, Oct-41
Mountain, Stanley J	Cross Keys / Newport	Huddersfield Apr-35
Murphy, Cornelius D 'Con'	Cross Keys	Leeds Jan-38, Nov-38, Dec-39, Nov-40, Oct-41, Feb-43, Feb-44, Nov-45
Nicholas, Michael J	Aberavon	Warrington +Feb-75, Jan-77, +Mar-79
O'Brien, Chris	Fairwater	Bridgend BD Oct-84
O'Neill, William	Cardiff	Warrington Dec-08, Dec-09
Oliver, George	Pontypool	Hull Dec-22 Pontypridd Apr-27
Orchard, Leonard	Newbridge	Keighley Apr-35
Orford, Edwin J 'Sandy'		Wakefield T Dec-39, Nov-40, Oct-41, Feb-44
Osmond, Frank F	Newport	Swinton Feb-49, Mar-50, Oct-50, Sep-51

Owen, Gareth		Oldham Mar-81
Owen, Roger	New Dock Stars (Llanelli)	St Helens +Nov-81
Owens, George	Swansea	Wigan Feb-23, Oct-23
Owens, Isaac A 'Ike'	RAF / Maesteg	Leeds Mar-45, Nov-45, Oct-46, Nov-46, Dec-47, Sep-48 Huddersfield Feb-49
Paddison, Thomas J	Merthyr Tydfil	Merthyr Tydfil Dec-08
Parker, Gwyn	Neath	Huddersfield Jan-28, Mar-31, Jan-32
Parker, Tommy	Aberavon	Wigan Nov-28
Parry, Don		Blackpool B Feb-80, Mar-81, Nov-81
Parsons, George	Newport	St Helens Feb-49, Oct-50, Sep-51, Sep-52, Sep-53
Pearce, P Gary	Llanelli	Ryedale York Nov-92
Perrett, Mark		Halifax Feb-95, Jun-96
Phillips, Bryn	Aberavon	Huddersfield Apr-26
Phillips, Douglas V	Swansea	Oldham Nov-45, Oct-46, Nov-46 Belle Vue R Feb-49, Sep-51
Phillips, L Owen	Swansea	Swinton Sep-51, Sep-53
Phillips, Rowland D	Neath	Warrington Nov-92 Workington T Feb-95, Oct-95, Jun-96
Powell, Daio		Wakefield T Feb-95
Powell, Stan	Risca	St Helens Mar-45
Preece, Chris		Bradford N Oct-84
Prendiville, Paul	Bynea	Hull +Mar-79, Feb-80, +Nov-81, Oct-84
Price, Gareth	Llanelli	Leeds Nov-45, Oct-46, Nov-46, Sep-47
Price, H Raymond	Abertillery	Belle Vue R Sep-52 Warrington Sep-53
Price, Terry G	Llanelli	Bradford N Nov-68, Oct-69
Pritchard, Gordon	Newport	Barrow +May-78 Cardiff City BD Nov-81
Prosser, David R	Neath	York Nov-36 Leeds Jan-38, Oct-41, Feb-43, Feb-44
Prosser, Robert	Newport	Salford Nov-68, Oct-69
Pugh, Norman	Swansea	Oldham Apr-35, Feb-36, Nov-36
Quinnell, L Scott	Llanelli	Wigan Oct-95
Radford, Brian	Aberavon	Bradford N Sep-52
Ray, Stephen	Pill Harriers	Warrington Nov-32
Rees, Charles	Penygraig	Salford Jan-12
Rees, Dai	Penygraig	Salford Dec-08
Rees, Dai	Abertillery	Halifax Feb-23, Oct-23, Feb-25, Sep-25, Apr-26, Mar-31
Rees, Graham T	Maesteg	St Helens Nov-68, Oct-69, Feb-70
Rees, Harry R	Loughor	Batley Oct-23, Feb-25
Rees, Lewis M	Cardiff	Oldham Apr-35, Feb-36, Jan-38
Rees, Rhys	Swansea	Merthyr Tydfil Apr-08, Apr-10
Rees, William 'Billo'	Amman United	Swinton Apr-26, Apr-27, Jan-28, Nov-28
Richards, Maurice CR	Cardiff	Salford Jan-77
Richards, Rees	Aberavon	Wigan Feb-14
Ring, Johnny	Aberavon	Wigan Feb-25, Sep-25, Apr-27, Jan-28, Nov-28
Ringer, Paul	Llanelli	Cardiff City BD Nov-81
Risman, Augustus JF 'Gus'	Cardiff Scottish	Salford Mar-31, Jan-32, Feb-36, Nov-36, Jan-38, Nov-38, Dec-39, Nov-40, Oct-41, Feb-44, Mar-45, Nov-45
Risman, John		Workington T Mar-79
Roffey, Fred L	Ebbw Vale	Wigan Jan-21 St Helens Apr-26

Name	Origin	Clubs
Rogers, John H	Cardiff	Huddersfield Feb-14, Dec-22
Rosser, Melvyn A	Penarth	Leeds Apr-26 York Mar-31, Nov-32
Rowe, Peter	Swansea	Wigan Oct-69, +Sep-75 Huddersfield Jan-77, Mar-79
Ruddick, George	Brecon	Broughton R Apr-08, Dec-08, Apr-10
Rule, Steve		Salford Mar-81
Sage, Charles	Mountain Ash	Hunslet Feb-25, Sep-25
Sandham, William	Neath	Hull KR Jan-12
Saunders, WJ 'Bill'	Ebbw Vale	Ebbw Vale Apr-08
Scourfield, Thomas B	Torquay Athletic / London Welsh	Huddersfield Apr-35
Seldon, Chris	Army / Pontypridd	St Helens Feb-80
Shaw, Glyndwr 'Glyn'	Neath	Widnes Feb-80, Nov-81 Wigan Oct-84
Shea, Jeremiah	Newport	Wigan Dec-22, Feb-23
Shugars, Frank H	Penygraig	Warrington Dec-09, Apr-10, Dec-10, Apr-11, Jan-12
Skerrett, Kelvin		Wigan Feb-95, Oct-95
Skerrett, Trevor		Wakefield T Mar-79 Hull Mar-81, Oct-84
Staines, Charles	Army / Bridgend	Castleford Sep-48
Standing, Colin	Bridgend	Wigan Feb-70
Stephens, Frank	Cardiff	Wigan Jan-28, Nov-28
Stephens, Gareth		Hull Jun-96
Sullivan, Anthony C		St Helens Nov-92, Feb-95, Oct-95
Sullivan, Clive A	Army	Hull Nov-68, Oct-69, Feb-70 Hull KR Jun-75, Sep-75, May-78, Mar-79
Sullivan, Jim	Cardiff	Wigan Dec-22, Feb-23, Oct-23, Feb-25, Sep-25, Apr-26, Apr-27, Jan-28, Nov-28, Mar-31, Jan-32, Nov-32, Feb-36, Nov-36, Jan-38, Nov-38, Dec-39
Talbot, Fred	Ebbw Vale	Huddersfield Apr-35
Thomas, Dai	Aberdare	Halifax Apr-08, Dec-08
Thomas, Evan J	Plll Harriers	Salford Apr-11, Feb 14
Thomas, Harold W	Neath	Salford Nov-38
Thomas, Johnny	Cardiff	Wigan Apr-08, Dec-08, Apr-10, Apr-11, Feb-13, Feb-14
Thomas, Les M	Llanelli	Oldham Sep-47, Dec-47
Thomas, Edward 'Ned'	Llanelli	Oldham Feb-23
Thomas, Phillip	Tredegar	Leeds Apr-08, Hull KR Dec-09, Dec-10
Thomas, Willie S	Aberavon	Salford Apr-11
Thomas, William 'Billie'	Swansea	York Mar-31
Thomas, W George	Newport	Warrington Jan-12
Thomas, W Gwyn	Cardiff-London Welsh	Wigan Feb-14, Jan-21
Thomas, W Trevor	Abertillery	Oldham Jan-32, Nov-32 Wigan Nov-40
Thompson, Joseph F	Cross Keys	Leeds Oct-23, Feb-25, Sep-25, Apr-26, Jan-28, Mar-31, Nov-32
Towill, Idris A	Bridgend	Huddersfield Jan-32
Treasure, David		Oldham Jun-75, Sep-75
Treharne, Llewellyn	Tredegar	Wigan Apr-08
Turner, Glyn	Ebbw Vale	Hull KR +Feb-75, +Sep-75 Hull May-78

Walters, Emlyn	Neath	Bradford N Nov-40, Oct-41, Feb-43, Feb-44, Sep-47
Walters, Graham	Army / Kidwelly	Hull Feb-80, Mar-81 Bridgend BD Oct-84
Wanbon, Robert	Aberavon	St Helens +Nov-68, Oct-69, Feb-70 Warrington Jun-75
Ward, Edward H 'Ted'	Llanelli	Wigan Sep-47, Dec-47, Sep-48, Feb-49
Warlow, D John	Llanelli	St Helens Nov-68
Watkins, Emlyn	Blaina	Leeds Apr-27
Watkins, David	Newport	Salford Nov-68, Feb-75, Jun-75, Sep-75, Jan-77, May-78
Watkins, W 'Billy'	Cross Keys	Salford Jan-32, Nov-32, Apr-35, Feb-36, Nov-36
Watkins, Edward	Cardiff	Wigan Oct-41, Feb-43, Mar-45
Watson, Ian		Salford Jun-96
Webster, Richard E	Swansea	Salford Jun-96
Whitcombe, Frank	Army	Broughton R Nov-38, Bradford N Dec-39, Nov-40, Oct-41, Feb-43, Feb-44, Nov-45, Oct-46, Nov-46
White, Leslie L 'Les'	Pontyclun	Pontypridd Jan-28 Hunslet Nov-28, Mar-31, Jan-32, Nov-32
Whitney, Harold	Naval Harlequins (Plymouth)	Salford Jan-21
Wilkins, Ray	Aberavon	Workington T +Jan-77
Williams, Brinley	Llanelli	Batley Jan-21, Dec-22
Williams, Cliff	Newport	Hunslet Feb-70
Williams, Eddie	Neath	Huddersfield Nov-28
Williams, Frank	Swansea	Halifax Feb-14
Williams, W Leslie T 'Les'	Cardiff	Hunslet Mar-50, Sep-51, Sep-52, Sep-53
Williams, Richard L 'Dickie'	Mountain Ash	Leeds Dec-47, Feb-49, Mar-50, Oct-50, Sep-51
Williams, Sidney A	Aberavon	Salford Nov-40, Feb-43, Sep-47, Sep-52
Williams, Thomas J	Llanelli	Oldham Feb-13
Williams, W.A. 'Billy'	Crumlin	Salford Jan-32
Williams, W.J. 'Billy'	Pontypool	Halifax Dec-08, Dec-09, Apr-10, Dec-10
Willicombe, David	Cardiff IAC	Halifax +Feb-70 Wigan Feb-75, Jun-75, May-78
Willis, Fred	Pontypool	Batley Jan-21
Wilson, Danny J	Cardiff	Swinton Mar-81, Nov-81, Oct-84
Wilson, Francis H	Cardiff	St Helens Nov-68, Oct-69, Feb-70, Feb-75, +Jun-75, Sep-75
Winslade, Charles H	Maesteg	Oldham Sep-53
Woods, Paul	Pontypool	Widnes Jan-77, May-78 Rochdale H Mar-79 Hull Feb-80, Mar-81
Woods, Thomas	Pontypool	Wigan Dec-22, Feb-23
Young, David	Cardiff	Salford Nov-92, Feb-95, Oct-95
Young, W Frank	Cardiff	Leeds Dec-09, Apr-10

Bibliography

Books

Billot, John: History of Welsh International Rugby (Cardiff, 1999)
Boucher, David: Steel, Skill & Survival (Ebbw Vale, 2000)
Caplan, Phil & Smith, Peter: Leeds RLFC 100 Greats (Stroud, 2001)
Carline, Steve: Parkside (Outwood, 2022)
Cartwright, Brian: A 'Ton' Full of Memories (Batley, 1986)
Chadwick, Stanley: Claret and Gold (Huddersfield, 1946)
Coffey, John: Strike (Leeds, 2012)
Coslett, Kel & Appleton, Mike: A Welsh Saint (Skipton, 2010)
Davies, DE: Cardiff Rugby Club: History and Statistics 1876-1975 (Cardiff, 1975)
Davies, Jonathan: Code Breaker (London, 1996)
Delaney, Trevor: The International Grounds of Rugby League (Keighley, 1995)
Dowson, Neil: 140 Years of the Wire (Warrington, 2016)
Evans, Howard & Atkinson, Phil: War Games: Rugby Union during the Second World War (Cardiff, 2019)
Fletcher, Raymond: Hull RLFC 100 Greats (Stroud, 2002)
Foster, Simon, Gate, Robert & Lush, Peter: Trevor Foster: The life of a rugby league legend (London, 2005)
Fuller, Eddie & Slater, Gary: Warrington RLFC 100 Greats (Stroud, 2002)
Gate, Robert: Gone North, two volumes, (Sowerby Bridge, 1986 and 1988)
The Struggle for the Ashes II (Sowerby Bridge, 1996)
Thrum Hallers 100 Greats (Stroud, 2004)
Rugby League Lions: 100 Years of Test Matches (Skipton, 2008)
Billy Boston: Rugby League Footballer (London, 2009)
Godwin, Terry: The International Rugby Championship 1883-1983 (London, 1984)
Golden, Ian: A Welsh Crusade (London, 2009)
Gronow, David: Huddersfield RLFC 100 Greats (Stroud, 2008)
Hardcastle, Andrew: The Thrum Hall Story (Halifax, 1986)
Thrum Hall Greats (Halifax, 1994)
Harris, Iestyn: There and Back (Edinburgh, 2005)
Holliday, Joe: Workington Town Hall of Fame (Workington, 2016)
Huitson, Dave, Nutter, Keith & Andrews, Steve: Keeping the Dream Alive (Barrow, 2008)
Jenkins, John M, Pierce, Duncan, Auty, Timothy: Who's Who of Welsh International Rugby Players (Bath, 2018)
Jones, Neil: From the Valleys to Headingley (London, 2022)
Latham, Mike: They played for Leigh (Adlington, 1991)
Latham, Mike & Gate, Robert: They played for Wigan (Adlington, 1992)
Lush, Peter: Ahead of his time (London, 2022)
Lush, Peter & Bamford, Maurice: Big Jim (London, 2013)
Lush, Peter & Farrar, Dave: Tries in the Valleys (London, 1998)
Mather, Tom: Best in the Northern Union (London, 2010)
Melling, Phil: Man of Amman (Llandysul, 1994)
Nicholas, Mike with Salter, Gary: From Swyn-y-Mor to Seattle (London, 2014)
Morris, Graham: Salford RLFC 100 Greats (Stroud, 2001)
Salford City Reds: A Willows Century (Skipton, 2002)
Rugby League in Manchester (Stroud, 2003)
The King of Brilliance (London, 2011)
Wigan RLFC 100 Greats (Stroud, 2005)

Richards, Huw: The Red and the White (London, 2009)
Richards, Huw, Stead, Peter & Williams, Gareth: More Heart and Soul: The Character of Welsh Rugby (Cardiff, 1999)
Roberts, Jane & Chris: The Greatest Sacrifice (Leeds, 2018)
Ross, David: Wales: History of a Nation (Glasgow, 2005)
Rylance, Mike: Trinity (Brighouse, 2013)
Samuel, Bill: Rugby: Body and Soul (Edinburgh, 1986)
Saxton, Irvin: History of Rugby League; booklets 1895–96 to 1979–80 (Pontefract)
Service, Alex: Saints in their Glory (St Helens, 1985)
The March of the Saints (St Helens, 1988)
St Helens RLFC 100 Greats (Stroud, 2006)
Slater, Gary: Jack Fish: A Rugby League Superstar (London, 2012)
Smith, David B & Williams, Gareth: Fields of Praise (Cardiff, 1980)
Thomas, Wayne: A Century of Welsh Rugby Players (1979)
Tingle, Richard & Service, Alex: The flying Sullivans (2001)
Walker, Brian: Roughyeds: The story (Oldham, 2004)
Waring, Eddie: England to Australia and New Zealand (Leeds, 1947)
Watkins, David: An Autobiography (London, 1980)
Wild, Stephen M: The Lions of Swinton (Swinton, 1999)
Swinton Lions RLFC: 150 years
Williams, Graham & Lush, Peter: Peter Fox: The Players' Coach (London, 2008)
Williams, Nigel: Bradford Northern (Bradford, 1989)
Winstanley, Jack: The Illustrated History of Wigan RLFC (Wigan, 1988)

Articles

Farrar, Dave: When Wales toured Australasia, Our Game No11
Gate, Robert: Truly a man of steel, Code 13 No4
Behold a mystery of a Welsh forward, Rugby League Journal No82
James, David: Wales versus New Zealand 1 January 1908, Code 13 No12
'Knightrider', A.G. 'Ginger' Thomas, Rugby League Magazine No22
Latham, Michael: South London? On your bike, Forty-20 May 2016
Miller, Dr Allen, A Rugby League Diary 1898-1938, Rugby League Journal No8
Morris, Graham, Glory for Wales at the Willows, Rugby League Journal No26
Other Nationalities: Part One 1904-1933, Rugby League journal No32
Schleppi, Dr John: Rugby League: the war years, Code 13 Nos 2, 3, 10, 12
Waring, Eddie: 'Land of My Fathers' Disappoints, Rugby League Review April 1948

Roy Francis had an excellent career as a player in rugby league, including being the first black player to play for Great Britain.

At **Hull,** he became player-coach in 1951 – he is believed to be the first black coach of a senior professional team in any sport in Great Britain – and used his experience of rehabilitating injured soldiers in the War to become an outstanding, innovative coach. He built a team based on young players who won the Championship twice, reached two Challenge Cup Finals and four Yorkshire Cup Finals. He built his teams around fitness, pace and a strong pack.

In 1963, he joined **Leeds**. He gradually rebuilt the team, introduced young talent and, after finishing top of the league table twice, won the Challenge Cup in 1968. The team's Yorkshire Cup win the same

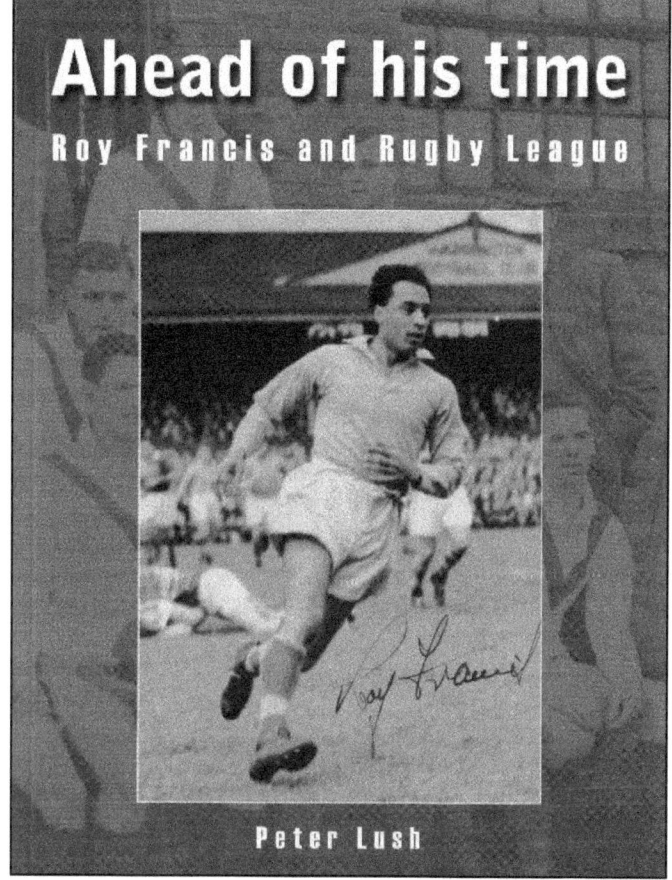

year meant that Roy had won every major domestic club honour as a coach.

In 1969 he became coach of **North Sydney** and, after two problematic years in Australia, returned home. A short spell at Hull in 1972 was followed by winning the Premiership with Leeds in 1975 and saving **Bradford** from relegation in 1976. He retired in 1977.

Based on detailed research, this book looks at Roy's playing and coaching careers and the development of his work. He was considered years ahead of his time and is now being recognised for his ideas, as well as the success he achieved. He died in 1989 at the age of 70. With a foreword by Great Britain and Wales international player **Jim Mills**, who played for Roy in Australia, every rugby league fan will find this book of interest.

Published in April 2022 @ £14.95, 184 page paperback.
ISBN: 9781909885295
Order from London League Publications Ltd (www.llpshop.co.uk), Amazon, AbeBooks, EBay or from any bookshop.

From The Valleys to Headingley
Leeds Welsh Rugby League players

By Neil Jones

Leeds Rugby League Club is one of the most famous names in the sport with many notable players playing on the hallowed field of Headingley since turning professional in 1895.

Since the launch of the Northern Union in 1895, Welshmen have played an important role in the many successes the club has had over the years. More than 150 Welsh players have represented the club. Many won honours and trophies while playing for Leeds.

This book commemorates the many Welshmen who came north to wear the famous blue and amber jersey. It includes many famous names such as **Frank 'Bucket' Young**, **Joe Thompson**, **Richard 'Dickie' Williams** and the legendary 'Golden Boy' **Lewis Jones**, considered by many to be the greatest player in the club's history. In more recent times, **Iestyn Harris** played a vital role in re-establishing Leeds as a major force in their new guise of the Rhinos.

The book records those players who were successful with Leeds, but also includes those that did not achieve the success they had hoped for when they turned professional and came north, such as **Edgar Tottle**, **Patrick Greaney** and **Enoch Hughes**.

This book details the lives and careers of every Welsh player to have played for the club, be it for the first team or academy level.

With a foreword by **Tony Fisher**, a Great Britain and Wales international, this book will be of interest to all rugby league fans.

Published in August 2022 @ £13.95.

186 page paperback illustrated with over 40 photos.
ISBN: 9781909885301

Order from London League Publications Ltd (www.llpshop.co.uk), Amazon, AbeBooks, EBay or from any bookshop.

In a league of his own
– The Brian Lockwood Story
By Phil Hodgson

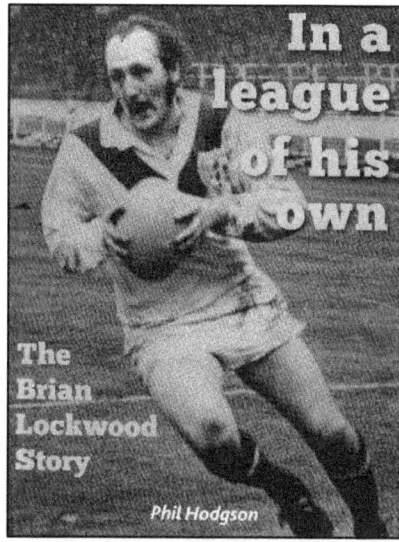

Brian Lockwood is indisputably one of the finest rugby league players, indeed sportsmen, of the last 60 years. Superb skills as a ball-playing forward, with the rugby intelligence to make maximum use of his talents – and, crucially, of those of the men around him – helped him famously create the vital try for Mike Stephenson against Australia that played a huge part in Great Britain winning the World Cup in 1972.

While not perhaps blessed with the natural speed to outpace all-comers over the length of a rugby league pitch, he was certainly fast enough over the important first 10 metres, creating countless scoring opportunities for team-mates in the international arena with Great Britain and England, for Yorkshire, and at club level.

His domestic career included over 10 years with his hometown club **Castleford**, followed by stints at Australian outfits Canterbury-Bankstown and Balmain and, back in England, with **Wakefield Trinity**, **Hull KR, Oldham** and **Widnes**. Rock solid in defence, he could more than hold his own in the hard-bitten physical era of the 1960s, 1970s and early 1980s.

Brian Lockwood, a member of a famous rugby league family, entered the *Guinness Book of Records* as, at the time, the only player to have appeared at Wembley on six occasions, where he never lost. He lifted the Challenge Cup twice with Castleford, helped topple Australia in the first test in 1973, and returned to the Twin Towers in 1980, where he won the Lance Todd Trophy as man-of-the-match for his display in Hull KR's victory over Hull FC, before going back to the stadium in 1981 and 1982 with Widnes – the cup kings.

After hanging up his boots, he coached down under with Maryborough and, in Yorkshire, at Batley and Huddersfield while continuing to build up a series of successful public houses – all the while acquiring many hilarious anecdotes – with his wife Anne and supportive family.

In a League of his own - The Brian Lockwood Story is a vivid account of a special man and family in what was a special era for British rugby league.

Published in October 2022 @ £14.95. Book details: 148 page paperback illustrated with over 40 photos. ISBN: 9781909885264

Available from the publisher at www.llpshop.co.uk , Amazon, AbeBooks and E-Bay, and can be ordered from any bookshop. An E-Book for Kindle users is also available on Amazon.

A Northern Union Man
The life of Harold Wagstaff

By Robert Gate & Graham Williams

Harold Wagstaff, known as the 'Prince of Centres', was one of the key players in the development of rugby league in the early twentieth century.

He made his debut for the Huddersfield first team in November 1906, at the age of 15, having previously played for Underbank. He joined the professional game at an important time for the sport. The number of players had been reduced to 13, and other rule changes made, including the introduction of play-the-ball after a tackle. This made Northern Union rugby a more open game, and Wagstaff and the Huddersfield team took full advantage of the changes.

He played for Yorkshire in 1908, and in January 1909 made his Great Britain debut against Australia, the first player aged under 18 to play for his country. He was made captain of Huddersfield in 1911, and under his direction the club won the Challenge Cup three times, the Northern Rugby League Championship three times, the Yorkshire League six times and the Yorkshire Cup five times. They won 'All Four Cups' in 1914–15, and were known as the 'Team of all the Talents'.

For Great Britain, Wagstaff captained the 1914 and 1920 Lions tours to Australia and New Zealand. This included the 1914 'Rorke's Drift' test, when a Great Britain team reduced to 10 men through injuries hung on to beat the Australians and win the Ashes.

However, it was not just his success that made him one of the sport's greatest players. It was the way he played the game, seeing the sport as a passing and handling game, rarely kicking the ball. He was made a founder member of the Rugby League Hall of Fame in 1988.

This book, as well as contributions from the two authors, includes an autobiographical newspaper series that Wagstaff wrote in the 1930s, excerpts from an autobiographical series published in 1921 and contributions from other rugby league writers, including Tony Collins and Harry Edgar. It is book that every rugby league fan will enjoy.

Published in July 2019 at £12.95. Special offer: £12.50 post free in the UK available direct from London League Publications Ltd, www.llpshop.co.uk. Also available on Amazon, E-Bay and Abe Books, or from any bookshop. Also available as an E-Book for Kindle from Amazon.